Approaches to Teaching Proust's Fiction and Criticism

Edited by

Elyane Dezon-Jones

and

Inge Crosman Wimmers

D1523313

The Modern Language Association of America
New York   2003

For information about obtaining permission to reprint material from
MLA book publications, send your request by mail (see address below),
e-mail (permissions@mla.org), or fax (646 458-0030).

Library of Congress Cataloging-in-Publication Data

Approaches to teaching Proust's fiction and criticism / edited by
Elyane Dezon-Jones and Inge Crosman Wimmers.
p. cm. — (Approaches to teaching world literature ; 80)
Includes bibliographical references and index.
ISBN 0-87352-908-1 (hardcover : alk. paper) — ISBN 0-87352-909-X (pbk. : alk. paper)
1. Proust, Marcel, 1871–1922—Study and teaching. 2. Proust, Marcel, 1871–1922—
Criticism and interpretation. I. Dezon-Jones, Elyane.
II. Wimmers, Inge Crosman, 1940– III. Series.
PQ2631.R63A523 2003
843'.912—dc22   2003016374
ISSN 1059-1133

Cover illustrations on the paperback edition are taken from the front of two notebooks
used by Proust. Courtesy of the Bibliothèque Nationale de France.

Printed on recycled paper

Published by The Modern Language Association of America
26 Broadway, New York, New York 10004-1789
www.mla.org

Approaches to Teaching Proust's Fiction and Criticism

Approaches to Teaching
World Literature

Joseph Gibaldi, series editor

For a complete listing of titles,
see the last pages of this book.

CONTENTS

PREFACE TO THE SERIES

In *The Art of Teaching* Gilbert Highet wrote, "Bad teaching wastes a great deal of effort, and spoils many lives which might have been full of energy and happiness." All too many teachers have failed in their work, Highet argued, simply "because they have not thought about it." We hope that the Approaches to Teaching World Literature series, sponsored by the Modern Language Association's Publications Committee, will not only improve the craft—as well as the art—of teaching but also encourage serious and continuing discussion of the aims and methods of teaching literature.

The principal objective of the series is to collect within each volume different points of view on teaching a specific literary work, a literary tradition, or a writer widely taught at the undergraduate level. The preparation of each volume begins with a wide-ranging survey of instructors, thus enabling us to include in the volume the philosophies and approaches, thoughts and methods of scores of experienced teachers. The result is a sourcebook of material, information, and ideas on teaching the subject of the volume to undergraduates. The series is intended to serve nonspecialists as well as specialists, inexperienced as well as experienced teachers, graduate students who wish to learn effective ways of teaching as well as senior professors who wish to compare their own approaches with the approaches of colleagues in other schools. Of course, no volume in the series can ever substitute for erudition, intelligence, creativity, and sensitivity in teaching. We hope merely that each book will point readers in useful directions; at most each will offer only a first step in the long journey to successful teaching.

Joseph Gibaldi
Series Editor

PREFACE TO THE VOLUME

Marcel Proust is living proof of the literary lesson that the narrator gives Albertine in *La Prisonnière (The Captive)*: "les grands littérateurs n'ont jamais fait qu'une seule œuvre, ou plutôt refracté à travers des milieux divers, une même beauté qu'ils apportent au monde" (3: 877); ("the great men of letters have never created more than a single work, or rather have never done more than refract through various media an identical beauty which they bring into the world"; 5: 505–06).[1] Although there are many ways of interpreting Proust's work, critics generally agree that in French literature there is a before and an after *A la recherche du temps perdu*. As a critic himself, Proust was instrumental in questioning the nineteenth-century theories that shaped his aesthetics. He revolutionized fiction writing with a novel that challenged all the rules of the genre and is still used today as the ultimate testing ground by various schools of criticism—ranging from textual to gender and cultural studies. Combining in one text social, aesthetic, ethical, philosophical, and sexual concerns, *A la recherche du temps perdu* tells the story of a life remembered—the life of a hero-narrator whose status still puzzles many first-time readers. The acknowledged complexity and the unusual length of the book may even deter some from discovering the many rewards of teaching Proust's fiction.

And yet scholarly output on Proust's works is at an all-time high—and has been ever since his works entered the public domain in the 1980s. The following two decades produced six new editions in French and two new translations into English. Proust has gone public in other ways as well. In newsletters and chat groups on the Web, in cartoons, movies, and popularizing publications directly or loosely related to *A la recherche du temps perdu*, Proust is rapidly becoming a household name.

In academic circles, he is seen as both a canonical and a subversive author. His works are taught not only in the context of French literature and culture but also in a number of diverse courses, as was shown by the MLA survey conducted for this volume. The volume's goal is to provide those considering teaching Proust's fiction and criticism with practical tools and a range of current perspectives.

In the introduction, Inge Crosman Wimmers discusses the challenging originality of *A la recherche du temps perdu*, explores the book's complex relation to Proust's other writings, and gives an overview of the critical reactions his works provoked. Because the publication history of *A la recherche du temps perdu* is as complex as the novel's genesis, we provide, in part 1, under the heading "The Instructor's Library," a guide to the many editions a teacher may choose from, both in French and English. Since the corpus of critical studies on Proust is possibly surpassed only by those devoted to Shakespeare, it is difficult to choose material that is objectively representative of such diversity. We offer a selected guide to, among other resources, Proust biographies and bibliographies, essay collections, guides to reading Proust, and special journal issues as well as entire journals devoted to Proust. In addition, the introduction discusses a number of important studies of Proust, and the essays in part 2 draw from many specific critical works. In the section "Aids to Teaching," we give an up-to-date survey of audiovisual materials and the addresses of useful Web sites, as well as detailed information on the Institut des Textes et Manuscrits Modernes (ITEM) and the Kolb-Proust Archive.

In part 2, "Approaches," the first section comprises essays that contextualize Proust's writings. The authors analyze the historical background and the social, political, and cultural circumstances, including the artistic world, in which Proust lived and wrote. They portray him as a man very much of his times and stress the important role that the Dreyfus affair and the First World War played in his development as a novelist. They also emphasize Proust's sensitivity to the aesthetic theories of his time, which affected his overall conception of art.

The next section proposes interpretive perspectives on topics of particular interest to the survey participants who answered the MLA questionnaire: the significance of names in the *Recherche*, the importance of reading in Proust's work, the function of memory and intertextuality, the representation of homosexuality, and the treatment of the novel in various film adaptations.

The final section offers ways of teaching Proust's fiction and criticism in specific settings, at different levels, and through diverse pedagogical approaches, including explication de texte, the use of technology, and the pairing of text and other art forms. Through theory and praxis, the contributors show that Proust's work can be used and enjoyed in all kinds of courses, from basic surveys to advanced graduate seminars in French literature, as well as in interdisciplinary contexts.

We have included a bibliography of works by Proust in part 1, "Materials," after the section on editions, to guide readers through the labyrinth of first, posthumous, critical, and revised editions of Proust's works, in French and in English.

We wish to thank the participants in the MLA survey, as well as our students and colleagues at Brown University and Washington University, who supported us in many ways. We give sincere thanks to Christine Hitchcock and Jennifer Gage for their much appreciated help. We are particularly grateful to Joseph Gibaldi for his guidance, patience, and unflagging enthusiasm for this project.

Elyane Dezon-Jones

NOTE

[1]*A la recherche du temps perdu*, ed. Tadié, 1987–89; *In Search of Lost Time*, ed. Enright, 1993.

Introduction: Why Proust Now?

What makes Proust's novel unique? What gives it its special appeal and makes it seem contemporary? Critics have characterized it as modern or postmodern, yet what exactly is it that gives one the impression that *A la recherche du temps perdu* charts a new course for the novel? Proust himself realized that he was onto something new and was unable or unwilling to confine his work in progress to a given genre, hesitating for a while by referring to it as an "important work" (*Corr.* 8: 39; my trans.). In 1908, Proust jots down some thoughts in a notebook and wonders what form his work should take: "Faut-il en faire un roman? Une étude philosophique? Suis-je romancier?" (*Carnet* 61) ("Should I write a novel? a philosophical study? Am I a novelist?"; my trans.). From 1913 on, though, he will use the word "roman" ("novel") to qualify *A la recherche du temps perdu*: "un important ouvrage, disons un roman, car c'est une espèce de roman" (*Corr.* 12: 79) ("an important work, let us call it a novel, for it is a kind of novel"; my trans.). Proust's initial hesitancy may be explained, in part, by the fact that the *Recherche* grew out of a work of literary criticism (*Contre Sainte-Beuve*), preceded by translations of and a critical essay on John Ruskin, a set of literary pastiches, and sketches on artists and writers. Proust was obviously eager to incorporate some of the aesthetic views developed previously into his new oeuvre, whatever shape it might take.

From the start, this innovative novel transgressed the well-established boundaries of its genre by absorbing into the framework of first-person narration the gnomic discourses of the essay, thereby closely weaving together the fictional and nonfictional, the personal and the general. In reading it, one is confronted with a dual perspective, that of the essayist focused on aesthetic, philosophical, and psychological beliefs and that of the novelist presenting such insights through narrative form—a story with characters in a concrete setting, living in time and space, and subject to social and historical forces, that is, a life in context where a person's own experiences constitute reality. It is the narrator's dual role as essayist and storyteller that has created the biggest interpretive problem, since the ideational commentary is almost always attributed to Proust.

Although *A la recherche du temps perdu* tells the story of a life remembered, it is not the author's. Proust was infuriated when the critic Francis Chevassu, in his review of 8 December 1913 in *Le Figaro*, described *Du côté de chez Swann* as "une nonchalante et pittoresque autobiographie" ("a nonchalant and picturesque autobiography"; my trans.). The same year, Proust wrote many letters to explain his intentions and to make a clear distinction between himself and "the gentleman who says I" (*Corr.* 12: 92; my trans.) in the novel: "I see readers," he protested, "imagining that I am writing the story of my life" (*Corr.* 18: 464; my trans.). Yet he sometimes blurred the line between author and fictional persona, leaving one to wonder who the "I" actually is. A telling example is the following passage from a letter of November 1913, addressed to René Blum:

C'est un livre extrêmement réel mais supporté en quelque sorte, pour imiter la mémoire involontaire . . . par un pédoncule de réminiscences. Ainsi une partie du livre est une partie de ma vie que j'avais oubliée et que tout d'un coup je retrouve en mangeant un peu de madeleine que j'ai fait tremper dans du thé, saveur qui me ravit avant que je l'aie reconnue et identifiée pour en avoir pris jadis tous les matins.

(*Corr.* 12: 295–96)

It is an extremely realistic book, but supported, so to speak, in imitation of involuntary memory . . . by a stem of reminiscences. Thus one part of the book is a part of my life, which I had forgotten and which suddenly I find again while eating a bit of madeleine that I have dipped into some tea, a taste that overjoys me before I have recognized and identified it as what I used to have every morning a long time ago.   (my trans.)

In the 1970s, Roland Barthes pointed out that the boundaries in *A la recherche du temps perdu* are so slippery that it is impossible for the reader to settle on a single genre: novel or essay? fiction or autobiography? As a way out, he proposed to view Proust's novel as a "third form" or "rhapsody," given its "sewn together" quality (*Essais* 316–17). More recently, Dorrit Cohn, in a chapter entitled "Proust's Generic Ambiguity" (58–78), took another close look at the novel's allusiveness. In asking what seems to her the most crucial question, Is it fiction, autobiography or both?, she invoked Philippe Lejeune's discussion of the "autobiographical pact" (Cohn 59–60). In view of Lejeune's model of autobiographical writing, the *Recherche* is found wanting since there are no generic markers and since the narrator's name is suspended only tentatively, being invoked hypothetically two-thirds through the novel. Equally disconcerting are the narrator's illusionist games of anchoring fiction in reality—presenting, for instance, some artists as well known (Bergotte, Elstir) when, in fact, they have no historical existence and introducing historical figures into the midst of a fictional setting (Zola at the Verdurins).

Since the novel has been subjected to diverse readings (which identify the work as autobiography, fictional narrative, hybrid work, a rhapsodic "third form," a deconstructive work), it seems best to approach *A la recherche du temps perdu* with an open mind, sensitive to its implied poetics, which asks readers to be ready to cross borders between fiction and autobiography, to be able to embrace both without seeing them as a textual dilemma. This approach calls for a certain flexibility on our part, a willingness to juggle frames of reference and to be subject to different kinds of communication as we are immersed in one text. No one can know for certain what Proust intended. Perhaps he simply refused to be boxed in by generic boundaries, eager both to engage in fabulation and to speak in his own voice when it came to sharing insights of universal import. It is, perhaps, the freedom that comes from crossing not only generic but also ontological borders that carries Proust well into the new millennium.

It is also a new conception of reality that makes this novel distinctive and that gives it its lasting appeal. Proust envisioned reality as nonstatic and thus as unable to be rendered through realist representation. In the Proustian world, reference is not simply to a given object or state of affairs but to a personal construction that reflects the very inflections of one's being. Proust, as well as his protagonist who aspires to become a writer, is in search of a style able to convey such a complex reality, in the narrator's words, "la réalité telle que nous l'avons sentie" (4: 459) ("reality as we have felt it to be" [6: 277]). But what aspects of style could exemplify such a worldview and impress this new aesthetics on the reader?

As early as 1924, Benjamin Crémieux described Proust's innovative style as "surimpressionistic" (83). This adjective is well chosen, since it refers to a style able to capture the many layers of inner life: simultaneous sensory impressions, emotions, feelings, thoughts, reminiscences, and imaginary input. This revolutionary poetics subjects us, as we read, to a new order of things by exemplifying the discovery of existential structures, the very architecture of our lives. The novel's central stylistic feature, metaphor, by its very design plays a crucial role in conveying the complexity of inner life, since it presents readers with associations among different semantic domains. In fact, Proust's entire narrative favors association instead of a more conventional logical and chronological order: a given event or a character's present situation is compared with similar ones elsewhere in the novel; the past suddenly intrudes into the present through involuntary memory and a solicitous narrator makes us conscious of ourselves by inviting us, as readers of his novel, to find our own connections as we mine our lives for similar experiences. This process is reinforced by the narrator's frequent interpolation of general conclusions that have universal implications.

By setting in motion the interaction between the world of the text and the world of the reader and by designing a narrative with multiple dimensions and variable points of contact, Proust has created a hypertextual work par excellence: a novel in constant movement and open to diverse readings. A la recherche du temps perdu is a dynamic text whose worldview and aesthetics are in harmony with the spirit of our electronic age, since it encourages us to seek new connections and to explore that which is aleatory.

Is it any wonder, then, that at the start of the new millennium, interest in Proust is steadily growing and the author of A la recherche du temps perdu is noticeably reaching a broader public? In fact, he is something of a cultural phenomenon, judging by the frequent mention in the media of his name, his oeuvre and the various works and activities it has inspired, including new films; theatrical stagings; a play; and such popularizing publications as Alain de Botton's How Proust Can Change Your Life, Stéphane Heuet's comic-book versions of "Combray" and of A l'ombre des jeunes filles en fleurs, and Estelle Monbrun's murder mystery Meurtre chez Tante Léonie (Murder chez Proust). Equally noteworthy are the proliferation of information and of chat groups devoted to Proust on the Internet and the recent access to Le Temps retrouvé online. Mementos surface everywhere, including bookmarks, T-shirts, scarves, watches, calendars, posters, CDs, videos, and countless other items that bring the author of *A la recherche du temps perdu* to public attention.

For specialists in Proust, the last decade has been challenging: new editions and translations of his work appear regularly, yet another biography is released, and critical works abound. As we take stock, it is apparent that Proust has survived all critical approaches. Critics have found evidence for their views in the wondrously open work that is *A la recherche du temps perdu*. Borrowing insights from philosophy, psychology, and science and combining social, aesthetic, and ethical concerns, the novel is an interdisciplinary tour de force. Obviously, its appeal is a lasting one, and it enjoys renewed and growing interest as time goes by.

Some of the most renowned critics and writers have paid homage to Proust. Leo Spitzer and Gérard Genette (*Figures 3*) focused on Proust's style and narrative technique. For Paul Ricoeur (*Temps et récit*), *A la recherche du temps perdu* was nothing less than an experience of living in time, a *Zeiterlebnis*. And Barthes, who in the 1960s approached Proust's novel from a structuralist perspective (Barthes, "Introduction à l'analyse"; "An Introduction"), gave it a more personal reading in the 1970s, citing pathos as a central force (*Essais*). More recently, André Aciman opted for a similar interpretation:

> But the figure who lies at the heart of today's Proust revival is the intimate Proust, the Proust who perfected the studied unveiling of spontaneous feelings. Proust invented a language, a style, a rhythm, and a vision that gave memory and introspection an aesthetic scope and magnitude no author had conferred on either before. He allowed intimacy itself to become an art form.   (82)

Theodor Adorno introduces a striking biological metaphor to describe Proust's malleable work:

> [T]he whole, resistant to abstract outlines, crystallizes out of *intertwined* individual presentations. Each of them conceals within itself constellations of what ultimately emerges as the idea of the novel. Great musicians of Proust's era, like Alban Berg, knew that living totality is achieved only through *rank vegetal proliferation*.   (174)

What could come closer to depicting the postmodern dimension of the novel than this biological image, whose present-day theoretical equivalent is the rhizome (Deleuze and Guattari "Mille plateaux"; "A Thousand Plateaus")?

There are yet other unexplored territories to be charted as we read and reread Proust's rich and multifarious novel. It is a generous work, without restricting boundaries, one that invites interdisciplinary voyages. We must make the most of new possibilities of reading now open to us. Technological innovations enable us to call up all the cross-references, variants, and sketches related to a certain theme or character or to explore further all cultural references, including works of art—actually letting us see a painting or hear a piece of music mentioned in the text by clicking on a choice from an electronic menu. These resources make us realize that literary works are what Gabriele Schwab has called "imaginary ethnographies" that initiate us into other worlds and help us understand them (39).

Looking back at the diverse reactions to Proust's oeuvre and anticipating future readings, one may safely conclude that there is something in it for almost everyone. For this reason various schools of thought have used Proust's writings as a testing ground. A number of approaches that his work invites are presented in this volume; we hope that they will inspire students and teachers to develop their own interpretations.

Inge Crosman Wimmers

Part One

MATERIALS

Editions

French Editions

There are three defining moments in the editing of Proust's *A la recherche du temps perdu*: the first edition, between 1913 and 1927, which presented "le texte nu"; the first critical edition, prepared by Pierre Clarac and André Ferré for Gallimard's Bibliothèque de la Pléiade series in the 1950s; and the new editions in the late 1980s.

In their articles, scholars generally refer to the "new" Pléiade edition of *A la recherche du temps perdu* (under the general editorship of Jean-Yves Tadié, 1987–89), which includes many sketches (*esquisses*) from the manuscripts and useful indexes. But students and teachers usually prefer the inexpensive paperback editions that became available about the same time, after Proust's published work fell into the public domain. Today we have the choice of three versions of the text: the Garnier-Flammarion edition in ten volumes, directed by Jean Milly (1984–87); the Folio edition in eight volumes (1988–89); or the Livre de poche classique edition in seven volumes (1992–93), which takes into account Nathalie Mauriac's discovery of the shorter version of *Albertine disparue* in 1987. There are differences in the text of the novel, established, presented, and annotated by seasoned Proust scholars, who have studied his manuscripts at the Bibliothèque Nationale in Paris. Each editor has his or her own theoretical approach, but all of them offer a general literary preface, numerous historical notes, helpful "résumés," and detailed information about the critical reception of the work.

The complex publication history of *A la recherche du temps perdu* makes it difficult to recommend one edition over another without taking a clear stand on the question of the copy-text. To make an informed choice, it is necessay to keep in mind that, after a few "écrits de jeunesse" ("early works"), which appeared in *Le Mensuel*, *Le Banquet*, and *La Revue blanche*, Proust published in 1896 a collection of sketches and short stories entitled *Les Plaisirs et les jours*. Until 1900, he worked on a "novel," which was published posthumously by Pierre Clarac and André Ferré, in 1952, as *Jean Santeuil*. For the first time, the question of the authorization of the text arose. It would later fuel passionate critical debates. In these fragments—which Proust abandoned in order to translate two texts by John Ruskin, *La Bible d'Amiens* (*The Bible of Amiens*), published in 1904, and *Sésame et les lys* (*Sesame and Lilies*) published in 1906—there are indeed traces of what will become parts of *A la recherche du temps perdu* after 1908 (see Marc-Lipianski).

In between, Proust wrote articles, reviews, and pastiches. The essays in which he condemns the biographical approach favored by nineteenth-century French critics were collected and published posthumously in 1954 by Bernard de Fallois under the title *Contre Sainte-Beuve*. A very different version was published, under the same title, by Pierre Clarac in 1971. This type of textual reconstruction is now deemed problematic.

A *la recherche du temps perdu* slowly evolved from an initial "conversation avec maman" ("conversation with my mother") about literature and criticism—including Charles-Augustin Sainte-Beuve's theories (see Brun, *Nouvelle directions* 19). *Du côté de chez Swann* (*Swann's Way*) was finally published in November 1913 by the publisher Grasset, at the author's expense. It was supposed to be the first volume of a trilogy that would have included *Le Côté de Guermantes* and *Le Temps retrouvé*. But in 1914 the First World War broke out, and, the same year, a proposal from the Nouvelle Revue Française, combined with the accidental death of Proust's secretary, Alfred Agostinelli, had far-reaching consequences on the evolution of the novel. Proust kept expanding it (introducing the Albertine cycle and the development on Sodom and Gomorrah) to the point that Jacques Copeau exclaimed in despair, "Mais c'est un nouveau livre!" (*Corr.* 18: 226) ("But it is a new book!"; our trans.). And it was indeed. The projected second volume, *Le Côté de Guermantes* (*The Guermantes' Way*) was to be published as the third, with so many additions that it had to be divided into *Le Côté de Guermantes* 1 (1920) and *Le Côté de Guermantes* 2 (1921). It followed *A l'ombre des jeunes filles en fleurs* (*Within a Budding Grove*), which had won the Goncourt Prize in 1919; *Sodome et Gomorrhe* 1 was attached to *Le Côté de Guermantes* 2, then *Sodome et Gomorrhe* 2 (*Sodom and Gomorrah*) appeared separately in 1922. In November of that year, Proust died while correcting the proofs of what he called *Sodome et Gomorrhe* 3 / *La Prisonnière* (*The Captive*).

The remaining volumes of his novel were edited by his brother Robert Proust and by Jacques Rivière, the director of the Nouvelle Revue Française. In a letter to Gaston Gallimard, dated 3 July 1922, Proust had ruled out *La Fugitive* (*The Fugitive*) because a book by Rabindranath Tagore was about to be published in France under that very title (*Corr.* 21: 331). Proust's wishes—if not his latest corrections—were respected, and the volume appeared in 1925, under the title *Albertine disparue*. Pierre Clarac and André Ferré, the editors of the 1954 Pléiade edition, restored *La Fugitive* as a title but, having no access to other documents, followed Robert Proust's copy-text. In 1987, Nathalie Mauriac and Etienne Wolff published a shorter version of *Albertine disparue*, based on the typescript corrected by Marcel Proust himself, which was discovered in the papers of Suzy Mante-Proust, Proust's niece, after her death (see C. Mauriac 332).

The Livre de poche classique edition of *A la recherche du temps perdu* presents both versions edited by Nathalie Mauriac Dyer: the short one—favoring "une fin précipitée" (Mauriac Dyer 100) ("a hasty ending"; our trans.)—as the author left it after crossing out about 250 pages, under the title *Albertine disparue* / *Sodome et Gomorrhe* 4; and the long one, *La Fugitive* / Cahiers d'Albertine disparue. Because this edition is the most complete—and the cheapest—it is the most useful in the classroom. The Garnier-Flammarion edition, revised by Jean Milly in 2003, also provides both versions of *Albertine disparue*, with a horizontal line in the margin indicating the passages that Proust suppressed on the last typescript he corrected. Any edition can be combined with Germaine Brée's edition of "Combray," which many teachers have enjoyed using over the years because of the helpful English annotation of the French text. We do recommend, however, exposing students to *Swann's Way* in its integrality, as a first step toward appreciating the uniqueness of *A la recherche du temps perdu*.

English Translations

In September 1920, the *Atheneum* announced that "Messrs Chatto and Windus, as publishers, and Mr Scott-Moncrieff, as author, have almost ready the first installment of M. Marcel Proust's *Remembrance of Things Past* in the English translation. The title of his initial volume is *Swann's Way*" (see Carter, *Marcel Proust* 794). Proust, misinformed by his friend Sydney Schiff, who wanted to translate the *Recherche* himself, protested against what he perceived as "nonsense" and exchanged a few nasty letters on the subject with Gaston Gallimard and Charles Kenneth Scott-Moncrieff (see *Corr.* 21: 476, 499). And yet this first translation, using the second line of Shakespeare's sonnet 30, "remembrance of things past," as a title, would become the standard British English version of the *Recherche* for fifty years. The last volume, *Le Temps retrouvé*, was translated as *The Past Recaptured* by Frederick A. Blossom and as *Time Regained* by Stephen Hudson (the pseudonym of Sydney Schiff) after the death of Scott-Moncrieff in 1930. The whole text is based on the Nouvelle Revue Française (N. R. F.) edition of 1919–27 and is still perceived as a lyrical and inspired rendering of the Proustian text.

In 1981, Terence Kilmartin produced a "reworking, on the basis of the [1954] Pléiade edition of Scott Moncrieff's version of the first six sections of *A la recherche*—or the first eleven volumes of the twelve volume English edition" (Introduction x), incorporating Andreas Mayor's 1970 translation of *Le Temps retrouvé*. Kilmartin chose to keep the title *Remembrance of Things Past* for his three-volume edition published by Random House to remain faithful to Scott-Moncrieff's spirit. This translation was well received by the critics and widely used until the beginning of the 1990s.

In 1992, the Scott-Moncrieff and Kilmartin translation was rerevised by D. J. Enright and published, in 1993, as *In Search of Lost Time* by Random House. In a note, Enright, the editor and translator, explains that he "has taken into account the second Pléiade edition of *A la recherche du temps perdu* published in four volumes between 1987 and 1989 under the direction of Jean-Yves Tadié" (xx). He decided to stay closer to the original titles of the different volumes of the *Recherche*. For example, he preferred the more explicit *Sodom and Gomorrah* to the former *Cities of the Plain*. For practical reasons quotations in this volume are taken from this Modern Library paperback edition. But we encourage teachers to compare it with the new translation published under the supervision of Christopher Prendergast for the Penguin Press in 2003. They will note, for instance, that Lydia Davis chose *The Way by Swann's* as the title of the first volume and James Grieve *In the Shadow of Young Girls in Flower* for the second. Stimulating discussions have been generated by these differences, as well as by the decision to entrust the translation to a team rather than to a single translator (engdep1.philo.ulg.ac.be/download/2002-2003/proust/penguinproust.htm).

English translations of Proust's other writings are more or less readily available. *Les Plaisirs et les jours*, which was published in 1896 by Calmann-Lévy, with a preface by Anatole France, illustrations by Madeleine Lemaire, and music by Reynaldo Hahn, was translated into English by Louise Varese in 1948, under the title *Pleasures and Regrets*. *Jean Santeuil* was translated by Gerard Manley Hopkins and published by Simon and Schuster in 1956 (then reprinted by the Penguin Press in 1985). In the 1980s, three publications are noteworthy: *On Art and Literature, 1896–1903*, translated by Sylvia Townsend Warner; *On Reading Ruskin*, translated and edited by Jean Autret; and *Against Sainte-Beuve and Other Essays*, translated and edited by James Sturrock.

The first four volumes of the *Correspondance de Marcel Proust*, edited in French by Philip Kolb, are available in English under the title *Selected Letters* (1983–2000). It is an indispensable tool for teachers, students, and scholars alike.

NOTE

Except where stated otherwise, quotations from *A la recherche du temps perdu* in this volume are taken from the new Pléiade edition (gen. ed. Tadié. Gallimard, 1987–89). Quotations from *In Search of Lost Time* are taken from the Modern Library paperback (rev. and ed. Enright).

Quotations from Proust's correspondence are taken from *Correspondance de Marcel Proust* (*Corr.*; ed. Kolb); their English translation, when it exists, is taken from *Selected Letters* (ed. Kolb). Unless stated otherwise, quotations from *Contre Sainte-Beuve* are from Clarac and Sandre's edition.

Bibliography of Works by Proust

A la recherche du temps perdu

In French

First editions
>   Du côté de chez Swann. Paris: Grasset, 1913.
>   A la recherche du temps perdu. 13 vols. Paris: N. R. F., 1918–27.

Critical editions of the Recherche

>Bibliothèque de la Pléiade. Ed. Pierre Clarac and André Ferré. Pref. André Maurois. 3 vols. Paris: Gallimard, 1954.
>
>Bibliothèque de la Pléiade. Ed. Jean-Yves Tadié. 4 vols. Paris: Gallimard, 1987–89.

Paperback editions of the Recherche

>Le Livre de poche. 8 vols. Paris: Hachette, 1965–68.
>
>Folio. Paris: Gallimard, 1972. (Same text as 1954 Pléiade ed.)
>
>G-F. Ed. Jean Milly, with an introd., notes, and bibliog. 10 vols. Paris: Flammarion, 1984–87.
>
>Bouquins. Ed. Bernard Raffalli. 3 vols. Paris: Laffont, 1987.
>
>Folio. 8 vols. Paris: Gallimard, 1988–89. (Same text as the 1987–89 new Pléiade ed.)
>
>Le Livre de poche classique. 7 vols. Paris: Hachette, 1992–93. Rev., with *Albertine disparue / La Fugitive*, ed. Nathalie Mauriac.
>
>Quarto. Paris: Gallimard, 1999. (Same text as the 1987–89 new Pléiade ed., without the *esquisses* [sketches] and editorial notes.)

In English

Swann's Way. Trans. C. K. Scott-Moncrieff. London: Chatto; New York: Holt, 1922. *Time Regained*. Trans. Stephen Hudson [Sydney Schiff]. London: Chatto, 1931. *The Past Recaptured*. Trans. Frederick A. Blossom. New York: Boni, 1932.

Remembrance of Things Past. Trans. C. K. Scott-Moncrieff and Terence Kilmartin. 3 vols. New York: Random, 1981. (Based on the 1954 Pléiade edition.)

In Search of Lost Time. Trans., rev. D. J. Enright. 6 vols. London: Vintage, 1992; New York: Mod. Lib., 1993, diff. pag. (Based on the new Pléiade edition.)

In Search of Lost Time. Gen. ed. C. Prendergast. London: Penguin, 2003.

Partial Editions with English Annotations

Combray. Ed. Germaine Brée. New York: Prentice, 1952.

Un Amour de Swann. Ed. William S. Bell. New York: Macmillan, 1965.

Early Drafts

Alden, Douglas, ed. *Marcel Proust's Grasset Proofs: Commentary and Variants.* Chapel Hill: U of North Carolina Dept. of Romance Lang., 1978.

Bales, Richard, ed. *Bricquebec: Prototype d' "A l'ombre des jeunes filles en fleurs."* Oxford: Clarendon, 1989.

Bonnet, Henri, and Bernard Brun, eds. *Matinée chez la Princesse de Guermantes.* Paris: Gallimard, 1982.

Winton [Finch], Alison. *Proust's Additions: The Making of* A la recherche du temps perdu. New York: Cambridge UP, 1977.

Correspondence

In French

Correspondance de Marcel Proust. Ed. Philip Kolb. 21 vols. Paris: Plon, 1970-93.

In English

Selected Letters. Vol. 1, 1880–1908. Ed. Philip Kolb. Trans. Ralph Manheim. Garden City: Doubleday, 1983. Vol. 2, 1904–09. Trans. Terence Kilmartin. London: Collins, 1989. Vol. 3, 1905–17. Trans. Terence Kilmartin. New York: Harper, 1992. Vol. 4, 1918–22. Trans. Joanna Kilmartin. New York: Harper, 2000.

Other Works by Proust

In French

First editions of Proust's literary criticism
  Les Plaisirs et les jours. Pref. Anatole France, illus. Madeleine Lemaire, and music pieces by Reynaldo Hahn. Paris: Calmann, 1896.
  Pastiches et mélanges. Paris: N. R. F., 1919.

Proust's translations of John Ruskin
  La Bible d'Amiens. Paris: Mercure, 1904.
  Sésame et les lys. Paris: Mercure, 1906. Ed. Antoine Compagnon. Brussels: Complexe, 1987.

Posthumous works
  Chroniques. Paris: N. R. F., 1927.
  Jean Santeuil. Ed. Bernard de Fallois. Pref. André Maurois. Paris: Gallimard, 1952.
  Contre Sainte-Beuve; suivi de *Nouveaux melanges.* Ed. Bernard de Fallois. Paris: Gallimard, 1954.

Critical editions
  Jean Santeuil. *Précédé de* Les Plaisirs et les jours. Ed. Pierre Clarac and Yves Sandre. Bibliothèque de la Pléiade 228. Paris: Gallimard, 1971.
  Contre Sainte-Beuve. *Précédé de* Pastiches et mélanges, *et suivi de* Essais et articles. Ed. Pierre Clarac and Yves Sandre. Bibliothèque de la Pléiade 229. Paris: Gallimard, 1971.

Textes retrouvés. Ed. Philip Kolb. Paris: Gallimard, 1971.
Le Carnet de 1908. Ed. Philip Kolb. Paris: Gallimard, 1976.
L'Indifférent. Ed. Philip Kolb. Paris: Gallimard, 1978. Rpt. from *La Vie contemporaine*, March 1896.
Ecrits de jeunesse. Paris: Institut Marcel Proust, 1991.
Carnets. Ed. Florence Callu and Antoine Compagnon. Paris: Gallimard, 2002.

In English

Pleasures and Regrets. Trans. Louise Varese. New York: Crown, 1948.
On Art and Literature, 1896-1903. Trans. S. T. Warner. New York: Carroll, 1984.
Jean Santeuil. Trans. Gerard Hopkins. New York: Simon and Schuster, 1956; Harmondsworth: Penguin, 1985.
On Reading Ruskin. Trans. and ed. Jean Autret. New Haven: Yale UP, 1987.
Against Sainte-Beuve *and Other Essays.* Trans. and ed. J. Sturrock. Harmondsworth: Penguin, 1988.

The Instructor's Library

All the contributors to this collection provided ample bibliographic data with their essays, and most of them felt it was not easy to choose among the overwhelming scholarship on Proust's fiction and criticism. The long list of works cited at the end of the volume reflects their desire to be as exhaustive as possible. As editors, we were confronted with the same problem, and to provide the most objective help to instructors in search of resources, we have chosen to offer a selected guide to biographical, bibliographic, background, and critical materials. Our introduction also discusses a number of important studies of Proust.

Two biographies were recently published, making George Duncan Painter's 1959 *Marcel Proust* somewhat outdated, although it was a groundbreaking study at the time and still remains a good source of basic information on Proust's life. William Carter's detailed *Marcel Proust* provides everything a reader needs to know about Proust's physical and emotional state "au jour le jour," as well as original insights about his family, entourage, and writing habits. Written in an elegant style, it never confuses Marcel the narrator with Proust the author and draws extensively from the correspondence and primary sources. The notes and the index are impeccable. Jean-Yves Tadié's *Marcel Proust* is more academic in tone and contains an excellent bibliography of previous biographical studies (see *Marcel Proust: A Biography* for the translation). Of interest also is Edmund White's interpretive biographical volume *Marcel Proust*.

Among general bibliographic works we found the following titles particularly helpful: Henri Bonnet, *Marcel Proust de 1907 à 1914*, with a general bibliography; Victor Graham, *Bibliographie des études sur Marcel Proust et son œuvre*; Douglas W. Alden, "Marcel Proust"; René Rancœur, "Bibliographie de Marcel Proust"; Janet C. Stock, *Marcel Proust: A Reference Guide, 1950–1970*; Annick Bouillaguet, *Marcel Proust: bilan critique*; Kazuyoshi Yoshikawa, *Index général de la* Correspondance de Marcel Proust.

We also recommend several collections of essays: René Girard, *Proust: A Collection of Critical Essays*; Jean-Yves Tadié, *Lectures de Proust*; John Cocking, *Proust: Collected Essays on the Writer and His Art*; Barbara Bucknall, *Critical Essays on Marcel Proust*; William C. Carter, *The UAB Marcel Proust Symposium*; Mary Ann Caws and Eugène Nicole, *Reading Proust Now*; Richard Bales, *The Cambridge Companion to Proust*; Armine Mortimer and Katherine Kolb, *Proust in Perspective: Visions and Revisions*.

Helpful tools to accompany the reading of the *Recherche* are Jacques Nathan, *Citations, références et allusions dans* A la recherche du temps perdu; Pauline Newman, *Dictionnaire des idées dans l'œuvre de Marcel Proust*; Maxine A. Vogely, *A Proust Dictionary*; Etienne Brunet, *Le Vocabulaire de Proust*; Terence Kilmartin, *A Reader's Guide to* Remembrance of Things Past.

Worth mentioning among the many reviews, journals, and periodicals that devoted an issue to Proust in 1971, the hundredth anniversary of Proust's birth, are *Europe* (Feb.–Mar.); *Adam International Review* (nos. 349–51); *L'Esprit créateur* (Spring); *Les Nouvelles Littéraires* (June); and *Revue d'histoire littéraire de la France* (Fall). In November 2000, *Le Magazine littéraire* published an up-to-date special issue on Proust.

Two annual journals, the *Bulletin de la Société des Amis de Marcel Proust* and the *Bulletin d'informations proustiennes* (BIP), publish highly specialized studies, as does *Cahiers Marcel Proust*. This irregular journal has published eighteen volumes since 1921, which include *Etudes proustiennes 1–6*, and has been published by Gallimard since 1973.

Dictionnaire Marcel Proust, edited by Annick Bouillaguet and Brian Rogers, is forthcoming in 2004 from Champion.

Aids to Teaching

Audiovisual Materials

The media resources for teaching Proust are rich and varied and lend themselves to the supplementation of different kinds of courses. Among them are Heuet's comic book version of several parts of Proust's novel and two CD-ROMS—one entitled *Proust: Œuvres romanesques complètes*, the other, *Marcel Proust: une découverte multimedia de l'œuvre de Marcel Proust*, created in conjunction with a major Proust exhibition, "Proust l'écriture et les arts" (Tadié) held at the Bibliothèque Nationale de France from 9 November 1999 to 6 February 2000. The CD produced for the exhibit offers many resources, including background information on Proust and his times; informative short essays; a bibliography; interviews (which may simply be read or actually listened to while viewing the person speaking); paintings and music related to Proust; and information on people, places, characters, and themes that students may access through an intricate network of cross-references. To complement this CD-ROM, the exhibition catalog, prepared by Tadié and Florence Callu, for the Bibliothèque Nationale de France in conjunction with the Musée d'Orsay, is a useful tool, since it includes excellent reproductions and informative articles. In addition, a small "cahier pédagogique," prepared by Catherine Lefrançois-Tourret and Denis Gombert, also contains some reproductions and offers pedagogical guidelines for further projects.

Equally useful are a number of documentaries devoted to Proust's life and works. One of the most stimulating is *Marcel Proust: A Writer's Life* (60 min.), which presents interviews with Iris Murdoch, Shelby Foote, and Roger Shattuck, as well as archival footage of some of Proust's contemporaries, including Jean Cocteau, François Mauriac, and Céleste Albaret. More archival interviews appear in a 1962 black-and-white film, *Portrait souvenir: Marcel Proust*, produced by Roger Stéphane and Roland Darbois. Besides Albaret, Cocteau, and Mauriac, the interviewees include Emmanuel Berl, Daniel Halévy, le duc de Gramont, Jacques de Lacretelle, le marquis de Lauris, Mme André Maurois, M. et Mme Paul Morand, and Philippe Soupault. The series Ten Great Writers of the Modern World includes a video on Proust under the title *Marcel Proust: Remembrance of Things Past*—with a dramatization of the "Matinée Guermantes" and interpretive comments by Michel Butor and Terence Kilmartin (60 min.). Also of interest is a program, prepared by BBC Enterprises, entitled *102, Boulevard Haussmann*; written by Alan Bennett, directed by Udayan Prasad, and produced by Innes Lloyd, it features Alan Bates as Marcel Proust. Another excellent program, *Proust vivant: Marcel Proust du côté des lecteurs* was produced by French and German television in September 2000; it consists of interviews, conducted by Thierry Thomas, with twelve readers from various walks of life (among them a taxi driver, a painter, a scientist, an actress, a composer, and Proust's great grandniece), all talking about the impact of Proust's novel on their lives.

Dramatizations and adaptations also enhance the teaching of Proust. *Céleste* by Percy Adlon gives viewers intimate insight into what it must have been like to live and work in Proust's household. It captures, moreover, the Proustian atmosphere of the novel with its attention to detail, light, sound, and movement. *Un Amour de Swann* (*Swann in Love*), by Volker Schlöndorff, focuses primarily on that part of the novel though the film draws on other parts of *A la recherche du temps perdu* to shed light on later aspects of Swann's life. Two more recent films, *Le Temps retrouvé* (*Time Regained*), directed by Raoul Ruiz, and *La Captive* (*The Captive*), directed by Chantal Akerman, lend themselves particularly well to the teaching of Proust (see Rebecca Graves's essay "Proust and the Cinema," in this volume). In addition to films, a recent adaptation for the theater by Harold Pinter and Di Trevis, *Remembrance of Things Past*, which opened at London's Cottesloe Theatre on 23 November 2000, is now available in print. Pinter's earlier *The Proust Screenplay* is still in print. This version and some of the films mentioned above are discussed by Roger Shattuck in the chapter "Filming the Unfilmable" (*Proust's Way* 192–206).

As of 2001, Proust's masterpiece is available on 36 CDs or audiocassettes, issued by Naxos AudioBooks.

Proust Online

For pedagogical purposes, the Kolb-Proust Archive (www.library.uiuc.edu) is one of the most useful resources, giving general information on Proust, a selected bibliography to Proust studies, an inventory of the Proust letters, the Proust questionnaire, and links to other Proust sites (see Virginie Greene and Caroline Szylowicz's essay on the Kolb-Proust Archive in this volume).

For general access to the Proust collection at the Bibliothèque Nationale de France, the following Web site is very useful: gallica.bnf.fr/proust/FondsProust. htm. Gallica is also an excellent source for images and texts in French from the nineteenth century and for accessing materials (including paintings, illustrations, and the like) to accompany the reading and teaching of Proust.

The Proust manuscripts can be consulted online through the Bibliothèque Nationale and the Institut des Textes et Manuscrits Modernes (www.item. ens.fr/proust.html; see Bernard Brun in this volume). Parts of the novel will soon be available online; the text of *Le Temps retrouvé* (the manuscript version and its transcription) may be accessed through gallica.bnf.fr/proust/manuscrit. htm.

For an Internet link to the Société des Amis de Marcel Proust et des Amis de Combray (where one can obtain information on the society's activities, the maison de Tante Léonie, the Institut Marcel Proust International, and the *Bulletin Marcel Proust*), use the following address: www.alma-inter.fr/proust/.

Any of the major search engines (Alta Vista, Google, Yahoo) can provide information on Proust and Proust-related items and activities. An online connection to *Proust Said That*—an English-language electronic magazine written for and by Proust amateurs and enthusiasts—may be reached through the Kolb-Proust Archive.

Frantext contains 3,500 French texts from the sixteenth to the twentieth centuries, including the 1954 Pléiade edition of *A la recherche du temps perdu* (subscription required).

For access to dictionaries, a CD-ROM is now available, "L'Atelier historique de la langue française," which includes seven of the most prestigious dictionaries, among them *Le Dictionnaire Littré*, *Le Dictionnaire de l'Académie Française*, and *Le Dictionnaire de La Curne*. The Project for American and

French Research on the Treasury of the French Language is another excellent resource: humanities.uchicago.edu/orgs/ARTFL.

Chris Taylor's *Marcel Proust: Ephemera Site*, described as "an informal site dedicated to publishing English translations of Marcel Proust's lesser known writings," is a useful service for those who do not know French (www.yorktaylors.free-online.co.uk).

Other Internet sites with substantial resources on Proust include the following: www.tempsperdu.com (exclusively devoted to Proust, includes a chronology of the novel; lists of characters; links to critical works, reviews, study guides, and to many other relevant sites); www.julesferry.com/biblio.html (for access to electronic texts of *Du côté de chez Swann* and *Les Plaisirs et les jours*); www.promo.net/pg (for access to Project Gutenberg, including electronic texts of *Du côté de chez Swann* and *A l'ombre des jeunes filles en fleurs*); and www.diplomatie.gouv.fr (searching keyword "Proust" provides access to cultural pages of the French Ministry of Foreign Affairs, with links to many literary resources).

Proust at the Institut des Textes et Manuscrits Modernes

Bernard Brun

Those manuscripts of Marcel Proust that are not found in private collections are preserved in the department of manuscripts of the Bibliothèque Nationale de France (BNF). They are no longer accessible to the public but can be consulted in microfilm format (http://gallica.bnf.fr/Proust.html).

The correspondence that is not held in private collections is preserved, along with other documents, in the Rare Book and Special Collections Library of the University of Illinois, Urbana. The inventory can be consulted at the Web site: www.library.uiuc.edu/rbx (databases: Proust).

These two institutions work in collaboration with the Proust team of the Institut des Textes et Manuscrits Modernes (ITEM) of the Centre National de la Recherche Scientifique housed in the Ecole Normale Supérieure (ENS) in Paris. The institute's Web site is http.www.item.ens.fr/proust.html.

The mission of the Proust team is to process the BNF's Proust collection and, more specifically, the documents connected with the writing of *A la recherche du temps perdu* (loose leaves, notebooks containing notes and drafts, typescripts, proofs, original editions). The team's computerized inventories of materials and their contents have made it possible to use a classification scheme that differs from the thematic or simply narrative system imposed by the BNF catalog. The invention of a standardized system of transcription and the collection, correction, and computerization of existing transcriptions have made it possible to publish previously unpublished material. *Matinée chez la Princesse de Guermantes,* an early version of the *Recherche*, came out in 1982; the *Cahiers Marcel Proust* (Gallimard) published a number of works between 1974 and 1987; and many new editions of the novel (G-F Flammarion, Bibliothèque de la Pléiade, Folio Bouquins, Livre de poche classique) are available.

The Proust team's documentation center has for years opened its doors to students, researchers, and scholars, both French and foreign, who wish to work on Proust's manuscripts and, more generally, on textual genesis. The center contains microfilms of manuscripts held at the BNF, inventories, and transcriptions in digitized form or hard copy. It is also endowed with another collection of microfilms, the French literary journals contemporary to Marcel Proust (1872–1915). The specialized library brings together monographs, theses, periodicals, and offprints on the problems of textual genesis and works closely with the extremely rich holdings of the library of the ENS, including, for example, most of the works that Marcel Proust was likely to have read, between 1880 and 1920, in original editions. Computerized files make it possible to find one's way easily in these collections and in the team's various projects, which include digitized transcriptions, the reconstitution of Marcel Proust's library, and a dictionary of quotations.

Various publications have resulted from the work of the Proust team, and two periodicals in particular present the team's findings: the *Bulletin d'informations proustiennes* (which has published 33 issues since 1975) and the *Sêrie Marcel Proust* (lettres *Modernes Minard*), which has published three issues since 1992.

The team, made up of two researchers (Bernard Brun and Nathalie Mauriac Dyer) and of temporary staff, is affiliated with the Universities of Paris III, Paris IV, Paris VII, and Marne-la-Vallée and participates in the activities of the Société des Amis de Marcel Proust (based in Illiers-Combray, France).

Genetic Approaches to Proust's Manuscripts

Nathalie Mauriac Dyer

Although research, not teaching, is the core mission of the Centre National de la Recherche Scientifique (CNRS), the thirty-year-old Proust program of the Institut des Textes et Manuscrits Modernes (ITEM) has become an important resource for Proust scholars. In a small room on the fourth floor at the Ecole Normale Supérieure, researchers from France, the United States, Japan, Italy, Switzerland, the United Kingdom, Germany, and other countries have access to a unique array of resources and tools: all the available editions of Proust's works; the complete *Correspondance*, edited by Philip Kolb; a substantial research library of specialized and often hard-to-find critical essays, periodicals, articles, and dissertations; the complete microfilmed collection of Proust's manuscripts (whose originals are housed at the Bibliothèque Nationale de France); the copyrighted inventory of the seventy-five *cahiers* (or notebooks) of *A la recherche du temps perdu*, an inventory recently completed in cooperation with the University of Paris III that allows the quick search of a theme or character—an invaluable help in navigating the *Recherche*'s complex web of writing. Everyone is welcome to participate in the Proust program's two seminars held each month. The first, through a series of lectures given by professors and doctoral and postdoctoral students, is focused on an annual theme. Recent themes have included intertextuality; *Sodome and Gomorrhe*, and the state of Proust's genetic studies. The other, led by the CNRS researchers Bernard Brun and me, is more specifically related to the scientific mission of ITEM and CNRS programs: the reading, classifying, and interpreting of the manuscripts of *A la recherche du temps perdu*. Brun, who has been responsible for the ITEM Proust program since the death of its cocreator, Claudine Quémar, in the late 1970s, edits the annual *Bulletin d'informations proustiennes*, which publishes current research on Proust, emphasizing the genetic approach but reflecting the work done in both seminars.

The corpus of *esquisses* (sketches and drafts) that Jean-Yves Tadié's new Pléiade edition of *A la recherche du temps perdu* presents at the end of each of its four volumes introduces the reader to the vast scope of Proust's preparatory work for his novel as "cathedral" (4: 610). Some have criticized the new Pléiade edition for submerging Proust's text and aesthetic achievement under a welter of manuscripts. Yet the manuscript material is far more complex than the *esquisses* suggest: the seventy-five notebooks are not conveniently divided into narrative units that correspond to sequences of the definitive text or that show the writer had been methodically working according to a single, fixed plan. Nor are they as homogenous in form and content as they might seem to be, because the new Pléiade editors have chosen to remove all traces of the writing process: crossed-out passages, marginal comments or developments, duplicated versions, and the like. Finally, the *esquisses* give only extracts from representative folios chosen out of several thousands. Therefore, the researchers who use the Pléiade *esquisses* to validate or invalidate some critical stand, be it thematic, stylistic, psychoanalytic, or other, ought to keep in mind that they are dealing with only partial textual evidence. It is always a good idea to go back to the original manuscript material, which ITEM (under the aegis of the Bibliothèque Nationale de France, the copyright holder) is always ready to provide to scholars. Thus they will discover, for any chosen passage, not just the variant readings but the passage's immediate narrative context and, if they exist, any unpublished revisions Proust made.

Since 1997, the Proust team at ITEM has begun the task of gathering, harmonizing, reviewing, and digitizing the already impressive number of available, if scattered, transcriptions: Cahiers 28, 59, 60, 61, 62, 71, and 75 have already been made available in either diplomatic or semidiplomatic form for the use of scholars (thanks to the work of Guilherme Da Silva, Francine Goujon, participants of the seminars, and me). Although this material can form the basis of various assignments at the undergraduate level, the transcription and commentary of a cahier or group of cahiers constitute an appropriate dissertation topic. Students who have to master the philological approach and expertise that lead to a valid critical edition also discover, hands-on, what genetic criticism is really about in Proust studies. What becomes of reading and interpreting a literary text when one is faced with its multidimensional strata? Any transcription of a given cahier has to take into account the genetic dimension of its previous and future versions, as most cahiers are only transitional stages, the result of or basis for transferring, copying, developing, and reorganizing material.

For instance, the first part of Cahier 71 (1913) is partly made up of narrative elements borrowed from Cahier 64 (1910–11). These elements will in turn be absorbed in Cahier 46 (1914), whereas further developments in Cahier 71 will later feed the writing of Cahiers 55 and 53 (1914–15). Since Cahier 53 itself owes a lot to Cahier 50 (1910–11), one can see how, put together, Proust's cahiers constitute a mute hypertext, whose links await critical emphasis to retrace the writer's creative gestures. Only a collective effort of transcription can achieve a complete representation of Proust's written web. The collected "avant text" of *A la recherche du temps perdu* would be an impressive ensemble, which could be approached quite independently from any supposed definitive text, as a labyrinth of evolving aesthetic formations; an avant text would invite nonlinear readings, which would help formulate the stages of the (paradigmatic or syntagmatic) process of creating a textual collage. If the rules for such genetic criticism are yet to be written, students today can join in helping scholars write them.

The prospect of describing the vast substrata of *A la recherche du temps perdu* may seem a distant dream, but it is important to make clear to students some of the basic yet challenging facts of the text's history. If we exclude the seminal and formative years when Proust was writing *Jean Santeuil* (1895–99) and translating Ruskin (1900–06), the *Recherche* is a work whose genesis extended over a period of at least fourteen years (1908–22) and never reached its conclusion. The author delivered completed and definitive parts of his novel— in 1913, 1918, 1920, 1921, and 1922—while other parts were still in progress and were sometimes undergoing major changes. *A la recherche du temps perdu* is a text that never fully knows how it will get where it is going (even if it knows it is going to *Le Temps retrouvé*, for Proust kept claiming he had written the last chapter of his book at the same time as the first), a text that our reader's eye only retrospectively, and in part mistakenly, sees in the mythical, unified framework of "l'œuvre." In the years of the First World War that interrupted the publication of *A la recherche du temps perdu* after its first volume, the novel blossomed from the three volumes planned (*Du côté de chez Swann, Le Côté de Guermantes, Le Temps retrouvé*) to five volumes published (*Du côté de chez Swann, A l'ombre des jeunes filles en fleurs, Le Côté de Guermantes 1, Le Côté de Guermantes 2 / Sodome et Gomorrhe 1, Sodome et Go-*

morrhe 2), which introduced new characters and episodes and resulted in un-avoidable aesthetic and stylistic discrepancies between its prewar and postwar parts. The scope of this narrative development, somewhat unforeseen by the writer himself, adds an enigmatic dimension to the play of echoes among volumes so characteristic of Proust's art: some hints in *Du côté de chez Swann,* for instance, may have been originally intended to prefigure episodes that, through later stages of the genesis of the text, would take a different form.

Curiously enough, with the untimely death of Proust in 1922 in the middle of the revision of *Sodome et Gomorrhe* 3, the first posthumous editors introduced a new twist in genetic chronology. Because the drastic alterations imposed by Proust in 1922 on the version of his 1916–17 manuscript hindered all publication of the following volumes of *Sodome et Gomorrhe* and of *Le Temps retrouvé,* editors ignored them (see the edition of *Albertine disparue* published by Grasset in 1987). Rather than let the *Recherche* appear unfinished, they published the earlier uncorrected 1916–17 version (under the titles *Albertine disparue* and *Le Temps retrouvé*). As a result, *A la recherche du temps perdu* today looks like a puzzle of temporalities, a sort of monster, intertwining different stages of development in eight volumes: a prewar volume, followed five to nine years later by four postwar volumes, followed by three wartime volumes (*La Prisonnière, Albertine disparue, Le Temps retrouvé*), as if the form of the work happened to mimic its circular structure. These accidents of publication, whether they be due to history, personal contingencies, or the mysteries of creation, forbid us to view Proust's masterpiece as a unified work: even if all the cahiers had disappeared or had been destroyed, the genetic dimension of *A la recherche du temps perdu* would remain key to an informed reading of it. The genetic approach constitutes the critical basis from which to ponder anew the recurrent question of the novel's aesthetic form.

The Kolb-Proust Archive for Research

Virginie Greene and Caroline Szylowicz

The Kolb-Proust Archive for Research was established in 1993 at the Library of the University of Illinois, Urbana (www.library.uiuc.edu/kolbp). Its main goal is to make available to researchers and students the documents and data gathered by Philip Kolb during more than fifty years of work devoted to editing Marcel Proust's correspondence. This goal involves both preserving physical documents and digitizing information to create an extensive and interactive online research tool.

The physical archive contains Philip Kolb's original collection of research materials: different editions of Proust's works; memoirs, biographies, and directories relevant to Proust and his time (e.g., *Almanach de Gotha,* Edmond de Goncourt and Jules de Goncourt's *Journal*); the most important French newspapers and journals from the 1870s to the 1920s (often in microfilm form); birth, death, and marriage certificates of some of Proust's correspondents; and photocopies and transcriptions of letters by and to Proust, sorted by correspondent.

This collection continues to grow with the addition of newly published works relevant to the activity of the archive. In addition, the library maintains an extensive collection of Proustiana through systematic acquisitions. Original autograph letters by and to Proust, manuscript fragments, and rare editions are housed in the Rare Book and Special Collections Library.

At the heart of the collection lies Kolb's life work: forty thousand handwritten index cards on which he recorded information he found in the letters of Proust and in many other sources and which he used to annotate Proust's correspondence. The cards include a chronology of Proust's life and contemporary events, a biobibliography of real and fictitious people mentioned in the correspondence, a bibliography of Proust's writings and of criticism published on his works during his lifetime, a file of literary citations, a file of places mentioned in the correspondence, and a detailed chronological index to the correspondence. Parts of the card files are already available on the Kolb-Proust Archive's Web site.

How can students and teachers use the archive? Because of space and staff constraints, visits to the Kolb-Proust Archive can only be made by appointment, but researchers and students are welcome. The Proustiana collection is available to the library patrons in the same way as any other library items. Original manuscripts and rare editions are submitted to the policies of the rare book room. Loan and photocopy requests can be handled through the library's interlibrary loan service. However, copyright restrictions may apply to some materials. The Web site, being freely accessible, is probably the most useful resource for beginners and nonspecialists.

From the comments and queries sent to the archive during the last four years, it appears that students use its Web site for three main purposes: to learn basic things about Marcel Proust's life and work, to find bibliographic information on primary or secondary materials, and to find how to have access to Proust's works online (which is easy enough) or to sources or criticism online (which is generally not possible). The archive, because of its nature and history, lends itself best to exercises or research oriented toward historicized and contextualized readings of Proust. The archive resources could certainly be used for creating course activities on themes such as Proust and the Dreyfus affair, Proust and *Le Figaro*, Proust and the stock market, Proust and new technologies (i.e., telephone, car, airplane, bicycle). Far from encouraging students to surf instead of read and to seek precooked packages of knowledge instead of think critically, the archive may help them to realize the difference between a document and a reference to a document, an original and a copy, a text and its glosses. Most of the students who visited the Web site had read the *Recherche*, at least partially, and liked it. This should reassure us of the possibilities of teaching Proust today and tomorrow.

Part Two

APPROACHES

Introduction

Respondents answering the MLA survey about teaching Proust's fiction and criticism pointed out that they needed to contextualize *A la recherche du temps perdu* to stimulate their students' interest in cultural issues as well as in more traditional thematic and stylistic questions. They deplored that only excerpts—and often the same excerpts—were taught in the classroom, without reference to Proust's other works, and they stressed the importance of linking the *Recherche* to his earlier writings, such as *Les Plaisirs et les jours* or *Jean Santeuil*, and to his lesser-known articles, pastiches, and essays. Agreeing that Proust can be approached from numerous and sometimes conflicting perspectives, they indicated that they would like to have a collection of essays providing them with a variety of current interpretations and pedagogical techniques. An enthusiasm for transmitting the joy of reading and teaching Proust constitutes the common thread linking the contributions in this volume. We hope that enthusiasm will be shared by many.

As time passes, it is more and more essential to give an overview of the historical events and cultural currents that surrounded the birth of *A la recherche du temps perdu* and thus to allow the reader to grasp its full sociocultural significance and exquisite complexity. This goal is what the first section of part 2, "Contexts," is meant to help teachers achieve. In "Proust: A Man of His Times," William C. Carter questions the myth of Proust the recluse to show how deeply Proust was involved in the social life of the belle époque, how attentive he was to technological progress, and how much he integrated what he saw and whom he met into the fabric of his novel. Without ignoring the incapacitating illness that plagued him all his life, Carter gives us the portrait of a man in full, an original artist who was still very much a product of his time.

At the turn of the century, the Dreyfus affair had a dramatic and lasting influence on French politics and social relations in general. Joseph Brami explains that it also defines the way in which the narrator of *A la recherche du temps perdu* sees himself and others. He explores the impact of anti-Semitism on salon life and private relationships and convincingly ties the narrator's vocation to the question of Jewish identity.

Just as important for the development of *A la recherche du temps perdu* is the First World War. In "Cataclysm at One Remove," Edward J. Hughes sheds light on Proust's strategies of representation, analyzing in depth the metaphors of upheaval and dislocation asssociated with the war. Contrasting Charlus's degradation with Saint-Loup's heroism, examining the butler's manipulation of Françoise through the vocabulary of conquest, defeat, and humiliation, Hughes concludes that social class is a key issue in the pages dealing with the war.

Most of the *Recherche* was written between those two historical events, the Dreyfus affair and the First World War, and the book tells the story of a narrator involved in both. It was a time of drastic changes on the political scene, and "Proust was not indifferent to politics" (Lewis 126). Does he "present his theory of art as a response to the nationalism of Maurice Barrès" (Lewis 128)? Proust participated in the heated debate about the separation of church and state by publishing an article entitled "La Mort des cathédrales" in *Le Figaro* of 16 August 1904. He also kept informed about rapidly changing trends in the arts, as his correspondence clearly suggests. Emphasizing his debt to John Ruskin and William Morris, Françoise Leriche argues that Proust's aesthetics are closer to the movement of art nouveau, characterized by arabesques, fluidity, and repetition, than to the impressionistic rendition of reality that was fashionable at the beginning of the twentieth century or to the cubist school that was to prevail in painting after the First World War.

References to paintings, in particular Botticelli's and Carpaccio's, are woven into the *Recherche* to demonstrate the opposing nature of love and art. But the references' main function, according to Kazuyoshi Yoshikawa, is to support a theoretical framework, which Proust elaborated over the years as he studied Ruskin's reproductions of art works. In the same way, Proust uses Jan Vermeer's *View of Delft*, praised by the critic Jean-Louis Vaudoyer in 1921, in a quintessential moment of confrontation between art and life, when the fictitious novelist Bergotte dies in *La Prisonnière*.

In "Seeing Proust Seeing," Mary Ann Caws broadens the perspective and stresses the interdisciplinarity that is at the core of *A la recherche du temps perdu*. Not only painting but also the worlds of music, dance, ballet, opera, and fashion are conjured up by Proust to create a complete work of art. The novel can be read as a perfect repertoire of what was in and what was out in the visual arts, in Paris, at the time.

Proust is definitely in today, and Margaret E. Gray puts him in a postmodern perspective. Stressing the importance of vision, she proposes "a systematic postmodern road map" and humorously debunks the clichés about the bad reputation of the Proustian text. She gives astute clues on how to use cartoons, self-help books, and movies—along with theory—to help students swallow the madeleine.

Proust was not only a man of his times but a writer for all time. His work lends itself to diverse critical approaches, as the next section, "Interpretive Perspectives," emphasizes. The first three essays focus on aspects of the novel that get at the heart of its aesthetics. In "Coding and Decoding: Names in the *Recherche*," Eugène Nicole studies various aspects of the nature and function of names, including etymologies, their linguistic and cultural motivation and their role in the hero's apprenticeship and in the novel's overall design. That reading plays a central role in Proust's novel and criticism is well documented in Pascal A. Ifri's essay, "A Lesson in Reading: From *Contre Sainte-Beuve* to the *Recherche*." Through the hero-narrator's careful readings of novels, art, and music, students are initiated into both the fictional universe and the poetics of the novel. The insight afforded us through a close look at the workings of involuntary memory is crucial. Geneviève Henrot's essay, "In Search of Hidden Impressions," examines specific instances of stylistic and structural manifestations of involuntary memory in the *Recherche* and shows how they shed light on the complex relation between psychological laws and their textual representation. In doing so, Henrot uncovers a pattern of occultation and revelation.

Intertextuality is an important feature of Proust's novel: the hero is repeatedly exposed to works of art (literature, music, painting), and the narrator, in telling his story, frequently introduces artistic references. In "Proust's Esther," Emily Eells discusses various references in the novel to the biblical story of Esther—references that include the Old Testament, Racine's dramatization of the story, the tapestries in the Sens cathedral, a painting by Francken the Younger, and music by Reynaldo Hahn. The intertextual play between Proust's novel and works of narrative fiction is equally revealing. In "Intertextual Pedagogy: Proust and Flaubert," Mireille Naturel shows how Proust went beyond the Flaubert model as she examines his criticism and pastiches of Flaubert's works. Particularly instructive are her comparative readings of central scenes involving female characters from *L'Education sentimentale* and the *Recherche*.

Another significant dimension of Proust's novel is homosexuality, since it plays a central role in the fictional world and touches on important social and ethical issues. In "Homosexuality in the *Recherche*," Lawrence R. Schehr considers several approaches to teaching the novel's homoerotic relationships, first considering particular episodes before settling on his preferred method: focusing on Charlus throughout the novel and analyzing a seminal scene, the opening pages of *Sodome et Gomorrhe*, which he sees as the "operating system" for all that follows.

Since there have been several new releases of films based on the *Recherche*, Rebecca Graves's essay, "Proust and the Cinema," offers another important intertextual perspective. After briefly discussing the problems raised in general by film adaptations of literary texts, Graves presents a dialogic model for studying recent adaptations of the novel, in particular Le Temps retrouvé, directed by Raoul Ruiz and La Captive, directed by Chantal Akerman.

The section "Specific Teaching Contexts" takes into account that Proust's growing popularity has led to a flurry of new editions, translations, and interpretations. It is more and more of a challenge to find the right key for introducing his works in the classroom. One approach is close textual reading. Roger Shattuck proposes a modified version of the traditional explication de texte to engage students in an original reading of the narrator's reaction to his grandmother's death in *Le Côté de Guermantes*. Linking this particular episode to other scenes of intermission and digression, Shattuck demystifies Proust's narrative mastery for beginners and seasoned readers alike.

In "Peddling Proust," Michèle Magill contends that there is always a way to introduce Proust at any level of instruction and in any teaching context, whether a conversation class, a civilization course, or a seminar on translation. She gives concrete examples of how to gradually bait students into reading all of Proust with selected pages of *A la recherche du temps perdu,* combined with an interactive approach to the text.

In "Introducing Proust," Julie Solomon proposes segmenting "Combray" to guide students through an analysis of the temporal, spatial, and logical relations. The goal of this exercise is to make readers pay attention to the narrator's discursive strategies by taking them from one segment to the next. Solomon's approach recognizes the identity of the narrating subject and the distinction between hero and narrator. Since these narrative and structural features are important for understanding the poetics of the novel as a whole, this essay can be integrated into various levels and frameworks of teaching the *Recherche.*

After giving a brief practical guide to studies on Proust and architecture, J. Theodore Johnson shows how the "steeples of Martinville" episode in "Combray" can be used at different levels of instruction by specialists and nonspecialists. He sugggests a systematic comparison of the passages dealing with the church of Saint-Hilaire de Combray and that of Saint-André des Champs, to make students realize how fundamental the notion of structure is in this "cathedral-novel."

Christie McDonald discusses teaching Proust's novel in a graduate course, where she considers "theoretical questions through close textual readings." She stresses the importance of giving students a global view of Proust's method of composition and analyzes the impact of phenomenological studies, rhetorical approaches, and genetic criticism on a critical reappraisal of *A la recherche du temps perdu.*

In "What to Do with Montjouvain?," Brigitte Mahuzier explains how she deals with a crucial but problematic episode of "Combray" in a gender studies course. She shows us how teachers can "zap" back and forth through the text of *A la recherche du temps perdu* so students will gain a new understanding of Proust's closeted agenda.

Diane R. Leonard explores the road to Proust through Ruskin in "Teaching Proust Comparatively." Through the reading of selected pages from Ruskin's *Elements of Drawing, Modern Painters,* and *Seven Lamps of Architecture,* as well as the systematic use of illustrations, she reveals the immediate influence of Ruskin's critical theories on the articles that Proust was writing at the time and Ruskin's hidden presence throughout the text of the *Recherche.*

Like painting and architecture, music plays a major role in Proust's novel. Jean-Louis Pautrot surveys the musical context in which Proust worked and analyzes the complex relation between the author's musical tastes and the narrator's admiration for the masterpieces of the fictitious composer Vinteuil. He also reflects on how music influences Proust's writing, both philosophically and stylistically, and gives advice on how to fruitfully link music and literature in an interdisciplinary course.

In "A Place for the Madeleine," Susan Rava demonstrates that it makes pedagogical sense to include Proust's work in all kinds of humanities courses in the undergraduate curriculum. Basing her argument' on her experience as a teacher and on her theoretical position, which challenges the transmission model, she leads us through the steps of enjoying "Combray" in a nonspecialist's English-language course.

CONTEXTS

Proust: A Man of His Times

William C. Carter

A question often asked about A *la recherche du temps perdu* is, Why does it continue to speak to generation after generation in a voice that seems fresh and vigorous? Far from being the culminating opus of decadent literature, as some of Proust's early critics believed, this novel constitutes one of the most dynamic and open works ever written. How, then, does it remain so young? Although there are a number of pertinent answers to this question, an important—and often overlooked—answer is its modernity.

Marcel Proust lived from 1871 to 1922, an era that he characterized as "une époque de hâte" (*Corr.* 3: 210) (the "age of speed" [*Letters* 4: 290]). These exciting, momentous years encompassed the fin de siècle, belle époque, and the First World War. By the time Proust was forty, the gas-lit world of his youth had been transformed by electricity, central heating, the telephone, the automobile, and the airplane. When he began writing his novel, Paris streets bustled with an astonishing variety of pedestrians, ambulatory vendors, drivers and their horses, and increasing numbers of the new, self-propelling vehicles called automobiles. He could see the past and the future on parade as horse-drawn carriages made way for cars. Proust was very much a man of his times and was often ahead of his times. The new scientific inventions, especially those of mass communication and transportation, fascinated him. The telephone, bicycle, train, automobile, and airplane all appear in the novel, literally and metaphorically, and often fulfill important narrative functions. Part of the fascination of reading A *la recherche du temps perdu* derives from its vivid depiction of the major social, political, and technological forces that changed daily life and the way people perceived time and space. In the following passage, the narrator and Albertine are about to embark on their first excursion in an automobile:

Elle pensait bien que nous pourrions nous arrêter çà et là sur la route, mais croyait impossible de commencer par aller à Saint-Jean-de-la-Haise, c'est-à-dire dans une autre direction, et de faire une promenade qui semblait vouée à un jour différent. Elle apprit au contraire du mécanicien que rien n'était plus facile. . . . Nous le comprîmes dès que la voiture, s'élançant, franchit d'un seul bond vingt pas d'un excellent cheval. Les distances ne sont que le rapport de l'espace au temps et varient avec lui. Nous exprimons la difficulté que nous avons à nous rendre à un endroit, dans un système de lieues, de kilomètres, qui devient faux dès que cette difficulté diminue. L'art en est aussi modifié, puisqu'un village qui semblait dans un autre monde que tel autre, devient son voisin dans un paysage dont les dimensions sont changées. (3: 385)

Although she realized it would be possible to stop here and there on our way, she could not believe that we could start by going to Saint-Jean-de-la-Haise, that is to say in another direction, and then make an excursion which seemed to be reserved for a different day. She learned on the contrary from the driver that nothing could be easier. We realised this as soon as the vehicle, starting off, covered in one bound twenty paces of an excellent horse. Distances are only the relation of space to time and vary with it. We express the difficulty that we have in getting to a place in a system of miles or kilometers, which becomes false as soon as that difficulty decreases. Art is modified by it also, since a village, which seemed to be in a different world from some other village becomes its neighbor in a landscape whose dimensions are altered. (4: 537–38)

Proust shows how the telephone makes the narrator aware of the passage of time in a scene containing elements of comedy mixed with premonitions of tragedy, heightened by allusions to the underworld in *Le Côté de Guermantes*. Saint-Loup suggests that, since a telephone service has been established between Doncières and Paris, the narrator try calling his beloved grandmother, apart from whom he is vacationing for the first time. The narrator goes to the post office where he imagines the telephone operators as the

Toutes-Puissantes par qui les absents surgissent à notre côté sans qu'il soit permis de les apercevoir . . . les ironiques Furies qui, au moment que nous murmurions une confidence à une amie, avec l'espoir que personne ne nous entendait, nous crient cruellement: "J'écoute."; les servantes toujours irritées du Mystère, les ombrageuses Prêtresses de l'Invisible; les Demoiselles du téléphone! (2: 431–40)

All-Powerful by whose intervention the absent rise up at our side, without our being permitted to set eyes on them . . . the ironic Furies who, just as we were murmuring a confidence to a loved one, in the hope that

> no one would hear us, cry brutally: "I'm listening!"; the ever-irritable
> hand-maidens of the Mystery, the umbrageous priestesses of the Invisi-
> ble, the Young Ladies of the Telephone.   (3: 174)

He observes that the isolation of someone's voice by this new invention provides a "présence réelle" ("real presence") but also the premonition of "une
séparation éternelle" ("an eternal separation" [2: 432; 3: 175]). The first attempted call fails because the line is busy. Once the call goes through, he hears
his grandmother's voice: "vue sans le masque du visage" (2: 433) ("seen without the mask of her face" [3:176]). Made anxious by her suddenly revealed vul-
nerability, he cuts short his visit to Saint-Loup's garrison and hurries home to
find "sur le canapé, sous la lampe, rouge, lourde et vulgaire, malade, rêvassant,
promenant au-dessus d'un livre des yeux un peu fous, une vieille femme acca-
blée" (2: 440) ("sitting on the sofa beneath the lamp, red-faced, heavy and vul-
gar, sick, day-dreaming, letting her slightly crazed eyes wander over a book, an
overburdened old woman" [2: 185]), whom he does not recognize. Once he
sees her again every day, though, habit resumes its anesthetizing role and he
forgets the revelation made possible by the telephone. His fears of an eternal
separation, adumbrated by the telephone call, are soon realized by her death.

In September 1905, when Proust was thirty-four, his mother died. His
intense grief lasted until 1907, when a summer vacation at the Grand Hotel in
Cabourg brought about a dramatic change in him. Depressed and ill, he had in
recent months gotten out of bed only once a week, without dressing. After arriving at the seaside resort "the pure air joined with a deadly dose of caffeine"
allowed him to hire the driver Alfred Agostinelli and to "go out every day in a
closed car" (*Corr.* 7: 285–86; my trans.). Riding across the Normandy country-
side with Agostinelli in his red taxi was, Proust said, "like being shot out of a can-
non" (*Corr.* 7: 263; *Letters* 2: 325). As the taxi sped along the road toward Caen,
famous for its medieval churches, Proust watched the distant spires appear and
disappear against the horizon in constantly shifting perspectives and marveled
at the phenomenon of parallax and relativity so keenly felt in the automobile.
On his return to Paris, Proust wrote an article, originally in *Le Figaro*, "Impressions de route en automobile," about the motoring trips (Contre Sainte-Beuve
63–69). He later used this piece as the basis for the "steeples of Martinville"
episode in which the rapidly changing perspectives dazzle the narrator, who
wants to be a writer. Exhilarated by the experience of parallax, the narrator
quickly jots down his impressions in what is to be for decades his only completed text. Perhaps Proust gave this text such an important place in the novel
because it not only contained his version of the modernist technique of multiple perspectives that he was to expand to its psychological equivalent of multiple selves but also marked for him the time in 1907–08 when he began writing
in earnest the work that became a monumental achievement.

Toward the end of the nineteenth century, sports caught on rapidly in
France as a result of British influence. In 1892, a French rugby team went to

England and inaugurated the first international sports events, leading to the creation of the modern Olympic Games. The contests between the British and French were a great success and French enthusiasm for sports spread rapidly to all classes. In his novel, Proust noted the new vogue for sports and the decline of romantic ennui:

> Mais, surtout depuis la faveur dont jouissent les exercices physiques, l'oisiveté a pris une forme sportive, même en dehors des heures de sport et qui se traduit par une vivacité fébrile qui croit ne pas laisser à l'ennui le temps ni la place de se développer. (4: 277)

> But in these days especially, when physical exercise is so much in favour, there exists also, even outside the actual hours of sports, an athletic form of idleness which finds expression not in inertia but in a feverish vivacity that hopes to leave boredom neither time nor space to develop in.
> (6: 13)

Sports, the new machines of mass transportation, and moving pictures made people]aware of speed as never before. Chronophotography and the first movies, with their successive points of view, inspired cubist painters. In 1911, the painter Jean Metzinger explained how the cubists' multiple perspectives had added temporality to painting: "They have allowed themselves to move round the object, in order to give a concrete representation of it, made up of several successive aspects. Formerly a picture took possession of space, now it reigns also in time" (Kern 147). Proust's contemporary Jacques Rivière, considered by many to be the finest literary critic of the era, was the first to notice his affinity with the cubists: "une chose . . . qui m'est apparue pour la première fois, c'est votre relation avec le mouvement cubiste, et plus profondément votre profonde immersion dans la réalité esthétique contemporaine" (*Corr.* 21: 376) ("one thing apparent to me for the first time . . . is your relationship to the Cubist movement, and, more importantly, the depth of your immersion in the world of modern aesthetics" [*Letters* 4: 412]). Like the cubists, Proust depicts various aspects of an object seen in rapid succession, such as the steeples of Martinville or Albertine's face when the narrator bends over her to bestow a kiss, but unlike the cubists he presents such perspectives as a spontaneous and successive vision rather than as an intellectualized and recomposed vision: "dans ce court trajet de mes lèvres vers sa joue, c'est dix Albertines que je vis; cette seule jeune fille étant comme une déesse à plusieurs têtes, celle que j'avais vue en dernier, si je tentais de m'approcher d'elle, faisant place à une autre" (2: 660) ("now, during this brief journey of my lips towards her cheek, it was ten Albertines that I saw; this one girl being like a many-headed goddess, the head I had seen last, when I tried to approach it, gave way to another" [3: 499]).

Sports also influenced fashion, as the narrator observes when he sees Albertine pushing a bicycle along the beach. She and her friends appear so different in their sporting attire from anyone he has known that he describes them as looking as though they had come from another universe (2: 152; 2: 510). These girls represent the rise of the less conservative elements of the middle class, who are the first to deck themselves out in the recommended attire for sports activities: "leur accoutrement tranchait sur celui des autres jeunes filles de Balbec, parmi lesquelles quelques-unes . . . se livraient aux sports, mais sans adopter pour cela une tenue spéciale" (2: 146) ("their attire generally was in striking contrast to that of the other girls at Balbec, some of whom . . . went in for sports, but without adopting a special outfit" [2: 503]). Both epithets he chooses for Albertine mention the sporting aspect of her appearance and have strong erotic connotations: "la bacchante à bicyclette, la muse orgiaque du golf" (2: 228) ("the bacchante with the bicycle, the orgiastic muse of the golf-course" [2: 619]). The narrator reminds us constantly about Albertine's love of sports. The girl is aware that he does not share her tastes and calls him a lizard for being so sedentary (2: 231; 2: 623).

From the very first mention of Albertine, Proust establishes the fact that she is mobile and that speed is one of her essential traits. He does this through an ingenious use of the English word "fast." It is Gilberte who first speaks to the narrator of Albertine, a friend of hers from school, long before her appearance on the beach at Balbec: "la fameuse 'Albertine.' Elle sera sûrement très 'fast,' mais en attendant elle a une drôle de touche" (1: 503) ("the famous 'Albertine.' She's certain to be dreadfully 'fast' when she's older, but meanwhile she's an odd fish" [2: 116]).

We do not know what signs lead Gilberte to make the prediction that Albertine will be "fast," but Proust evidently chose the English word because of its double meaning: rapid movement through space and sexual promiscuity. When the narrator first sees Albertine and the little band of girls—unaware that he is seeing "the famous Albertine"—he wonders about their sexual mores because of their sporting attire, the golf clubs, and the bicycle, accoutrements and equipment that indicate agility, speed, and, for the narrator, undefined social categories. Because of Albertine's appearance—especially the bicycle and golf clubs—and her insolent manner, he makes the following assumption about the girls' sexual conduct:

> une fille aux yeux brillants, rieurs . . . sous un "polo" noir, enfoncé sur sa tête, qui poussait une bicyclette avec un dandinement de hanches si dégingandé, en employant des termes d'argot si voyous et criés si fort . . . je conclus plutôt que toutes ces filles appartenaient à la population qui fréquente les vélodromes, et devaient être les très jeunes maîtresses de coureurs cyclistes. En tout cas, dans aucune de mes suppositions, ne figurait celle qu'elles eussent pu être vertueuses.   (2: 151)

> a girl with brilliant, laughing eyes . . . a black polo-cap crammed on her head, who was pushing a bicycle with such an uninhibited swing of the

hips, and using slang terms so typical of the gutter and shouting so loudly
. . . that I concluded that these girls belonged to the population which
frequents the velodromes and must be the very juvenile mistresses of
racing cyclists. In any event, none of my suppositions embraced the possibility of their being virtuous.   (2: 509)

Stillness and mobility relate to art and desire in Proust's novel. Girls in
motion, most often seen on bicycles, arouse desire in the narrator. Albertine,
chief among the girls whom Proust calls "êtres de fuite" (3: 599) ("creatures of
flight" [5: 113]) always exhibits an enthusiasm for sports and bicycles, automobiles, and airplanes. Fast by nature, she becomes, through the narrator's obsessive jealousy, a truly volatile figure:

> Des yeux—par mensonge toujours immobiles et passifs—mais
> dynamiques, mesurables par les mètres ou kilomètres à franchir pour se
> trouver au rendez-vous voulu, implacablement voulu. . . . Entre vos
> mains mêmes, ces êtres-là sont des êtres de fuite. Pour comprendre les
> émotions qu'ils donnent et que d'autres êtres, même plus beaux, ne don-
> nent pas, il faut calculer qu'ils sont non pas immobiles, mais en mouve-
> ment, et ajouter à leur personne un signe correspondant à ce qu'en
> physique est le signe qui signifie vitesse.   (3: 599)

> Eyes mendaciously kept always immobile and passive, but none the less
> dynamic, measurable in the yards or miles to be traversed before they
> reach the desired, the implacably desired meeting-place. . . . Even when
> you hold them in your hands, such persons are fugitives. To understand
> the emotions which they arouse, and which others, even better-looking,
> do not, we must recognize that they are not immobile but in motion, and
> add to their person a sign corresponding to that which in physics denotes
> speed.   (5: 113–14)

The sign in physics that stands for speed is V, shorthand for velocity, a V
whose shape resembles that of wings, a motif often used in connection with
Albertine. The importance that Proust attaches to the erotic themes of capture
and flight can be seen in the titles he gave to the two volumes of the novel
where these notions dominate: *La Prisonnière* and *La Fugitive*—although a
recent manuscript discovery indicates that Proust's ultimate choice for the title
of the next to last volume of the *Recherche* was *Albertine disparue* (Mauriac
and Wolff 11).

Change and the reaction to change set the tone of the period. The First
World War—the first war in which common soldiers became the heroes and
also the first in which airplanes were used to launch bombs—accelerated the
process of transformation and provided the coup de grâce to the vestiges of the
French aristocracy. After the war, the duchesse de Guermantes's salon, once

the epitome of aristocratic elegance and snobbery, is described as a broken-down machine no longer "functioning" properly and unable to maintain its fierce exclusivity (4: 535; 6: 390). Even the aloof, glamorous faubourg Saint-Germain must yield to the force of time, as the narrator observes:

> Ainsi change la figure des choses de ce monde; ainsi le centre des empires, et le cadastre des fortunes, et la charte des situations, tout ce qui semblait définitif est-il perpétuellement remanié, et les yeux d'un homme qui a vécu peuvent-ils contempler le changement le plus complet là où justement il lui paraissait le plus impossible.   (4: 596)

> Thus it is that the pattern of the things of this world changes, that centres of empire, assessments of wealth, letters patent of social prestige, all that seemed to be forever fixed is constantly being re-fashioned, so that the eyes of a man who has lived can contemplate the most total transformation exactly where change would have seemed to him to be most impossible.   (6: 486)

The new heroes of the age of speed—the cyclist, the chauffeur, and the aviator—all appear in Proust's novel. Albertine the cyclist is a mysterious, erotic creature, while the aviator symbolizes the artist. At the beginning of the novel's climatic scene, the narrator, at last looking inward for the keys to his past, suddenly feels himself rising in flight: "comme un aviateur qui a jusque-là péniblement roulé à terre, 'décollant' brusquement, je m'élevais lentement vers les hauteurs silencieuses du souvenir" (4: 437) ("like an airman who hitherto has progressed laboriously along the ground, abruptly 'taking off' I soared slowly towards the silent heights of memory" [6: 243]). The earthbound, horizontal explorer who finally discovers how to become an airborne visionary is a key Proustian metaphor, symbolizing the vision, freedom, and individuality of the artist.

A la recherche du temps perdu is a novel with infinite possibilities built on the model of the universe. Du côté de chez Swann appeared in 1913, during the time that Einstein's theories were becoming widely known and were providing the first new model for the physical world since Newton (see Erickson; Carter, "Proust, Einstein"). In 1931, Edmund Wilson declared the Recherche the literary equivalent of Einstein's theory of relativity: "[Proust] has recreated the world of the novel from the point of view of relativity: he has supplied for the first time in literature an equivalent on the full scale for the new theory of physics" (Wilson 189). In doing so, Proust created new ways of looking at the world, making his dynamic, open-ended novel one of the most complex and stimulating optics that we have for viewing our own lives.

The Role of the Dreyfus Affair in the *Recherche*

Joseph Brami

The numerous references to the Dreyfus affair in *A la recherche du temps perdu* play a substantial role in shaping the overall meaning of the work. One of the most written-about events in French history, the affair burst onto the scene in 1894 when a French Jew, an army captain by the name of Alfred Dreyfus, was falsely accused of spying for Germany and sentenced to forced labor on Devil's Island. High-ranking military officials covered up the truth, with the exception of one man, Colonel Picquart, who stood up to the hierarchy, risking both his career and his honor. It was only after intellectuals such as Bernard Lazare, Emile Zola, and Anatole France launched a lengthy campaign in defense of truth and justice that the government eventually agreed to reexamine the case. For years, the country was torn into pro- and anti-Dreyfus camps. Because Dreyfus was Jewish, the affair brought on a huge wave of anti-Semitism that left its mark long after Dreyfus's name was cleared and he was reinstated in the army in 1906. For background material, I recommend Michael R. Marrus's *The Politics of Assimilation* or Jean-Denis Bredin's *L'Affaire* (*The Affair*), as well as Jean Cheyrasse's movie *Dreyfus ou l'intolérable vérité* or Yves Boisset's *L'Affaire Dreyfus*. Although Proust followed the affair closely and was clearly a Dreyfusard (*Corr.* 6: 155; 14: 309; 19: 530), he does not give a factual account of it in his novel. Rather, he uses the Dreyfus affair in the *Recherche* as a logical step in a process that will lead Marcel, the narrator, to his ultimate conception of literature in particular and of art in general.

The references to the affair in the *Recherche* barely cover fifty pages of the new Pléiade edition, only somewhat more than one or two hundredths of the entire work. Yet their thematic importance should not be underestimated. Such references occur throughout Marcel's entire recorded experience, again and again serving as a point of reflection. They are concentrated in *Le Côté de Guermantes* and in *Sodome et Gomorrhe*. But, in fact, the first one occurs in *A l'ombre des jeunes filles en fleurs*, when Marcel begins his visits with Mme Swann (1: 508; 2: 122–23), and the last is found almost at the end of *Le Temps retrouvé*, during a soirée at the prince de Guermantes's house (4: 536, 570; 6: 391, 446), long after the novel's general public has relegated the affair to the past.

Marcel is considered by his Dreyfusard friends, Swann, Saint-Loup, and Bloch to be "one of them." At one point, Swann jokingly remarks to Marcel and Saint-Loup that their being seen together will make people think they are talking as members of the Syndicate (a fictitious Jewish pro-Dreyfus group targeted by anti-Semitic, anti-Dreyfus rhetoric) (3: 96; 4: 132). In addition, Marcel is involved in disputes over the affair, even fighting several duels on its account (3: 10; 4: 11). Furthermore, whenever the Dreyfus affair is the subject of conversation around Marcel, he is the one who has initiated it, for example, with Saint-Loup and Rachel (2: 462; 3: 217), with Swann (2: 868; 3: 796), and with M. de Guermantes (3: 77; 4: 105). Even when he seems not to be partic- ipating in conversations about the affair, he is listening closely to what both sides have to say (2: 518, 530–31, 537–40, 541–43; 3: 297, 313–16, 323–27, 330–33). He shows a Dreyfusard sensitivity in his attention to the salon con- versations he hears. The primary focus throughout, however, is not on his own involvement in the conflict; allusions to duels, for example, are made in pass- ing, with no explicit analysis of his opinion.   Rather, Marcel's concern is the affair's impact on people around him.

The general picture of humanity that emerges from his observations is indeed bleak. Although the prince de Guermantes, under the influence of his wife, sets aside his hatred of Jews enough to change his mind about the affair once he is convinced of Dreyfus's innocence (3: 103–04, 106–10; 4: 142–43, 146–51),   he is the exception to the rule. And the rule, for Marcel, is that human behavior, as seen throughout the affair, is shallow and ugly.

Occurring just when Marcel is gaining access to Parisian salons (1: 508; 2: 122–23), the affair opens his eyes to the reality of life in society. Throughout his childhood and adolescence, he is fascinated with the Swanns and the Guer- mantes and enchanted with them and their social milieu. The Dreyfus affair is a catalyst that reveals to him basic human vanity. No one is exempt in the end: aristocrats and bourgeois, men and women, old people and young people, het- erosexuals and homosexuals, Catholics and Jews—all will come to reveal their cruelty, pettiness, and stupidity with regard to the Dreyfus affair.

During the affair, salon life is characterized solely according to whether one is pro- or anti-Dreyfus, Jewish or gentile, or openly associates with Jews. In other words, the usual patterns of snobbery depend on new dynamics, a phe- nomenon that displeases the leaders of social life in both camps. Mme de Guer- mantes, who is against Dreyfus, deplores the fact that everyone expects to be invited to her house because they are anti-Dreyfus and anti-Jewish (2: 535, 3: 321; 4: 157, 5: 779). Mme Verdurin, initially in favor of Dreyfus and eager to gain recognition for her salon, cuts short all discussion of the affair once she sees that the final political triumph of the Dreyfus camp is not going to bring her the desired social result (3: 278; 4: 384). Mme Swann, who believes in Dreyfus's innocence (2: 560; 3: 357), nonetheless beseeches her husband not to speak out on Dreyfus's behalf, since she is concerned that his Jewish origins and pro-Drey- fus opinions will hamper her social ascension (2: 549; 3: 341). For many people, Dreyfus's innocence or guilt—and the basic ethical questions it raises—is of no importance. Mme de Guermantes believes Dreyfus is innocent (2: 767; 3: 653) but does little more than make what she deems to be witty remarks about it:

> En tout cas, si ce Dreyfus est innocent . . . il ne le prouve guère. Quelles
> lettres idiotes, emphatiques, il écrit de son île! Je ne sais pas si M. Esther-
> hazy vaut mieux que lui mais il a un autre chic dans sa façon de tourner

les phrases, une autre couleur. Cela ne doit pas faire plaisir aux partisans de M. Dreyfus. Quel malheur pour eux qu'ils ne puissent pas changer d'innocent. (2: 536)

In any case, if this man Dreyfus is innocent . . . he has not done much to prove it. What idiotic turgid letters he writes from his island! I do not know whether M. Estherhazy is any better, but at least he has more of a knack of phrase-making, a different tone altogether. That can't be very welcome to the supporters of M. Dreyfus. What a pity for them that they cannot exchange innocents. (3: 322)

Men are targets of Marcel's critical view as well. M. de Norpois, who illustrates the art of speaking without saying anything, acknowledges that if indeed the army chief of staff did something wrong, then it means that something "singularly regrettable" happened (2: 539; 3: 326). Charlus's deep anti-Semitism leads him to consider that Dreyfus is innocent because as a Jew he cannot be considered French and therefore the question of his betrayal should not even be raised (2: 584; 3: 390).

Jews are also the subject of the narrator's observations of human weaknesses during the affair. Viewed against the anti-Semitism of the time, Marcel's stance is one of sensitivity to the Jewish condition. His sympathetic stance, however, still allows him ample room to criticize his Jewish characters' apparently self-blinding acceptance of their alienation as Jews. Bloch's father, for example, does not feel hurt by Mme Sazerat's anti-Semitism because she is pro-Dreyfus; in fact, he finds her point of view gratifying because, in his mind, it proves the sincerity of her opinion about Dreyfus (2: 585; 3: 392). Swann's behavior is not idealized either. Although his pro-Dreyfus feelings bring out a new awareness about his origins and lead him to wish to see innocence triumph before his death, he nonetheless refuses to sign a petition in favor of Dreyfus because he finds his own name too "Hebraic," thus adopting the typical attitude of an alienated Jew who does not want to make waves (3: 111; 4: 152). His daughter Gilberte will later go one step further. She becomes Mlle de Forcheville after her mother's remarriage, and her eagerness to hide her origins is so strong that no one dares to pronounce her father's name in her presence (4: 166; 5: 787).

It is important to make students realize that these reflections on the Dreyfus affair are part of the general experience of disillusionment that characterizes the hero-narrator's relationships to other people. Disillusionment plays a major role in the process of self-understanding, which will lead Marcel to realize his vocation as a writer in *Le Temps retrouvé*. Comparing Chateaubriand's evocation of a bird's song and the scent of mignonette to his description of the events during the French Revolution and the Empire, the narrator states that the remembered sensations have inspired pages of greater literary value than historical analysis because they reveal inner experiences of the self (4: 306; 6: 54). This passage is part of a five-page description of the confusion about the affair in the public mind, twenty years after it has ended. No one remembers exactly who was involved in the affair or what they did and in which of the opposing camps people once stood. Furthermore, no one has the slightest idea what being in one or the other camp meant then or what it means in the present for that matter. New political alliances have been formed; new opinions have been taken up. Dreyfusards who would in the old days have been identified as antinationalists can now play the nationalist tune, with their former involvement completely forgotten (4: 304–09; 6: 51–57). As the narrator points out:

> Les mots de dreyfusard et antidreyfusard n'avaient plus de sens, disaient les mêmes gens qui eussent été stupéfaits et révoltés si on leur avait dit que probablement dans quelques siècles, et peut-être moins, celui de boche n'aurait plus que la valeur de curiosité des mots sans-culottes ou chouan ou bleu.   (4: 306)

> The words Dreyfusard and anti-Dreyfusard no longer had any meaning then. But the very people who said this would have been dumbfounded and horrified if one had told them that probably in a few centuries, or perhaps even sooner, the word Boche would have the curiosity value of such words as *sans-culotte, chouan* and *bleu*.   (6: 54)

For Marcel, historical events as they unfold are less valuable to literary inspiration than reflective inner experience. What he sees through the affair, as it is playing itself out around him, is merely the frailty of the human ego, with its vanity, self-centeredness, and either willed or accidental blindness; in itself, the affair reveals nothing of lasting value. It only provides a further subject of reflection. It is this effort toward understanding and its perfect expression in "les anneaux nécessaires d'un beau style" (4: 468) ("the necessary links of a well-wrought style" [6: 290]) that he seeks as an artist. Listening to conversations about the affair in the various salons is a necessary waste of time for Marcel because it will allow him to realize his vocation as a writer:

> Et je compris que tous ces matériaux de l'œuvre littéraire, c'était ma vie passée. . . . Ainsi toute ma vie jusqu'à ce jour aurait et n'aurait pas pu être résumée sous ce titre: Une vocation.   (4: 478)

> And I understood that all these materials for a work of literature were simply my past life. . . . And thus my whole life up to this present day might and yet might not have been summed up under the title: A Vocation.
>   (6: 304)

Marcel's experience of the Dreyfus affair can be seen as a fundamental series of steps on his path to self-knowledge. It represents the very kind of shallowness that all his future literary efforts will attempt to avoid, a crucial negative phase in a dialectical movement of thought that will allow him to see that only in the endeavor toward a work of art will he reach a deep understanding of life and develop the ability to communicate it to others.

Cataclysm at One Remove:
The War in *Le Temps retrouvé*

Edward J. Hughes

In seeking to convey the complexity of the First World War, Proust's narrator uses a variety of strategies. Although he pays attention to social realism (he describes the atmosphere generated by the variegated appearance of international troops in Paris and air raids over the capital, for example), he also explores the psychological workings of collective conflict. He writes that the war is to be understood as an extension into the public domain of private desires and antagonisms and likens the machinations of political leaders such as King Constantine of Greece, Germany's William, and Ferdinand of Bulgaria to those of Albertine or Françoise (4: 350; 6: 117). The requirements of foreign policy are thus entangled with the story of Marcel's paranoia and misogyny. We might expect recent political, military, or economic history to be cited as causes for the war, yet the narrator is just as likely to propose the natural sciences or mathematics as sources of explanation. Thus, as the human or animal body is composed of myriad cells, he ventures,

> il existe d'énormes entassements organisés d'individus qu'on appelle nations; leur vie ne fait que répéter en les amplifiant la vie des cellules composantes; et qui n'est pas capable de comprendre le mystère, les réactions, les lois de celle-ci, ne prononcera que des mots vides quand il parlera des luttes entre nations.   (4: 350)

> there exist huge organized accumulations of individuals which are called nations: their life does no more than repeat on a larger scale the lives of their constituent cells, and anybody who is incapable of comprehending the mystery, the reactions, the laws of these smaller lives, will only make futile pronouncements when he talks about struggles between nations.
>   (6: 118)

In the same analogizing way, he likens international war to cataclysmic geologic transformations precipitated by tidal waves and glaciers (4: 351; 6: 118–19). Urgent hypothesizing and scientific speculation are his oblique ways of capturing the enormity of the war engulfing France.

Michael Sprinker argues that the war episode in *Le Temps retrouvé* is the most explicitly historical section of the work but asks how precisely history appears in the episode (160). Proust's tactic is to work impressionistically, filtering the war through key individuals and locations such as Charlus, the brothel that Charlus sets up in Jupien's name, Françoise, Saint-Loup, and wartime Paris.

For some—Charlus and Mme Verdurin, for example—the war barely troubles normal routine. Yet the narrator, keen to underscore just how precarious their pleasure taking is, again appeals to science, talking of the release of an explosive energy on a cosmic scale, "une masse un million de fois plus grande que le soleil, ayant en même temps détruit tout l'oxygène, toutes les substances dont nous vivons" (4: 351) ("a mass a million times greater than the sun, having in the process destroyed all our oxygen and all the substances on which we live" [6: 119]). Proust's catastrophe theory pushes him to get behind what he terms the apparent immutability of the sun to explore the planet's incessant, explosive activity.

To convey the urgency of his speculation and to contrast it with the motif of private hedonism—"les gens vont . . . à leur plaisir" (4: 351) ("People . . . go about their pleasures" [6: 119])—the narrator introduces abstract mathematical notions. Thus, regarding the pursuit of individual pleasure, the Verdurins and the Charluses of this world, he suggests, apply a multiplier every bit as great as the divisor they impose on the suffering of millions. The anecdotal confirmation of this magnification of private desire and the radical exclusion of the other comes with the story of Mme Verdurin's enjoying her croissant while faking a reaction to the sinking of the *Lusitania* (4: 352; 6: 120).

If science is a preferred vehicle for conveying the magnitude of events and for contesting the complacency of upper-class Parisians insulated from such events, another counterpoint to this selfishness comes in the sentimental cameo of Françoise's millionaire cousins. When the cousins' nephew is killed in battle, they give up their comfortable retirement to help run the cafe for the young widow. The narrator hails their tireless dishwashing and serving from morning to night as a service every bit as altruistic as that of men at the front. Indeed, the dedication of Françoise's cousins becomes symptomatic of French national greatness, as symbolized by the church of Saint-André des Champs (4: 424; 6: 226). Their exceptional dedication prompts an equally exceptional move on the part of the narrator, who protests that although everything in his novel is fictional, he will break that rule by paying tribute to the nation's heroes and heroines. The inference is that momentous contemporary events sweep fictional conventions aside:

> Et persuadé que leur modestie ne s'en offensera pas, pour la raison qu'ils ne liront jamais ce livre, c'est avec un enfantin plaisir et une profonde émotion que, ne pouvant citer les noms de tant d'autres qui durent agir de même et par qui la France a survécu, je transcris ici leur nom véritable: ils s'appellent, d'un nom si français d'ailleurs, Larivière.   (4: 424)

> And persuaded as I am that I shall not offend their modesty, for the reason that they will never read this book, it is both with childish pleasure and with a profound emotion that, being unable to record the names of so many others who undoubtedly acted in the same way, to all of whom France owes her survival, I transcribe here the real name of this family: they are called—and what name could be more French?—Larivière.
> (6: 225–26)

The narrator's avowedly emotional commemoration brings with it a celebration of Frenchness and a return to the cult of *la France profonde* that takes us back to Combray and its medieval churches. Indeed Saint-André des Champs becomes shorthand for the best in French patriotism and encompasses the efforts of people like the Larivières, Françoise, and Saint-Loup (4: 317). (Sprinker deftly reconstructs attitudes toward the war, from the selflessness of the Larivières to the selfishness of Morel and from the defeatism of Charlus to the patriotism of the Verdurins and the Bontemps [164]). In owning up to his "childish pleasure," the narrator indirectly signals the plurality of perspectives that he adopts in the war pages of *Le Temps retrouvé*: to the languages of science and cataclysm, we can now add sentimental nationalism. The moralizing tone adopted as he heaps praise on the Larivière couple spurs him on to contrast their sacrifice with the young man in a dinner jacket whose only care is to line up a male prostitute for later that evening.

Jupien's brothel will provide the venue for that meeting. Yet in describing it, the narrator is far from judgmental, reconstructing, rather, his first naive impressions. Surprised to see someone looking like Saint-Loup slipping out of the brothel, he remembers how Saint-Loup's name had been maliciously associated with a spy scandal and wonders if the brothel might be a nest of spies. On first entering the brothel, he overhears conversations between men that convince him a crime is about to be committed. Yet he soon discovers that talk of chains and beating people until they bleed is part of the masochistic ritual of the male brothel (4: 391; 6: 177).

The heroic Saint-Loup loses his war medal at the brothel, providing Proust with an ideal pretext for reflection on moral relativism. Significantly, brothel clients voice their praise for those few officers who sacrifice themselves for their men and thereby redeem a class seen as privileged and cowardly by the ordinary soldiers. Saint-Loup's homosexuality may meet with disapproval in society at large, but his heroism in battle enables the narrator to contest the received view that the rich are necessarily cosseted. This preoccupation with social strata came at a time of heightened class antagonism that was to lead especially to the strikes of 1917.

The debate on social privilege enters Marcel's home when Saint-Loup returns there in search of the missing medal, indirectly drawing Françoise and the butler into the moral maze. The narrator mentions caustically the desire of Françoise's nephew and the butler's son to avoid frontline service, a desire no less intense than Saint-Loup's will to fight. Yet what condemns Saint-Loup in the eyes of the domestic staff is his failure to adopt Germanophobic stereotypes: he admires the courage of the Germans and refuses to use the Boche label, whereas the butler plies Françoise with stories of German barbarism. Although these lurid stories terrorize Françoise, the narrator's mockery, directed at both himself and the domestics, carries an explicit if still jocular commentary on democratization and Republican ideology. Marcel tries in vain to correct the butler's mispronunciation of *envergure* (the butler, scanning the papers, has been warning Françoise of an enemy offensive on a new scale). The result is that each time Marcel enters the room, he seems to hear insistently repeated the incorrect version of the term *enverjure*, prompting him to reflect that this mere butler was appealing to the Declaration of the Rights of Man for the right to pronounce the term as he chooses, in a spirit of Republican egalitarianism that sets him on a par with his master (4: 421; 6: 220). Through the medium of friendly banter, then, very real class antagonisms are being worked into the novel.

Françoise's Germanophobia later lapses into the pacifism she demonstrated years earlier in Combray, but this lapse too is a response carefully nurtured by the butler, who, in undermining her, militates against the patriotic traditions of Saint-André des Champs. The prospect of an Allied victory (and Françoise's peace of mind) leaves him in despair for "[il avait] réduit la guerre 'mondiale,' comme tout le reste, à celle qu'il menait contre Françoise" (4: 422) ("He had reduced the 'world' war, like everything else, to the war which he was secretly waging against Françoise" [6: 222]). Here the narrator returns to his earlier hypothesis that war extends private antagonisms into the public realm, the scullery becoming a vantage point for the observation of international conflict and national identity.

The lurid language of conquest, defeat, and humiliation that features liberally in the butler's manipulation of Françoise extends in parodic form to Jupien's brothel, where Charlus's sessions with burly Parisians bemuse Marcel. Consideration of social class again provides the key: Charlus is keen to be handled by those he believes to be authentic, hard men from eastern Paris, so that aristocratic pleasure taking requires the radical otherness of working-class male culture (4: 403; 6: 195). Hence the young milkman is touted by Jupien as one of the great rogues of Belleville who killed his sergeant while serving in the African batallion. Jupien's lies feed the destructive fantasies that proliferate in Charlus's mind. And as Sprinker demonstrates, Charlus's degradation, along with Saint-Loup's heroic death, captures symbolically the end of aristocratic social power (162). The social ascent of Charlus's persecutor, Mme Verdurin— who is to become the princesse de Guermantes—is probably the most eye-catching event in a process of revolutionary social change.

Like the brothel, Paris under curfew sees a blurring of social classes as people congregate in blacked-out metro stations. Again, the narrator associates this convergence with sexual desire, the corridors of the metro station becoming spaces of instant gratification. In the absence of what the narrator labels the eternal *marivaudage* (light-hearted gallantries) of salon society, "les mains, les lèvres, les corps peuvent entrer en jeu les premiers" (4: 413) ("hands, lips, bodies may go into action at once" [6: 209]). A double force majeure, made up of war and libidinal desire, thus challenges civilized society: "le cadre social . . . qui entoure nos amours, nous n'y pensons presque pas" (4: 412) ("The social setting . . . which surrounds our love-making barely impinges upon our thoughts" [6: 208]). The natural sciences figure again as the narrator likens pleasure secured in extreme circumstances to natural phenomena such as eclipses, tidal bores, and volcanoes. Archaeology provides another vehicle of representation, the promiscuity of the Parisian metro triggering reference to the convulsive destruction of Sodom and to the graffito *Sodoma* discovered in the ruins of Pompeii. Sodom, Pompeii, and Paris thus provide a roll call of devastated cities marked by frank, reckless desire. The metaphors of upheaval elegantly if indirectly capture the radical social dislocation of the war.

Charlus is the source of the archaeological erudition here, and his own recklessness spells his decline, which complements the social rise of the Verdurins who spurn him. He likens the city under bombardment not only to Pompeii but also to Herculaneum, where the priests were engulfed by lava as they tried to rescue the sacred vessels. Charlus's oracular conclusion, "C'est toujours l'attachement à l'objet qui amène la mort du possesseur" (4: 386) ("Attachment to an object always brings death to its possessor" [6: 170]), provides one of the central psychological messages of the novel and could be read as indirectly signaling the demise of his class, which is wedded to ritual and tradition.

The motif of attachment to the object also surfaces when Gilberte writes to Marcel from war-torn Combray and explains what drove her to leave the safety of Paris. At the sight of "mon cher Tansonville menacé" (4: 334) ("my beloved Tansonville threatened" [6: 94]), she claims, she returns to defend the family estate and her father's art collection against the advancing German army. Proust reinforces the axis linking private and resoundingly public events when Gilberte explains that the memory of sites of their childhood have become major battle sites. Thus the hawthorn path, the scene of emotional conflict for young Marcel and Gilberte, is now a battleground of immense strategic importance, and the names Roussainville and Méséglise are as famous as Austerlitz and Valmy. The eight-month battle along Swann's way—a fictional transcription of Verdun (see 4: 335, 1214n2)—has cost 600,000 German lives. The clear inference is that a private adolescent lyricism is engulfed by history.

Here too, in keeping with Proust's habit of unsettling seemingly incontrovertible human motives, Gilberte's heroism is questioned. If her latest letter claims that she wanted to defend the family home against the enemy, she had written earlier of wanting to get away from Paris and the aerial bombardment. We see, then, her initial fear of the enemy mutating into courage. In signaling both Gilberte's feisty nationalism and her timidity, Proust fuels a relativism already evident in Saint-Loup, who is a hero of the battlefield and a regular in Jupien's brothel. The point Proust makes is that characteristics such as valor, cowardice, or sexual orientation cannot constitute the totality of the human subject. The effect is to unsettle tribal or class certainties such as nationalism or bourgeois heterosexual morality.

Although he questions Gilberte's patriotism, the narrator cultivates the mystique of war when he describes Saint-Loup's trip to see him. The young officer conveys, we are told, the almost supernatural aura surrounding all soldiers on leave. Their experiences are evoked as titanic struggles unfolding along "[les] rivages de la mort" (4: 336) ("the shores of death" [6: 97]), and they come across as ghosts haunting us with tales from beyond the grave. Saint-Loup carries a scar on his face "plus auguste et plus mystérieuse . . . que l'empreinte laissée sur la terre par le pied d'un géant" (4: 337) ("more august and more mysterious than the imprint left upon the earth by a giant's foot" [6: 97]). The vibrant fantasy confirms that while *Le Temps retrouvé* rarely offers historical documentation of the official variety, it conveys, tangentially and impressionistically, the momentousness of war.

Saint-Loup suggests that the tranformative impact of the conflict is also visible nearer home. Recalling a zeppelin raid over Paris the night before, he is enthusiastic about the great visual spectacle, likening the airmen to Valkyries climbing into the sky (4: 338; 6: 99). Wagnerian composition again promotes aestheticism as an oblique channel of representation of the war. Elsewhere, however, talk of high culture leads us circuitously back to social engagement. Charlus may criticize the French and British destruction of the Combray church that the Germans had been using as an observation post, his complaint being that the medieval church symbolized the history of France as well as his own ancestral past (4: 374; 6: 154). But the narrator rejects the aestheticism, arguing that human lives take precedence over cathedral stones. Proust thus reconstructs the ethical debate of the time that attracted key figures such as Maurice Barrès, who, while decrying the German bombardment of Rheims cathedral in September 1914, put the humble French foot soldier ahead of national monuments (see 4: 375, 1232n1).

Proust is a master of the art of indirectness. Even when he addresses the phenomenon of war obliquely, through zoological or geologic metaphors or aestheticism or as a transposition of Marcel's battles with Françoise or Albertine, he understands acutely the social upheaval of his day. We need to draw out the importance of these allegorical reflections when teaching the war episode in *Le Temps retrouvé*. Similarly, social class is a key issue in the war pages, the pedagogical challenge being to demonstrate how the tensions accompanying the demise of the aristocracy, the rise of the bourgeoisie, and perceptions working-class people have about their superiors and about the war are refracted through a small group of characters and locations. Similar tensions cluster around national identity, in which the fantasy of social cohesion served by Saint-André des Champs disintegrates, to be superseded by an emerging social reconfiguration that Proust sought to document.

Proust Art Nouveau?

Françoise Leriche

For decades, scholars have studied Proust's relation to the visual arts, mainly from two perspectives. Either they have tried to identify the sources that Proust used to create the imaginary paintings mentioned in *A la recherche du temps perdu*—that is, the actual paintings that inspired Elstir's works or the originals of the narrator's descriptions of landscapes, seascapes, or portraits (for instance, Monet's *Nympheas* has been proposed as a model for the water lilies on the Vivonne River [see Monnin-Hornung; Johnson, "Proust's 'Impressionism'"; Le Pichon; Chelet-Hester; Eells]). Or they have focused on describing the symbolic function of Elstir's paintings in the narrative, wondering whether the paintings express the aesthetics of metaphor later developed in *Le Temps retrouvé* or whether they illustrate a different Proustian aesthetic (Eissen; Leriche). Does the narrator's visit to Elstir's studio, in *A l'ombre des jeunes filles en fleurs*, represent an important stage in his apprenticeship, as Yasue Kato assumes, or is Elstir's masterpiece *The Harbour of Carquethuit* just a lure leading nowhere, as Theodore J. Johnson, Jr., has argued ("Proust's 'Impressionism'"; "Proust and Painting")?

My purpose here is to question the conclusions of studies that assume that since Elstir is an impressionist painter, Proust's style and aesthetics are impressionistic. As early as 1920, E. R. Curtius compared Proust's style to Monet's, and many critics followed his lead (Monnin-Hornung; Chantal). Johnson was the first scholar to reconsider seriously the two terms of this equation: Elstir's impressionism in *The Harbour of Carquethuit* and Proust's supposed impressionist style, as well as the notion of literary impressionism (Johnson, "Proust's 'Impressionism'"). Criticizing the thesis of a purely impressionist Proust, Johnson invites us to compare Proust's style to cubism—as did Jacques Rivière in 1926 and more recently Paola Placella Sommella, Claude Gandelman, and Taeko Uenishi, who thoroughly studied Proust's "cubist affinities" (Uenishi 83). Isabelle Serça makes an even stronger case, comparing Cézanne's techniques of fragmentation and Proust's massive use of parentheses. One could argue, however, that more readers are sensitive to the organicism of *A la recherche du temps perdu*, which stems from its long, enveloping sentences, and are less aware of its angles, ruptures, and discontinuity, which are so characteristic of cubism.

In *The Story of Art*, Ernst Gombrich stresses the fact that impressionism is not so much the dawn of modernism as the final avatar of realism:

> Some people may consider the Impressionists the first of the moderns, because they defied certain rules of painting as taught in the academies. But it is well to remember that the Impressionists did not differ in their aims from the traditions of art that had developed since the discovery of

nature in the Renaissance. They, too, wanted to paint nature as we see it and their quarrel with the conservative masters was not so much over the aim as over the means of achieving it. Their exploration of colour reflexes, their experiments with the effect of loose brush-work, aimed at creating an even more perfect replica of the visual impression.   (427)

"We" here simply means anyone who would be at the same place, looking at the same view. Impressionism in painting has never been a pictorial practice of metaphor; rather it has been the objective rendering of light and of the alteration of shapes resulting from the perception of light. But are impressionism and cubism the only alternatives in the visual arts at the beginning of the twentieth century? Is there no other expression of artistic sensibility between 1886—which marks the end of impressionism—and 1908–10, when the first manifestations of cubism appeared and when Proust was beginning to work on the *Recherche*? Of course, a literary, pictorial, or architectural style is always unique, but, at a given time, isn't there a community of tastes, an ideal of beauty that will allow art historians and literary critics to label certain artists and writers of the same generation? I argue that if Proust's work can be appreciated in the light of any aesthetic trend, it is neither impressionism nor cubism but art nouveau.

After being despised as *style nouille* for more than sixty years, art nouveau was reassessed with a vengeance in the 1980s and 1990s. Carefully studied by art historians from different backgrounds, it was the subject of many international exhibitions, in Berlin, Paris, London, and Washington, DC. Illustrated books, catalogs, and especially the videocassette and DVD *Art Nouveau: 1890–1914*, produced by Carroll Moore for the National Gallery of Art's 2001 exhibit in Washington, DC, can be used to introduce students to the pictorial and architectural characteristics of art nouveau.

An international movement in the visual arts that affected painting, graphic arts, architecture, and the applied arts, art nouveau developed between 1880 and 1914, roughly corresponding to Proust's formative years and to the genesis of *A la recherche du temps perdu*. Art nouveau has many facets: the Anglo-Saxon tradition, for example, is more ascetic than its Continental counterpart. But beyond some stylistic differences, there is a common philosophy inherited from John Ruskin, the British art critic and socialist thinker, whom Proust translated and studied from 1899 on. Ruskin noted the gap between a financial elite who could afford expensive works of art and ordinary people who did not have the means or leisure to visit museums and to be exposed to art. To address the needs of ordinary people, the artist's new mission was to create beauty for everyday objects. Inspiration had to be drawn from nature, the source of beauty and truth according to Ruskin's Romantic philosophy. The first manifestations of this new way of thinking about the function of art in society were the Arts and Crafts movement and William Morris's variation on Arthur Lasenby's famous Liberty style—which Proust mentions several times in his correspondence. In France, art nouveau had a second source of inspiration: the architect Eugène Viollet-le-Duc, who insisted on the necessity of using new materials such as iron and glass. Iron was no longer to be hidden behind stone or artificial decoration but was to be made highly visible. Instead of copying old styles (such as Gothic or neoclassic), the craftsmen and artists had to invent a new style for a new age, the age of iron—a style that would highlight the beauty of the materials and explore all their aesthetic possibilities. Proust was familiar with Viollet-le-Duc's theories, since the architect's name appears three times in *A la recherche du temps perdu* and eight times in Proust's general correspondence.

The common features of art nouveau productions—whatever their national and stylistic differences might be—are organicism, unity of conception, refusal of pastiche, and "art synthesis" (Bouillon 85). The stylistic features of Continental art nouveau, to which Proust was exposed, appeared in buildings, paintings, posters, and everyday-life objects characterized by the stylization of natural forms, the arabesque and serpentine line, bright colors, and baroque design (see Portoghesi, Quattrocchi, and Quilici). The *Art Nouveau* videocassette mentioned above includes excellent examples, such as the Hotel Tassel, by Victor Horta, in Brussels (sec. 6: "Nature") and Castel Bérenger, by Hector Guimard, in Paris (sec. 8: "The Total Work of Art"). The cassette shows that Horta and Guimard not only designed the buildings but also that they were responsible for the decoration of the walls, the mosaics on the floors, the staircase balusters, the furniture, the lamps, and even the doorknobs, so that no extraneous element would be introduced into the stylistic unity of the whole. Every detail was thought of as part of the whole; every curve, every color had to echo similar colors, similar curves.

Jean-Paul Bouillon claims that James McNeil Whistler, Pierre Bonnard, Edouard Vuillard, and Maurice Denis belong to the art nouveau school because of their flattening technique in drawing and their taste for decorative effects. For these artists, details have no intrinsic value but contribute to an overall aesthetic effect: their function is to create a rhythm, to evoke visual echoes (see Bouillon's analysis of Maurice Denis's 1892 *Madame Ranson au chat*, 45).

All these features may be applied to Proust's style and technique of composition. The unity of conception of *A la recherche du temps perdu* is a fact: Proust conceived the first and the last volumes at the same time, the whole novel being aimed "against Sainte-Beuve," as any study of his manuscripts will confirm. In December 1919, he repeated in a letter to Rosny the Elder what he had often stated before: "le dernier chapitre du dernier volume, encore non paru, a été écrit tout de suite après le premier chapitre du premier volume" (*Corr.* 18: 546) ("the last chapter of the last [volume, not yet published,] was written immediately after the first chapter of the first" [*Letters* 4: 107]).

Even when later, enormous developments were added, the fundamental binarism of the novel was reinforced. When Proust invented a new episode, he always created two antithetical movements, the second experience echoing the first. Thus in *A l'ombre des jeunes filles en fleurs*, the section "Nom de pays: le nom" (enchantment and reverie triggered by a name) is immediately followed by "Nom de Pays: le pays" (disappointment in the face of reality).

When the hero first attends a performance of *Phèdre* with La Berma in the title role, he experiences no aesthetic pleasure (1: 440–42; 2: 25–27), whereas the second time, he can fully appreciate the actress's invisible genius (2: 347–48; 3: 55–56). This revelation, in turn, echoes passages concerning Vinteuil's sonata; in the first 1910 draft dealing with the audition of the sonata (Cahier 69), Proust makes an explicit link between those two episodes, comparing music and acting, two forms of art *sine materia*. One can find many more examples of such deliberate choices. According to Proust, details that could be interpreted as realistic or based on personal memories have no actual autobiographical foundation; they have, instead, been invented as pure signifiers. For instance, he explained to Henri Ghéon that Madame Sazerat, a character in "Combray," never existed as a person: he created her and put her in front of a stained-glass window "pour accentuer l'impression humaine de l'église à telle heure" (*Corr.* 13: 24) ("in order to stress the sensation of humanity given by the church at a given time"; my trans.).

The unity of the novel is, moreover, reinforced by the first-person narrative, which enables Proust to combine descriptive perceptions of the world, introspective passages that psychologically analyze the self, philosophical meditation, and theoretical developments. One could argue that many instances of omniscience undermine the consistency of first-person narration, that they introduce a disconcerting dissonance or rupture. Omniscient narration increases markedly in the volumes rewritten after the First World War, that is, after 1918. Thus, if anything cubist can be found in the change from first-person point of view to omniscient narration, it is not embedded in Proust's writing technique but appeared rather late in the process of his creation—later than the period of art nouveau, the aesthetics of which surely influenced Proust during the years 1908–14. For example, in *Sodome et Gomorrhe 2*, one can find numerous instances of omniscient narration in passages concerning Charlus and Morel. Thus, though the hero was not present at the restaurant of Saint Mars le Vêtu (3: 395–99; 4: 550–57), the reader is given all the details of the luncheon involving these two characters. Similarly, during Morel's aborted visit to the prince de Guermantes, the hero, who was not present at the scene, nevertheless knows how frightened Morel felt when he saw Charlus's photograph in the prince's drawing room and how upset the prince himself was by failing to find anyone: "Il eut beau avec son valet, par crainte de cambriolage et revolver au poing, explorer toute la maison" (3: 468) ("in vain, he and his valet, fearful of burglary, and armed with revolvers, search the whole house" [4: 656]). These are two examples among many of additions to the post-1914 text of the *Recherche*.

Since the publication of *Du côté de chez Swann* in 1913, critics have emphasized the originality of the Proustian sentence: It is long, sinuous, and complex in structure, and the systematic addition of numerous parenthetical elements creates dynamic tensions in it (Serça 69). Compared by André Beaunier and Jacques-Emile Blanche to meandering arabesques, the Proustian sentence reproduces on paper the distinctive features of Continental art nouveau.

The dynamic tension of Proustian syntax can be attributed mainly to three rhetorical devices, which may be seen as literary equivalents of the common use of curves and arabesques in the visual arts: parenthetical adjunction, hyperbaton, and anaphoric rhythm effects. Whether or not it is indicated by dashes, the parenthetical adjunction aims at dislocating the sentence by inserting secondary information (circumstances, descriptive elements, comparisons) between its main components (subject and verb, adjective and noun, and the like). Another structuring device, the hyperbaton, consists in having the sentence rebound through apposition of words, just when it seemed to have come to an end. The combination of these techniques produces an ornamental and dynamic effect reminiscent of the arabesque, as the following example illustrates (parenthetical adjunction is indicated by italics, hyperbaton by boldface, and anaphor by underlining):

> C'étaient de ces chambres de province qui—*de même qu'en certains pays des parties entières de l'air ou de la mer sont illuminées ou parfumées par des myriades de protozoaires que nous ne voyons pas*—nous enchantent de mille **odeurs** qu'y dégagent les vertus, la sagesse, les habitudes, toute une vie secrète, invisible, surabondante et morale que l'atmosphère y tient en suspens; **odeurs** naturelles encore, certes, et couleur du temps comme celle de la campagne voisine, mais déjà casanières, humaines, et renfermées, *gelée exquise industrieuse et limpide de tous les fruits de l'année qui ont quitté le verger pour l'armoire; saisonnières* mais mobilières et domestiques, corrigeant le piquant de la gelée blanche par la douceur du pain chaud, oisives **et** ponctuelles comme une horloge de village, flaneuses **et** rangées, insoucieuses **et** prévoyantes, lingères, matinales, dévôtes, heureuses <u>d'une paix qui</u> n'apporte qu'un surcroit d'anxiété <u>et d'un prosaisme qui</u> sert de grand réservoir de poésie à celui qui les traverse sans y avoir vécu.
> (1: 48–49)

> They were rooms of that country order which—just as in certain climes whole tracts of air or ocean are illuminated or scented by myriads of protozoa which we cannot see—enchant us with the countless **odours** emanating from the virtues, wisdom, habits, a whole secret system of life, invisible, superabundant and profoundly moral, which their atmosphere holds in solution; **smells** natural enough indeed, and weather-tinted like those of the neighbouring countryside, but already humanized, domesticated, snug, an exquisite limpid jelly skillfully blended from all the fruits of the year which have left the orchard for the store-room, **smells** changing with the season, but plenishing and homely, offsetting the sharpness of hoarfrost with the sweetness of warm bread, **smells** lazy and punctual

as a village clock, roving **and** settled, heedless **and** provident, linen **smells**, morning **smells**, pious **smells**, rejoicing <u>in a peace which</u> brings only additional anxiety, <u>and in the prosaicness which</u> serves as a deep reservoir of poetry to the stranger who passes through their midst without having lived among them.   (1: 66–67)

Such a Proustian sentence is not constructed according to a classical, logical order but is twisted like the iron forged by Guimard or the Nancy-school artists. It is structurally powerful in its general design and in its detail through the mastery of a carefully thought-out syntax, an exuberant unfolding always linked to the whole as is the case in art nouveau.

Students should be reminded that the impressionists rejected drawing and lines and favored the juxtaposition of small color strokes. Cubists gave priority to structure, volumes, and shapes, but their recomposition of objects omitted details and movements leading to unity and harmony. Art nouveau stands not in-between but elsewhere—in a vertiginous movement trying to recapture the inner dynamism of life. Proust's art, in its attempt to catch the subtle movements of the human psyche through spiraling sentences, is the most obvious example of art nouveau in literature.

Proust and Painters

Kazuyoshi Yoshikawa

Paintings in *A la recherche du temps perdu* serve an important function. In "Un Amour de Swann," for example, a painting by Botticelli triggers Swann's love for Odette. The narrator tells us that at first Swann even feels "a sort of physical repulsion" (1: 276) for Odette: "Pour lui plaire elle avait un profil trop accusé, la peau trop fragile, les pommettes trop saillantes, les traits trop tirés. Ses yeux étaient beaux mais si grands qu'ils fléchissaient sous leur propre masse" (1: 193) ("Her profile was too sharp, her skin too delicate, her cheekbones were too prominent, her features too tightly drawn, to be attractive to him. Her eyes were beautiful, but so large they seemed to droop beneath their own weight" [1: 276]). One day, however, Swann realizes that Odette's figure resembles the image of Zipporah, Jethro's daughter, in Botticelli's painting in the Sistine Chapel: "laissant couler le long de ses joues ses cheveux qu'elle avait dénoués, fléchissant une jambe dans une attitude légèrement dansante" (1: 219) ("her loosened hair flowing down her cheeks, bending one knee in a slightly balletic pose" [1: 314]). Circumstances then turn around completely. He now comes to think of the woman who at first was not his type as "un chef-d'œuvre inestimable" (1: 221) ("an inestimably precious work of art" [1: 317]) and even goes so far as to display on his desk a copy of Botticelli's portrait of Zipporah in lieu of a photograph of Odette. Botticelli's painting thus serves not only as an important stimulus for Swann's love but also as an opportunity for the narrator to criticize Swann's understanding of the arts as "idolâtrie" ("idolatry").

Students might consider how Proust, who had never visited the Sistine Chapel, was able to describe in detail the portrait of Zipporah as it appears in Botticelli's *Life of Moses*. Proust had seen *The Works of John Ruskin* published as the library edition at the turn of the century, which featured a detail of Zipporah on the back of the title page to volume 23. Ideally, students should be provided with a reproduction of the work of art in question. I use the catalogue raisonné for each painter mentioned in the text under consideration.

A variation of Swann's love for Odette in "Un Amour de Swann" is the hero's love for Albertine. Once again, a work of art plays a central role in the love relationship; this time it is a painting by Carpaccio. In *Albertine disparue*, the hero suffers from a broken heart even after Albertine's death, and we find him trying to recover in Venice, where he is wrapped in his mother's love as if he were a child again. One day, as the hero visits the Academy Museum, his attention is fixed on the *Patriarche di Grado esorcisant un possédé* ("The Patriarch of Grado Exorcising a Demoniac"). As he looks at the cape worn by a Venetian aristocrat depicted in the painting, he is suddenly reminded of a coat with a similar pattern once worn by Albertine.

> Sur le dos d'un des compagnons de la Calza, reconnaissable aux broderies d'or et de perles qui inscrivent sur leur manche ou leur collet

l'emblème de la joyeuse confrérie à laquelle ils étaient affiliés, je venais de reconnaître le manteau qu'Albertine avait pour venir avec moi en voiture découverte à Versailles. . . . Toujours prête à tout, quand je lui avais demandé de partir, . . . elle avait jeté sur ses épaules un manteau de Fortuny. . . . (4: 226)

On the back of one of the *Compagni della Calza* identifiable from the emblem, embroidered in gold and pearls on their sleeves or their collars, of the merry confraternity to which they were affiliated, I had just recognized the cloak which Albertine had put on to come with me to Versailles in an open carriage. . . . Always ready for anything, when I had asked her to come out with me . . . she had flung over her shoulders a Fortuny cloak. . . . (5: 877)

In this way, the hero recalls his old love for Albertine through the coat designed by the Venetian designer Fortuny, who was inspired by Carpaccio's painting.

In the section before the above quotation, the narrator describes Carpaccio's painting in great detail, evoking the color of the sky, the shapes of chimneys, and various aspects of the people's clothing. One is inclined to express one's admiration for Proust's minute descriptions. However, as Jacques Nathan points out (200), this passage is closely inspired by the art historian Léon Rosenthal's *Carpaccio, biographie critique*, published in 1906. For example, Proust's "l'admirable ciel incarnat et violet" (4: 225) ("the marvellous rose-pink and violet sky" [5: 876]) is clearly borrowed from Rosenthal's expression "un ciel admirable, rouge, violet" (47) ("a marvellous red and violet sky"; my trans.). Another telling example is that of the chimney stacks seen against the sky, Proust's "ces hautes cheminées incrustées" (4: 225) ("the tall incrusted chimneys" [5: 876]), which is a version of Rosenthal's "les hautes cheminées . . . et leurs montants incrustés d'arabesques" ("the tall chimneys . . . and their tops incrusted with arabesques"; my trans.).

In another example, the hero sees in a painting "le barbier essuyer son rasoir, le nègre portant son tonneau" (4: 226) ("the barber wiping his razor, the negro humping his barrel" [5: 877]). This passage is taken from Rosenthal's "un barbier . . . essuie son rasoir et . . . un nègre se courbe sous le poids d'un tonneau" (51) ("a barber . . . wipes his razor . . . a Negro bends under the weight of a barrel"; my trans.). Here, Proust even repeats Rosenthal's error. As Annick Bouillaguet points out (134), the person who is "humping his barrel" on his back is not a black person at all. One can see that in the original painting his cheeks are white instead of black and that his legs look black because he is wearing black tights. When Proust wrote this passage in 1916, his memory of the painting had obviously grown foggy since he had seen it during his first stay in Venice in 1900. Rosenthal's study thus supplied Proust with a solid framework for reviving the image for *Albertine disparue*.

In the Proustian passage under discussion, the hero feels "comme une légère morsure" (4: 226) ("a slight gnawing" [5: 877]) at his heart. The author's application of the adjective "légère" ("slight") to "morsure" ("gnawing") may reveal his intent to show that the hero's broken heart has already healed. At the conclusion of this passage, the hero is "envahi pendant quelques instants par un sentiment trouble et bientôt dissipé de désir et de mélancolie" (3: 226) ("overcome for a few moments by a vague and soon dissipated feeling of desire and melancholy" [5: 877–78]). At the beginning of this passage, the narrator tells us that Carpaccio "faillit un jour ranimer mon amour pour Albertine" (4: 226) ("almost succeeded one day in reviving my love for Albertine" [5: 876]). In both cases, his love for Albertine is diminishing and Venice is presented as the place of liberation.

In contrast to the ephemeral love for Albertine, the hero finds eternal love symbolized by the love between mother and son. When he is studying the mosaic in St. Mark's baptistery for his research on Ruskin, his mother throws "un châle sur les épaules" (4: 226) ("a shawl over my shoulders" [5: 875]) to protect him from the cold. This scene of the mother in the baptistery is engraved in the hero's mind and remains with him long after her death. The passage describing this striking scene appears directly before the passage about the *Patriarche di Grado*:

> Une heure est venue pour moi où quand je me rappelle le baptistère, devant les flots du Jourdain où saint Jean immerge le Christ tandis que la gondole nous attendait devant la Piazzetta il ne m'est pas indifférent que dans cette fraîche pénombre, à côté de moi il y eût une femme drapée dans son deuil avec la ferveur respectueuse et enthousiaste de la femme âgée qu'on voit à Venise dans la *Sainte Ursule* de Carpaccio, et que cette femme aux joues rouges, aux yeux tristes, dans ses voiles noirs, et que rien ne pourra plus jamais faire sortir pour moi de ce sanctuaire doucement éclairé de Saint-Marc où je suis sûr de la retrouver parce qu'elle y a sa place réservée et immuable comme une mosaïque, ce soit ma mère.
> (4: 225)

> A time has now come when, remembering the baptistery of St Mark's—contemplating the waters of the Jordan in which St John immerses Christ, while the gondola awaited us at the landing-stage of the Piazzetta—it is no longer a matter of indifference to me that, beside me in that cool penumbra, there should have been a woman draped in her mourning with the respectful and enthusiastic fervour of the old woman in Carpaccio's *St Ursula* in the Accademia, and that that woman, with her red cheeks and sad eyes and in her black veils, whom nothing can ever remove from that softly lit sanctuary of St Mark's where I am always sure to find her because she has her place reserved there as immutably as a mosaic, should be my mother.
> (5: 876)

In this long sentence, the subordinate clause is divided into two parts, each written in a different tense. The first half indicates events of the past. It refers to the time when the narrator's mother was still alive and kneeled before the mosaic of the baptism of Christ in Saint Mark's baptistery. In comparing his mother to the aged woman in the *Legend of Saint Ursula*, he evokes the figure of the woman in black mourning clothes who kneels in prayer in front of Ursula lying on the casket in Carpaccio's *Martyrdom of the Pilgrims and the Funeral of St. Ursula*. It is interesting to note that an enlargement of this section of Carpaccio's painting showing the woman in mourning clothes appears in Rosenthal's work, to which Proust referred.

By comparison, in the latter half of the subordinate clause, the verbs are in the present tense. The same woman in mourning clothes, the woman "aux joues rouges, aux yeux tristes" ("with her red cheeks and sad eyes"), is mentioned. Now we are dealing not with the real mother but with a vivid image of her that has become engraved in the hero's mind "comme une mosaïque" ("like a mosaic").

This long passage focused on the mother inside the baptistery precedes the scene mentioned above where Albertine is remembered in front of the *Patriarche di Grado*. This juxtaposition is no coincidence. The vivid image of the mother that continues to live on in the hero's mind is intended to contrast with the image of Albertine, who is fading from his memory. Through these two paintings by Carpaccio, Proust depicts the contrast between two women who play important roles in the hero's emotional life. *Martyrdom of the Pilgrims and the Funeral of St. Ursula* recalls the mother's image etched eternally in the hero's mind, whereas *Patriarche di Grado exorcisant un possédé* evokes the image of Albertine, for whom his love is fading.

As we have seen, paintings play an important role in describing how love changes with the flow of time in both "Un Amour de Swann" and *Albertine disparue*. In a famous scene of *La Prisonnière*, as well, Proust expresses his belief that art transcends life. Bergotte, a novelist, falls ill when in his later years he goes to see an exhibition and draws his last breath in front of Vermeer's "petit pan de mur jaune" (3: 692–93) ("little patch of yellow wall" [5: 244]). This fragment of the *View of Delft* acquires an immortal, sacred glow through Bergotte's death.

Proust probably based this scene on an experience he had in 1921, when his friend the art critic Jean-Louis Vaudoyer took him to the Jeu de Paume Museum, where they saw Vermeer's masterpiece. To describe it, Proust freely adapts numerous passages from Vaudoyer's critique of the exhibition. For example, Vaudoyer writes, "[C]es maisons de briques, peintes dans une matière si précieuse, si massive, si pleine, que, si vous en isolez une petite surface en oubliant le sujet, vous croyez avoir sous les yeux aussi bien de la céramique que de la peinture" (515) ("these brick houses, painted in a substance that is so precious, so massive, so full, that if you isolate a small area and forget the context, you will think you are looking not just at painting but at ceramics"; my trans.). Indeed, the phrase "le petit pan de mur jaune" does not appear in the critic's review, but we can recognize the similarities in "une petite surface" ("a small area") of "maisons de briques" ("brick houses"). Vaudoyer's use of the word "céramique" is reminiscent of Proust's phrase "une précieuse œuvre d'art chinoise" (3: 692) ("some priceless specimen of Chinese art" [5: 244]). Further on, Proust writes that Bergotte "remarqua pour la première fois des petits personnages en bleu, que le sable était rose . . ." (3: 692) ("noticed for the first time some small figures in blue, that the sand was pink . . . [5: 244]). This is clearly borrowed from "cette étendue de sable rose-doré . . . où il y a une femme en tablier bleu" ("that expanse of pinkish-gold sand . . . with a woman in a blue smock"; my trans.), found in Vaudoyer's criticism.

However, Proust does not simply borrow phrases from Vaudoyer's article. In his description of the *View of Delft*, where the phrases are extremely similar to Vaudoyer's, Proust makes a point of giving credit where it is deserved. Twice he explicitly refers to a critical source: "un critique ayant écrit"; "grâce à l'article du critique" (3: 692) ("an art critic having written somewhere"; "thanks to the critic's article" [5: 244]). The number of phrases similar to Vaudoyer's and the repeated references to the critic suggest that Proust intended to reveal to his readers that this critic is none other than Vaudoyer. We can interpret Proust's indirect references to him as a way of paying homage to his friend, who not only advised him on "the mysterious Vermeer" but also took him to the Jeu de Paume Museum. Both in his novel and in his essay *Contre Sainte-Beuve*, Proust points out the importance of solitude in artistic creation and bitterly criticizes social relations. However, even in the solemn death scene of the novelist Bergotte, who had extolled the eternal nature of art, we find Proust praising his friend Vaudoyer and thus revealing his own attention to social obligations.

After having examined several examples of art in Proust's novel, we can conclude that much of his understanding of the arts was obtained through illustrated essays. Proust described Botticelli's figure of Zipporah after having seen a detail of *Life of Moses* in the library edition of Ruskin's works. To describe Carpaccio's painting, the novelist relied on Rosenthal's specialized book; and to describe Vermeer's work, he used Vaudoyer's critique of the exhibition. Proust was well aware of the leading research and criticism of the art world of his time, and he carefully incorporated some of these writings into his novel. Though *A la recherche du temps perdu* presents an imaginary world, it is not as closed off from reality as its author claims. The novel is open to and marked by the world in which Proust lived.

We have seen how the paintings of Botticelli, Carpaccio, and Vermeer highlight one of the main themes of *A la recherche du temps perdu*: the opposing nature of love and art—mortal love that is bound by time and immortal art that is free from the boundaries of time. Paintings also demonstrate the novel's artistic basis. In addition to those discussed in this essay, other paintings and artists play an important role in *A la recherche du temps perdu*: for instance, Giotto's *Vices and Virtues* provides an allegorical dimension for several of the novel's characters (e.g., 1: 80–81 [1: 112–13] and 2: 241 [2: 637–39]) and the styles of Claude Monet and James Whistler underlie some of the novel's impressionistic descriptions (see 1: 166–68 [1: 238–40] and 2: 162–63 [2: 523–26]). There are, moreover, compelling references to works by Gustave Moreau and El Greco (see my "Proust et Moreau," "Proust et le Greco," and "Proust et Vermeer"; see also Monnin-Hornung's *Proust et la peinture* and Sophie Bertho's *Proust et ses peintres*).

In making students aware of the important role art plays in the *Recherche*, it is helpful to select appropriate images to illustrate quotations from the text. Such images appeal to students and enable them to compare the works of art in question with Proust's use of them. Teachers can thus strengthen students' interest in the novel and guide them toward a better understanding of the writer's aesthetics.

Seeing Proust Seeing

Mary Ann Caws

The Multiman

Most famously lending his work and word to the relation between the visual and the imaginary arts, Marcel Proust somehow—almost miraculously—has turned out to embrace an even far wider field than we might have thought. Given the prevalence of visual imagery and the numerous actual references to sight and paintings in Proust's work, the art of visual effect in the *Recherche* facilitates the classroom and lecture use of slides, illustrations, images, and the like. Nonetheless, and just as important, music and dance are inescapably part of his world and, by extension, of our own since we have, in great numbers, become Proustian. This essay deals mainly with music and dance, which are as easy to illustrate as the arts more frequently spoken of. Stage sets, costumes, recordings, musical scores: all these enter into the larger Proustian world.

When teaching interdisciplinary art and literature courses, particularly in an urban context, it is crucial for the success of class discussions and work to have a writer such as Proust at the center. Such courses can work from this single author out to the wider cultural world, showing the context of the period through the various arts. I have found this approach especially gratifying in a large urban university, such as the Graduate Center, City University of New York, where I teach—for the worlds of music, dance, and spectacle are as important in this city as the museums are, so that all of Proust's wide interests can come into play.

Musical Building Stones

We can compare Proust's intertextual play with the constructions of Thomas Hardy, whose work with the stonemason's geometry was much admired by Proust (see 3: 878; 5: 507). The architectural keystone of a building noted by Hardy is visibly and conceptually akin in Proust both to the intimate and wide-spread presence of elements such as the little musical phrase the narrator hears and is obsessed by and to the way in which figures and emotions recur. Proust essentially constitutes the framework of the entire experience of reading, seeing, and building, and he passes on that experience.

The sonata and quartet forms are often present in what we see of Proust's imaginative creation. In the film *Céleste*, by Percy Adlon, the performance of the quartet in the bedroom of the hero-narrator is the key to the sensitivity of the film and its viewing. In actual fact, Proust invited the Poulet Quartet, with its members Gaston Poulet, Louis Ruyssen, Victor Gentil, and Amable Massis, to play for him Beethoven's Opus no. 130 quartet in B-flat major and Cesar Franck's quartet in D major for strings. He passed the evening stretched out on his green velvet sofa to listen, in the candlelight, and when the musicians had finished the performance, he asked them to repeat what they had already played—at two in the morning (see Carter, *Marcel Proust* 619–21). Such obsessive passion forms, along with the haunting strains calling that passion forth, the element that holds together Proust's work, life, and listening, just as the recurrence of the composer Vinteuil throughout the *Recherche* acts to gird architecturally the various elements of the immense text.

Opera

Proust's musical obsessions are felt everywhere in the *Recherche*. Proust preferred opera in all its high drama, Debussy's *Pelléas et Mélisande* being his favorite because of its melody and Maeterlinck's words. Any evening it was being played, Proust requested the operators of that miraculous machine called the *théâtrophone* to interrupt whatever he might have planned to do, so that he could listen to a concert, as he did on 21 February 1911 to a performance at the Opéra Comique. This musical telephone, the subject of one of Jules Chéret's famous posters, was available as early as 1881, when it was exhibited at the International Electrical Exhibition in Paris and it came into wide usage from 1890 to 1932. Placed under the stage and transmitted by telephone lines into a large black ear trumpet or telephones that were set up in cafes and restaurants or for private subscribers, the *théâtrophone* transmitted performances directly from eight concert halls in Paris, including the Paris Opera House, the Comédie Française, and the Opéra Comique.

Proust was haunted by the role of Pelléas, whose parts he would sing to himself. At times he would ascribe the role to his composer and musician friend Reynaldo Hahn, and he would figure as an imaginary "Markel," a combination of Marcel and Arkel, the father of Golaud (see *Corr.* 10: 261). "Il y a quelques lignes vraiment imprégnées de la fraîcheur de la mer et de l'odeur des roses que la brise lui apporte" (*Corr.* 10: 257) ("There are some phrases truly impregnated with the freshness of the sea and the smell of roses carried by the breeze"; my trans.) he wrote to Antoine Bibesco in March 1911. For Proust, who was an asthma sufferer, the scene of Pelléas issuing into the light from a dark vault (as in Beethoven's *Fidelio*) seems to have had a lasting effect. This scene, along with the delicacy and melancholy of the opera, is perhaps in part responsible for his affection for *Pelléas*.

Ballet

What a great watcher Proust was! When the Ballets Russes, Diaghilev's creation, came to Paris in 1910 for the second time, Proust was in the audience for opening night at the opera on 4 June. He was accompanied by Reynaldo Hahn as well as Jean-Louis Vaudoyer, the art critic. On this evening, the dancers Vaslav Nijinsky, Tamara Karsavina, and Ida Rubinstein were appearing in Alexander Borodin's *Prince Igor* and Rimsky-Korsakov's brightly colored *Schéhérazade*. The costumes and the decor, both by Léon Bakst, were orange, green, and blue. The principal dancers were adulated by Proust and the rest of Paris, Proust referring to Nijinsky as a "dancer of genius" (Tadié 543). About the set, he said "I never saw anything so beautiful" (Painter 2: 160). Tamara Karsavina, dressed in her dazzling costume by Bakst ("a painter of genius" [Tadié, *Biography* 543]) for *The Firebird (L'Oiseau de feu)*, was painted in the Auteuil studio of the society painter Jacques-Emile Blanche, the creator of the celebrated portrait of Proust with the flower in his buttonhole and the bright rosebud of lips beneath his moustache.

Nijinksy was the scandal of Paris for this 1910 season, and his famous death throes in Debussy's *Après-midi d'un faune (Afternoon of a Faun)*—based on Mallarmé's poem—were particular favorites of Proust. But in fact it was Bakst's stage design that so greatly appealed to Proust, more so than the dancing of Nijinsky or Rubinstein. Rubinstein also danced in Debussy's *Martyre de Saint-Sébastien (Martyrdom of St. Sebastien)*, which was based on a play by Gabriele D'Annunzio. But Proust preferred the sapphire ceiling in the sets by Bakst to the story or the dancing.

During the following summers, Proust would always attend the performances of the Ballets Russes, in his proverbial fur coat, while Diaghilev would sit in the master's box, eyeing the proceedings through his mother-of-pearl lorgnette. Beside Diaghilev, often, was Misia Sert, once married to Thadée Natanson, editor of the *Revue blanche*, where Proust could admire the writings of the poet Stéphane Mallarmé and the artwork of the painter Edouard Vuillard. So the cultural scene resembled the height of a symbolist performance, albeit more brightly colored. The performances were just like Proust's own work, in all its triumph of brilliant gossipy detail, subtle interpersonal relations, and extensive intertextual and interdisciplinary significance—exploding on the page and in the brain.

When Nijinsky danced in *Le Dieu bleu*—with music by Hahn, scenario by Jean Cocteau, and choreography by Michel Fokine—at the Théâtre du Châtelet on 13 May 1912, Proust was too ill to go. But when, in 1917, he attended one of the representations of Diaghilev's notorious ballet *Parade* with music by Eric Satie, he was able to marvel at the sets in their cubist blues and whites by Picasso, whom he had met for dinner at the Crillon, thanks to his friend Bibesco. So the worlds of symbolism and cubism came to inhabit Proust's novel, from which music is seldom absent, no more than is the dance of grand society.

Couture

There is little doubt that the painter with the greatest influence on Proust's novel, and perhaps on his imagination, was Carpaccio. Just as Carpaccio's Venice was the city with the greatest impact on the hero-narrator, the Venetian couturier Mariano de Fortuny in all his glory plays a major role in the novel (see Lydon). After all, it is an indoor gown by Fortuny that the narrator places on the shoulders of Albertine "comme l'ombre tentatrice de cette invisible Venise" (3: 895–96) ("like the tempting phantom of that invisible Venice" [5: 531]). The Countess Greffulhe, Proust's friend, had two Fortuny dresses, which Proust was able to study at close range (see *Corr.* 11: 154–55). When the narrator describes Carpaccio's *Patriarche di Grado exorcisant un possédé* ("Patriarch of Grado Exorcising a Demoniac"), in which one of the Compagnons de la Calza wears a cloak of Fortuny material, he brings the cloak's folds to the novel's pages, also evoking Whistler's Venice pictures (3: 225; 5: 876). When the gowns are described in *La Prisonnière*, they bring the elegance of painting to the worlds of literature and couture:

> Elles étaient plutôt à la façon des décors de Sert, de Bakst et de Benois, qui en ce moment évoquaient dans les Ballets russes les époques d'art les plus aimées, à l'aide d'œuvres d'art imprégnées de leur esprit et pourtant originales; ainsi les robes de Fortuny, fidèlement antiques mais puissamment originales, faisaient apparaître comme un décor, avec une plus grande force d'évocation même qu'un décor, puisque le décor restait à imaginer, la Venise tout encombrée d'Orient où elles auraient été portées, dont elles étaient, mieux qu'une relique dans la châsse de Saint-Marc, évocatrices du soleil et des turbans environnants la couleur fragmentée, mystérieuse et complémentaire. Tout avait péri de ce temps, mais tout renaissait, évoqué, pour les relier entre elles par la splendeur du paysage et le grouillement de la vie, par le surgissement parcellaire et survivant des étoffes des dogaresses. (3: 871–72)

> Like the theatrical designs of Sert, Bakst, and Benois, who at that moment were recreating in the Russian ballet the most cherished periods of art with the aid of works of art impregnated with their spirit and yet original, these Fortuny gowns, faithfully antique but markedly original brought before the eye and like a stage décor, and with an even greater evocative power since the décor was left to the imagination, that Venice saturated with oriental splendor where they would have been worn and of which they constituted, even more than a relic in the shrine of St. Mark, evocative as they were of the sunlight and the surrounding turbans, the fragmented, mysterious, and complementary color. Everything of those days had perished, but everything was being reborn, evoked and linked together by the splendour and the swarming life of the city, in the piecemeal reappearance of the still-surviving fabrics. (5: 497–98)

Although Mme Straus and Mme de Madrazo each offered to lend Proust her Fortuny coat, he refused, preferring to look at reproductions of Carpaccio's paintings (see *Corr.* 16: 57–58). The kind of fashion and sewing that go together to make up the greatness of the novel leads from that perverse yet comprehensible gesture of refusal to Proust's final comparison of building his work as Françoise has constructed her *bœuf-en-daube* and her clothing (3: 1090): piece placed upon piece, like a pattern in tissue paper laid upon cloth, or, in Proust's case, scraps of paper placed here and there, his "paperoles" laid one upon another, stuck every way on his proofs, to create the final version of his great text. What he omits, what he achieves by omission and tacking on, piecing together, will result in just a line or two, but all the same, he must have a few reproductions of the painter he so loves, Carpaccio.

That kind of obsession, like that of both a couturier and a simple seamstress, is contagious, luckily, for the readers who in their turn have to piece together all the diverse parts of the pattern so laid upon text and lives. It sews up all the separate strands of cultural context and writerly process into the great novel so enhanced by its different modes, from visual art to ballet to opera.

NOTE

This essay appears in a slightly different version in my *Marcel Proust*, Overlook Illustrated Lives (New York: Overlook, 2003).

"Maintenant, Regardez": Proust in a Postmodern Context

Margaret E. Gray

Cruel experience has taught me that one of the greatest challenges facing the teacher of Proust is the antipathy and prejudice students bring with them to the text. "But he's supposed to be so boring! so long-winded! And nothing happens!" Rather than fight these vast and insidious enemies, cultural hearsay and cliché, one might try to engage them as a teaching tool. Certain postmodern notions provide a basic framework for reducing the strangeness and otherness of the Proustian text and for demonstrating to students that Proust is not really so different after all. Proust is our friend; beneath what seems to be so alien, he is like us, runs the message of this postmodern approach. My purpose here is to explore ways in which such notions can prove useful in teaching Proust, primarily to undergraduates.

One important aspect of the postmodern, for instance, involves vision—different ways of seeing and multiple perspectives. Indeed, Proust himself was intrigued by multiple perspectives, as we see when we read that he sent Celeste, his housekeeper, to fetch a dozen pairs of eyeglasses for him to try. He kept one or two on his nightstand and never returned the others (Albaret 322). Could he have been trying to make a point for us—that different points of view are useful and should be retained rather than rejected? We might point here to the *Recherche* and the narrator's rapture at producing a description of the shifting perspectives of the "clochers de Martinville" episode (1: 177–80; 1: 196–99), where the lurching trajectory of Dr. Percepied's carriage produces an evolving scenario, a veritable choreography, of the three steeples in relation to one another: now posed on the plain, now separated in a jolt, now flinging themselves in the carriage's path, now hesitating on the horizon before vanishing, only to reappear. Perhaps Marcel's joy in writing this description derives not only from the act of artistic creation but also from the exercise in different perspectives it provides. It can therefore only be all the more Proustian for us to add yet another pair of eyeglasses, the postmodern, to his bedside collection. After all, as suggested in one of Proust's own images, lenses transform our vision, as when the oculist polishes them, sets them on our nose, and says, "Maintenant, regardez," and the world is suddenly entirely different (2: 623).

Postmodernism describes a contemporary, postindustrialized society and image-saturated culture, so let us imagine the owner of the nose on which those eyeglasses are placed. Who is today's reader of Proust—someone who reads for hours every day, like the young narrator himself in the Combray garden, losing track of the advancing afternoon? More likely, it is someone who surfs the Web for hours, inclined to agree with Anatole France, who, despite writing a preface for Proust's first published volume, *Les Plaisirs et les jours*, confessed that he didn't actually read Proust, for life was too short and Proust too long (qtd. in Tadié, *Biography* 849). In approaching Proust nowadays, one might begin by asking students to think about the mockery and dismissiveness with which Proust is associated in today's cultural climate. Depending on the level of the class, one might refer to Roland Barthes's effort, in *Mythologies,* to analyze the cultural significance of such simple objects as wine and cheese. Let's face it (one might say to the class), at this signifying level, in contemporary culture the Proust myth does mean tedium, verbosity, and minutiae. Students can be asked to find examples on the Internet or elsewhere of the cultural myth Proust represents and to interpret those examples for the class. My favorites include a *New Yorker* cartoon by Ed Arno of a woman saying to a book salesman, "I want something to get even for that new translation of Proust he gave me last year." Proust is understood here as sadistic punishment because he is unreadable; any gift of Proust can only inspire revenge in the receiver. In a parody by the columnist Russell Baker a man is overwhelmed with memories provoked by the scent of his shaving cream, while someone else pounds on the door, demanding, "Are you going to be in there all day?" The implication is that daily life in contemporary culture leaves no time for obsolete activities such as nostalgia and retrospection. Proust is not only punishment, he's a dinosaur.

Other examples, however, might demonstrate not the strangeness and difference of Proust but the effort to reduce such difference. Students can be shown the self-help book *How Proust Can Change Your Life,* in which Alain de Botton enlists Proust to provide advice in various arenas, producing such chapters as "How to Love Life Today," "How to Suffer Successfully," "How to Be a Good Friend," and "How to Be Happy in Love." Using this self-help approach, symptomatic of our age, one might suggest to students that Proust helps us correct our perspective; as Botton would put it, Proust teaches us how to see trivial things. Before students begin to read "Combray," they can be asked to keep in mind what is being described in the opening pages, why it might seem strange to them, and what new kind of perception is being proposed. Students might be asked to practice this different sort of detailed perception by recording in a journal their own experiences of the threshold between sleeping and waking. After students have read the madeleine scene, they can be asked to write about a similar experience of déjà-vu. For the scenes set in Mme Verdurin's salon, they can be asked to eavesdrop during a social event, recording conversation and their impressions; for the Montjouvain episode, where the narrator secretly witnesses a display of lesbian sadomasochism, students can be assigned to observe an event voyeuristically (a lunch date in a student cafeteria?), using, of course, judgment and discretion. Such exercises help students break down the barrier they may perceive between their lives and the events Proust wrote about.

Perhaps the ultimate expression to date of this embracing of Proust as "just one of us" is the comic-book adaptation of "Combray" by Stéphane Heuet, who set out to rescue Proust from imprisonment in a "ghetto of snobs," as he puts it (qtd. in Riding). Students can be asked to compare passages, asking themselves what interpretation of this or that episode in Proust's "Combray" is at work in Heuet's version? For instance, the comic-book version, if anything, makes Françoise more sinister in the *sale bête* episode. We see Marcel overhearing her fearsome cries and approaching the bloody scene through various rooms and corridors; we feel his hesitant trepidation, his reluctance at being drawn through his own fascination toward this source of evil (50; compare 1: 120; 1: 170). Curiously enough, very little of the comic aspect of this scene survives in the comic-book version. Similarly, students might compare the scene of Gilberte behind the hawthorns, where Heuet's abridged text indicates, simply, "Je la trouvais si belle . . ." (55) ("I thought her so beautiful . . ."). Students will enjoy discussing the nuances that are lost in Heuet's text by its omission of the remainder of that line, "que j'aurais voulu pouvoir revenir sur mes pas, pour lui crier en haussant les epaules: 'Comme je vous trouve laide, grotesque, comme vous me repugnez!'" (1: 140–41) ("that I should have liked to be able to retrace my steps so as to shake my fist at her and shout, 'I think you're hideous, grotesque; how I loathe you!'" [1: 155]). Such comparisons help sharpen student perceptions and appreciation of the original "Combray."

The postmodern also assists us in appreciating Proust's relation to his predecessors in the context of a literary tradition, particularly visible through the postmodern medium of pastiche. The architectural example often quoted in this connection is Philip Johnson's AT&T building (now owned by Sony) in Manhattan, with its mix of styles, from the broken roof and Chippendale pediment at the top to the Roman-arch entryway at the bottom. Understood by Fredric Jameson as an empty play with forms from the past detached from their contexts ("Consumer Society" 114), the pastiche helps us see in Proust an eclecticism of styles from a literary past, from the chatty *voici pourquoi* ("here's why") of Balzac to the almost sinister control of Flaubert. The Goncourt pastiche in *Le Temps retrouvé* provides students a highly visible example of negotiation with a literary past. Just what is being rejected in the narrator's discouraged reaction to the Goncourt journal? Students also enjoy Proust's pastiches, found in *Pastiches et mélanges*, based on the Lemoine affair, a news event that Proust found very "balzacien" (Sandre 694). Henri Lemoine, claiming (falsely) that he had discovered how to manufacture diamonds, extorted 64,000 pounds from the president of the De Beers diamond company, Sir Julius Werner. Originally, Lemoine's intention was to force a drop in the value of De Beers stock, which he would then buy up at a greatly reduced rate; but Werner discovered the truth, and Lemoine was eventually sentenced to six years in prison. Proust himself was a De Beers stockholder and initially anxious over the news of Lemoine's claim. In the Goncourt pastiche, he caricatures himself by circulating the rumor that a drop in diamond values has provoked the suicide of Marcel Proust: a false rumor corrected within a few paragraphs. Working on the quirky, mercurial form of the pastiche in class helps students appreciate Proust's often cheeky relation to his literary tradition and the importance of that relation to the evolution of his own style. A class competition on pastiching Proust gives students a heightened sense of the appropriation, internalization, and reproduction of voice that goes into the exercise.

Having assisted us in seeing the tangled and complex negotiation with a literary past carried on by the *Recherche,* our postmodern eyeglasses will also help us see the many ways in which Proust's writing anticipates what was to come later in French prose fiction, such as the *nouveau roman.* Here we might invoke François Lyotard's idea of the postmodern as a "futur antérieur," or what will have been. Dislodging the postmodern from any chronological relation to the modern, Lyotard instead considers the postmodern a moment of promise or possibility within the modern, a glimpsing of a certain sublime "unprésentable" (32) ("unpresentable"; my trans.). It is only in the future-perfect naming of what will have been, however—a round-trip through the future and back again—that we learn to recognize this moment of possibility. In this way, in going back to Proust now, we see the anticipation of what was to come; in going back to Proust through what has been written since, we realize that he shows us what will have been.

In this vein, students might learn to recognize Proust not only as an heir to Balzacian realism in his elaborate, detailed descriptions but also as a precursor to the *nouveaux romanciers* in his occasionally fantastic use of figuration. They will see how certain scenes, certain images, become hyperreal, almost hallucinatory, taking representation of the real to its very limit. One might point here to Alain Robbe-Grillet's *La Jalousie,* where elaborate, clinical, obsessive detail accumulates to the point of hallucination, as in the image of the centipede. The stain it leaves on the wall after being smashed by Franck—the neighbor who, the reader understands, is perhaps and perhaps not having an affair with the narrator's wife—becomes progressively larger, until it is as big as a dinner plate. Ultimately, the stain, emblem of the narrator's obsessive jealousy, spreads everywhere—to the sky, the valley, the study, the bedroom, the dining room, the road leading to the highway—and all these instances are narrated in the same clinical tenor (141).

Similarly, Proust's descriptions occasionally seem faithfully to replicate the world but, eventually, to go too far in doing so, accumulating to the point of crushing, or canceling, what they purport to describe. Narrative flow is interrupted, suspended, in Proust's writing, as mimetic description tips into hallucination, evoking a perpetual present schizophrenically divided from past and future, a present Jameson has specifically linked to the postmodern ("Consumer Society" 119). One might point here to the extended comparison in *Le Côté de Guermantes* of an elegant evening at the opera to a marine cave. The Guermantes and their guests are goddesses and tritons of the somber depths. Bald pates in the audience are compared to pebbles. The metaphor actually erupts into the scene itself, in the form of the princesse de Guermantes's crown of pearls and white seashells. The scene concludes with reference to an instant in which this *panorama éphémère* ("ephemeral panorama") is arrested in a sort of "instant éternel et tragique" (2: 338–54) ("eternal tragic instant" [3: 39–64]), almost as though the very weight of figuration had brought narrative momentum to a halt. A similar accumulation of descriptive detail occurs in the boardwalk scene where the narrator first lays eyes on Albertine and the "petite bande" (1: 145–50; 2: 503–14). We have a succession of disjointed images: the girls are compared to noble and serene Greek statues, to a luminous comet, to a machine recklessly released and careening along the boardwalk, to a group of birds about to take flight, and again to a Greek frieze or fresco depicting a procession. In descriptive passages such as these, the accumulation of imaged detail risks confounding and stalling narrative movement.

Such a use of images to redirect and confuse narrative levels, scrambling what Brian McHale calls the "minor" world of the metaphor and the "major" world of the novel (138), becomes particularly visible as narrative device in the post-1970 *nouveau nouveau roman*. Claude Simon's 1971 novel, *Les Corps conducteurs,* for instance, opens with a description of ten plastic mannequin legs in a store window; in the same paragraph, the narrative abruptly shifts to the operating-room scene of an amputated leg, the surgeon surrounded by a dozen young interns. Throughout the text, "conducting bodies" such as the image of the unattached leg act to reroute and redirect the text; the image has become the narrative's conducting mechanism. Students can be made to appreciate the subtlety and coercion of Proust's anticipation of this technique, all the more effective in that it is entwined within the conventions of realism.

As a final exercise for studying Proust in postmodern perspective, students will enjoy analyzing the semiotic implications of a batch of "Proust's Chocolate Chip Cookies Madeleine." Originally featured in the *Washington Post,* this recipe, it turns out, is nothing but the *Joy of Cooking* recipe for chocolate chip cookies, with one curious change: two minutes' less of that most Proustian of ingredients, time (qtd. in Johnson, *Proust Research*). Discussion might begin with the cultural resonance at work in this encounter between that most different, alien, and baffling of writers (putatively—now, of course, the class knows better) and that most intimate and familiar of banal childhood treats. Having noticed that the only thing Proustian about these cookies is their name, students can be challenged to consider the implications. What kind of negotiation is at work in this interplay of familiarity and otherness? What gestures of appropriation or resistance? What meanings can be ascribed to the subtraction of two minutes of cooking time? Is Proust being attacked or is he being appropriated? Is he being refused, kept at a safe distance, reduced to meaningless signifier, securely contained and quarantined elsewhere? Or is he being translated and integrated into the familiar, comforting, everyday routine of an old-fashioned, after-school kitchen treat? *Bon débat, et bon appétit!*

Coding and Decoding:
Names in the *Recherche*

Eugène Nicole

A well-researched field of Proustian criticism, the study of proper names in the *Recherche* has been mostly concerned with the question of their iconic properties, a fact that derives from the abundant, theme-specific discourse on proper names we find in Proust's novel. Unfolding in the narrative as part of the hero's apprenticeship, this discourse indicates Proust's well-known interest in language and, more specifically, his concern with the pragmatics of names. Thus, the *Recherche* illustrates the progressive erosion of the young hero's singular rapport with this class of signs. The importance Proust placed on this process is well documented. In a letter to Louis de Robert, in 1913, Proust mentions a possible triadic structure for his novel whose sections would have been entitled "The Age of Names," "The Age of Words," and "The Age of Things" (*Corr.* 12: 232).

Traces of this intellectually structured bildungsroman remain throughout the text. Thus the "Age of Names" is introduced by a narrator already able to theorize a semiotic—albeit idiosyncratic—opposition. Contrary to common names, he claims in "Nom de pays: Le nom" ("Place-Names: The Name"), proper nouns "présentent des personnes—et des villes qu'ils nous habituent à croire individuelles, uniques comme des personnes—une image confuse qui tire d'eux, de leur sonorité éclatante ou sombre, la couleur dont elle est peinte uniformément . . ." (1: 380) ("present to us—of persons and of towns which they accustom us to regard as individual, as unique, like persons—a confused picture, which draws from them, from the brightness or darkness of their tone, the colour of which it is uniformly painted" [1: 551]).

Practically all Proustian studies on names since the groundbreaking analyses of Roland Barthes ("Proust") and Gérard Genette ("Proust") in the 1970s have stressed that the examples the text offers as illustrations of this passage do not entirely conform to the phenomenon of synesthesia to which it alludes. Rather, in most cases, the context produces the synesthesia. For example, before having met any of the Guermantes, the young hero states that they appeared to him "toujours enveloppés du mystère des temps mérovingiens et baignant comme dans un coucher de soleil dans la lumière orangée qui émane de cette syllabe: 'antes'" (1: 169) ("invariably wrapped in the mystery of the Merovingian age and bathed, as in the sunset, in the amber light which glowed from the resounding syllable 'antes'" [1: 242]).

As Jean Milly points out, it seems obvious that the synesthesia antes/orangé relies much less on the nasal vowel common to both signifiers than on the metaphorical connotations linking the "Merovingian age," the "sunset," and the orange color ("Sur quelques noms" 67). Referential elements may also be embedded in such constructs, as in the following reverie: "Coutances, cathédrale normande, que sa diphtongue finale, grasse et jaunissante, couronne par une tour de beurre" (1: 381–82) ("Coutances, a Norman cathedral which its final consonants, rich and yellowing, crowned with a tower of butter" [1: 552]). The synesthesia that now interprets the same nasal vowel as "grasse et jaunissante" ("rich and yellowing") is obviously reinforced by or derives from this "tour de beurre," which, in fact, alludes to the name of the right tower of Rouen's cathedral. Other instances of contextual motivation rely on the so-called eponymic process, a practice typical of Plato's *Cratylus*, that consists of bestowing meaning on names that are not supposed to have any by finding in them a word endowed with meaning. Thus, "Quim*perlé* . . . s'*emperle*" (1: 382). In yet another passage, the hero dreams he enters "comme au milieu d'une pluie de *perles*, dans le frais gazouillis des égouttements de Quim*perlé*" (2: 21) ("as into a shower of pearls, into the cool babbling water of watery Quim*perlé*" [2: 324]).

Whatever the technique he uses, the young hero of the *Recherche* may be said to be a distant offspring of Cratylus, the character who in the Socratic dialogue of the same title argues against his opponent, Hermogenes, that names have been fashioned in such a way that their form reflects the essence of what they designate. In "Proust et les noms," Barthes recognized this filiation and, claiming that it is the novelist's duty to create the right names, went so far as to praise Proust for having done so (157). Genette, however, makes it clear that it would be totally erroneous to speak of "Proustian cratylism" (*Mimologiques* 328n4). Indeed, as Barthes himself had noted (152), the young hero's onomastic reveries will prove to be illusory constructs of his imagination and a source of repeated disappointments. These disappointments are highlighted in a number of passages ranging from "Noms de pays: le pays" ("Place-Names: The Place") in the second part of *A l'ombre des jeunes filles en fleurs* to *Sodome et Gomorrhe* 3. Arriving in Balbec, the hero experiences a dramatic collapse of the imaginary content he attaches to names (2: 19–22; 2: 321–25). Somewhat later, after listening to the duke's genealogies in *Le Côté de Guermantes* (2: 725–30; 3: 593–600), aristocratic names he had thought to be radically different from one another turn out to be intricately related. Later, during his second summer in Balbec, his automobile outings link places and villages around the resort in a similar way (3: 493–97; 4: 692–98). The final blow given to the prestige of names happens, as Genette points out (*Mimologiques* 325), in the form of a purely linguistic experience, when the hero listens to Brichot's etymologies (3: 280–84, 314–29, 484–86; 4: 396–401, 434–36, 679–81), which counter with the authority of science his own etymological musings.

A more balanced appraisal of these passages has since been offered by Antoine Compagnon, in his *Proust entre deux siècles*. He argues that the hero's disenchantment when confronted with real places in "Noms de pays: le pays" ("Name-Places: The Place") makes it unlikely that the hero needs this supplementary lesson to reject Cratylus's ideas and embrace Hermogenes's. For Compagnon, Brichot's etymologies confirm the hero's necessary disenchantment, but they also blur the duality of names and things, endowing names with another, new "layer" (235) and, in the more specialized Norman corpus (3: 484–86; 4: 679–81), nurturing a new, substitutive reverie that feeds on the evocation of legendary Norman invaders. Compagnon, however, does not only consider Brichot's etymologies in relation to the pragmatics of names. Assessing the extent of Proust's interest in toponymy—then a relatively new branch of onomastics—and documenting the sources of Proust's erudition in the field, Compagnon is mainly concerned with a related and equally important aspect of the question: How should we interpret the massive presence of such a "foreign body" in the Proustian fiction (253)?

Joseph Vendryès, who raised the issue as early as 1940 in an article that is perhaps the first to be entirely devoted to this topic, "Marcel Proust et les noms propres," interpreted Brichot's etymologies as a satire of academic pedantry—Brichot's model being a professor of ancient philosophy at the Sorbonne, Victor Brochard, whose name, it has been often noted, bears some resemblance to his fictive counterpart. Compagnon does not deny the parodic character of Brichot's etymologies; for him the professor's mania constitutes the degradation of a branch of knowledge in a novel, which he claims attempted to fuse all fields of knowledge (*Proust* 252). Not unlike the duke's genealogies, Brichot's etymologies and to a lesser extent those the curé of Combray had proposed earlier in the narrative (1: 101, 105–07, 117; 1: 142–47) would then constitute, Compagnon argues, traces of an opposite drive fighting against the organic unity of the work (253).

Onomastic reveries, as I have already noted, imply a relation between a name and a context. In this respect, they are variations on the *topos onomatos* Aristotle defines in his *Rhetoric* (1400b; 323) as a concocted reading of the proper name (Nicole, "L'Onomastique" 251–52). The same is true of their less poetic counterparts Verdurin/ordures (1: 283; 1: 409); Saint-Euverte/verte (3: 99; 4: 136).

In all these examples the names are being decoded. But, as Barthes remarks, insofar as the novelist is concerned with the form of the names he or she invents or "borrows" ("Proust et les noms" 154) (as Proust did, for example, from French toponymy, Illiers residents, the *Almanach de Gotha*, or Saint-Simon's *Memoirs*), he or she engages in a reverse, symmetrical, more or less intuitive and more or less apparent coding process. Quasi-transparent names, such as Larivière, Legrandin, and La Vivonne, are exceptions. Most of the time, morphophonological analyses will be in order if one wants to explain the "general semantic connotation" of the name (see Valesio 49). The endings of the names Legrandin and La Vivonne are good examples.

The "logothetic" function as defined by Christian Moraru (125) may also be approached at the level of diachrony. Onomastic variation in the drafts of the *Recherche* not only suggests that names are an intrinsic component of the creative process as a whole; in some instances it also helps us make more informed guesses about the values attached to the novelist's final choices. In the letter presenting the manuscript he was sending to Gallimard in 1912, Proust explains: "A la fin du premier volume (troisième partie) vous verrez un M. de Fleurus (ou de Gurcy, j'ai changé plusieurs fois les noms) dont il a été vaguement question comme amant de Mme Swann" (*Corr.* 12: 287) ("At the end of the first volume [third part], you will see a M. de Fleurus [or de Gurcy, I have changed the names several times] who was vaguely referred to as Mrs. Swann's lover"; my trans.).

When one considers the successive (and at times concomitant) designations of this character, evident in the drafts, it is clear that these changes represent interesting variants of a common form. In the case of Charlus, more specifically, two roughly consecutive series can be retraced: Guercy, Guerchy, Quercy, Gurcy/Fleurus, Charlus. One cannot entirely explain, of course, why the second pattern replaced the first one; moreover, mentions of Gurcy still appear in Grasset's proofs of 1913, together with the newer form of Fleurus. However, the final choice of Charlus represents a better solution to the designation of Palamède de Guermantes: a semilatinized version of Charles, it projects on the character an archaic or outmoded connotation, but its ending is also given an explicit derogatory connotation when Charlus is denigrated as a "douairière en us" (4: 346; 6: 112); this name, moreover, links Charlus to Charles Swann (both failed to accomplish any work of art); it also helps its transformation into a common noun (or antonomasia) effected in the diegesis in occurrences such as *un Charlus* and *les Charlus* that appear in *Sodome et Gomorrhe* and refer to homosexuality (Nicole, "Personnage" 214–15). In 1918–19 Proust will also align on Charlus the name of his protégé. Previously named Bobby Santois, he became Charlie Morel after this late revision.

Let us note that onomastic systems implying a common textual feature involve many characters. The presence of the *ber* syllable in several onomastic signifiers (Bergotte, Robert, Gilberte, Albertine, La Berma, etc.) has been linked to Proust's grandmother's maiden name (Berncastel) or more plausibly to the Merovingian names Proust came across in his readings of the historian Augustin Thierry (Richard, "Proust et la nuit" 23). The same pattern appears in connection with elements of the diegesis: the presence of the syllable *ber*, both in Gilberte and Albertine, will lead to the confusion of their names in the Venetian telegram (4: 220–23; 5: 869–73).

If one takes a close look at the changes affecting a given name in the drafts of the *Recherche*, some may seem to be unrelated (Montargis, Beauvais, Saint-Loup); others present evidence of morphophonological links such as the designations of the Combray River (La Claire, Le Loir, La Gracieuse, La Pinsonne, La Vivette, La Vivonne) or those of the musician Vinteuil (Bourget, Lignon, Vington, Vinteuil, or, rarely, Vindeuil). The choice of Balbec is interesting since the evolution of this name is closely linked to its signified. The place it designates already figures in *Jean Santeuil*, where its name fluctuates between Keregrimen, Beg Doc, and Beg-Meil, "small village of the Concarneau Bay," which, notes Maurice Bardèche, will give Balbec "its double Breton syllables" (1: 60). This comparison does not take into account the more complex diachrony that characterizes Proust's drafts. The forms include a series of elements borrowed from Norman toponyms (Bricquebec, Bouillebec, Bolbec, Querqueville) or slightly modified from them (Cricquebec, Briquebec). Some instances of Querqueville (the most common form in the notebooks until 1913) coexist with the *bec* ending forms, prevailing in the Grasset's proofs of 1913 and 1914. At this point, however, the Persian character of the Balbec church appears to have been reinforced in the narrative (Nicole, "Genèses" 118–19). Bricquebec is almost systematically replaced by Bolbec or Balbec. The names are thus reduced to two bisyllabic signifiers. This helps to explain the final choice of Balbec, which reflects in its "syllabes hétéroclites" (1: 381) ("incongruous syllables" [1: 552]) the dual Persian-gothic style of the monument, while by homophony it invites an association with such names as Usbeck in Montesquieu's *Lettres persanes* or the Lebanese Baalbek, as Genette has pointed out (*Mimologiques* 319n1).

This last example reminds us that a name's remotivation in the *Recherche* also relies on cultural associations. These may be perceived in relation to the onomastic code or subcodes of the language. Relying heavily on real names, Proustian onomastics as a whole conforms to the French onomastic code which, although it retains more archaic forms, conforms to the phonological code. Barthes was right in this regard when he posited a "francophonic plausibility" in names such as Guermantes, Villeparisis, Laumes, and Argencourt. Of course, more documented knowledge of the genesis of the text goes contrary to Barthes's claim that the novel's onomastics, systematically structured, triggered the entire process of writing ("Proust" 156). Barthes's reading of a subtly coded opposition between the aristocrats and the commoners should not be discarded. Yet other peripheral systems of names must be considered in relation to the French onomastic code. For instance, besides the Norman toponyms already mentioned, a name like Stermaria (Cauderan, Penhoet, Silaria,

Kermaria, Stermaria in the drafts) results from Proust's search for a character-istically Breton form, whose ultimate choice serves to bind the signifier more closely to the character, since *Ster* (water) applies particularly well to the young woman, whom the narrator obsessively associates with water or with a Breton island. Special attention was also given to characters of Jewish origin (see, for example, the case of Nissim Bernard in *Le Côté de Guermantes* [2: 132–33; 2: 482–84]). In the case of Swann, this origin is alluded to only in the pronuncia-tion of his name, which departs from the usual, English-sounding one. The same relation to a name of Jewish origin applies to Bloch (in a reversed way), who will not entirely free himself from his cultural roots by adopting the name of Jacques du Rozier. Rachel appears in the Grasset's proofs of 1914; the same document shows the name Gebzeltern being changed to Israel in the scene that describes the first outburst of Charlus's anti-Semitism (2: 123; 2: 470).

Most cultural onomastic associations are based on intertextuality or eponymy (Pasco 283). Some associations are tempting to establish (*Swan Lake* because of Swann and Odette) but do not appear to have a precise symbolic value in the novel's contents, unless one finds a way to determine that value through elaborate and at times far-fetched connections, as Michel Butor face-tiously does in "Les Sept Femmes de Gilbert le Mauvais." As an example of eponymic associations, Allan H. Pasco offers the case of the déclassé Mme de Villeparisis, who bears the Christian name "Madeleine," "that of the quinte-sential fallen woman, subsequently restored" (283).

It seems obvious that Proust's carefully chosen onomastics call for a number of linguistic, textual, and cultural associations. In addressing this question, a teacher might prefer to adopt a conservative view, while keeping in mind Proust's own theory of reading as expressed in *Contre Sainte-Beuve*:

> Et c'est là, en effet, un des grands et merveilleux caractères des beaux livres (et qui nous fera comprendre le rôle à la fois essentiel et limité que la lecture peut jouer dans notre vie spirituelle) que pour l'auteur ils pour-raient s'appeler "Conclusions" et pour le lecteur "Incitations."   (176)

> Indeed it is one of the great and wonderful characteristics of good books (which will give us to see the role at once essential and limited that read-ing may play in our spiritual lives) that for the author they may be called "Conclusions" but for the reader "Incitements."

(Against Sainte-Beuve 210)

A Lesson in Reading:
From *Contre Sainte-Beuve* to the *Recherche*

Pascal A. Ifri

Teaching Proust is teaching how to read an author who reflects on reading and gives lessons in reading throughout his writings. Reading is the thread connecting most of the essays and texts that constitute *Contre Sainte-Beuve* and *Pastiches et mélanges*, while *A la recherche du temps perdu* is, among many other things, a complex reading lesson.

Started in 1908 and never completed, *Contre Sainte-Beuve* actually developed into the *Recherche*, as shown by Maurice Bardèche, Henri Bonnet, and Almuth Grésillon, among others. First published by Gallimard and edited by de Fallois under the title *Contre Sainte-Beuve* in 1954, thirty-two years after Proust's death, the book is composed of fragments denouncing Charles Sainte-Beuve's critical method and proposing a better method for reading authors such as Gérard de Nerval, Charles Baudelaire, Honoré de Balzac, and Gustave Flaubert. The 1954 edition also includes several texts, written around the same time, that are in fact earlier versions of passages of the future novel, as well as various essays on art and literature. The 1971 edition, by Pierre Clarac and Yves Sandre, keeps only the critical texts written in response to Sainte-Beuve's method under the title *Contre Sainte-Beuve*, but it contains two additional sections: "Pastiches et mélanges," and "Essais et articles."

In *Contre Sainte-Beuve* Proust blames Sainte-Beuve for judging writers more on their human and social qualities than on their works. In so doing, he presents some theories that will reappear in *Le Temps retrouvé*. The most famous one, to which *Contre Sainte-Beuve* is often reduced even though it offers many other insights on literature, defines a book as

> le produit d'un autre moi que celui que nous manifestons dans nos habitudes, dans la société, dans nos vices. Ce moi-là, si nous voulons essayer de le comprendre, c'est au fond de nous-même, en essayant de le recréer en nous, que nous pouvons y parvenir.   (Contre Sainte-Beuve 221–22)

> the product of a self other than that which we display in our habits, in company, in our vices. If we want to try and understand this self, it is deep inside us, by trying to recreate it within us, that we may succeed.
>
> (Against Sainte-Beuve 12)

This conception of literature affects the way Proust approaches the authors he discusses and helps him discover their unique qualities. For example, here is the conclusion to his study of Nerval:

Mais tout compte fait, il n'y a que l'inexprimable, que ce qu'on croyait ne pas réussir à faire entrer dans un livre qui y reste. C'est quelque chose de vague et d'obsédant comme le souvenir. C'est une atmosphère. L'atmosphère bleuâtre et pourprée de *Sylvie*. Cet inexprimable-là, quand nous ne l'avons pas ressenti nous nous flattons que notre œuvre vaudra celle de ceux qui l'ont ressenti, puisque en somme les mot sont les mêmes. Seulement ce n'est pas dans les mots, ce n'est pas exprimé, c'est tout mêlé entre les mots, comme la brume d'un matin de Chantilly.

(Contre Sainte-Beuve 242)

But when all is said and done it is only the inexpressible, only what one thought one would not succeed in putting into a book, which survives. It is something vague and obsessive like the memory. It is an atmosphere. The bluey, purplish atmosphere of *Sylvie*. When we have not experienced this inexpressible something, we flatter ourselves that our own work is the equal of that of those who have experienced it, for the words after all are the same. Only it is not in the words, it is not expressed, it is mixed in between the words, like the mist on a morning in Chantilly.

(Against Sainte-Beuve 32–33)

Besides *Contre Sainte-Beuve*, Clarac and Sandre compile various texts by Proust and collect them in two sections. The first, *Pastiches et mélanges*, was written around the same time or a few years earlier than *Contre Sainte-Beuve*. The second, *Essais et articles*, includes writings he composed at various stages of his life. Most of these texts offer direct or indirect observations about reading or reflect the author's ideas on the subject, including the pastiches, which are nothing but, in his words, "de la critique littéraire *en action*" (Contre Sainte-Beuve 821) ("literary criticism *in action*"; my trans.). In fact, if Proust is such a good *pasticheur*, it is not so much because he can reproduce the stylistic particularities of the authors he imitates, but mainly because he captures their inner voices, the intangible qualities that make each one distinct. As Jean Milly puts it, "Le mécanisme du pastiche consiste avant tout à retenir et prolonger la musique des phrases de l'écrivain" (*Proust* 20) ("above all the mechanism of the pastiche consists in retaining and prolonging the music of the sentences of the writer"; my trans.).

However, the most interesting text in *Pastiches et mélanges* on the subject of reading is one of two titled "Journées de lecture," the one Proust used for the preface of his translation of John Ruskin's *Sesame and Lilies* under the title "Sur la lecture." This text describes in detail some of the author's most pleasurable reading experiences and contains a number of ideas about literature and reading that will be developed in the *Recherche*:

La lecture est au seuil de la vie spirituelle; elle peut nous y introduire: elle ne la constitue pas. (Contre Sainte-Beuve 178)

Reading is on the threshold of the spiritual life; it can introduce us to it:
it does not constitute it.   (Against Sainte-Beuve 211)

la lecture est pour nous l'incitatrice dont les clefs magiques nous ouvrent
au fond de nous-même la porte des demeures où nous n'aurions pas su
pénétrer. . . .   (Contre Sainte-Beuve 180)

reading is for us the instigator whose magic keys have opened the door
to those dwelling-places deep within us that we would not have known
how to enter. . . .   (Against Sainte-Beuve 213)

Since parts of *Contre Sainte-Beuve* eventually turned into the *Recherche*, it
is not surprising that reading is also a central theme in Proust's novel. If the latter can be summed up as a vast amplification of the statement "Marcel devient
écrivain" (Genette, *Figures 3* 75) ("Marcel becomes a writer"; my trans.), it is
also a lesson in reading (Ifri 202–18). Since the narrator ultimately aims at
helping his readers discover their own truths, he must make sure they read his
text correctly and thus he teaches them how to read. He does it by using
negative examples of bad readers and by providing reading models. The bad
readers include Norpois and Brichot, who are unable to understand true art
because they are prisoners of their condescension and supporters of a utilitar-
ian literature; Saint-Loup, who "n'était pas assez intelligent pour comprendre
que la valeur intellectuelle n'a rien à voir avec l'adhésion à une certaine for-
mule esthétique" (2: 93) ("was not intelligent enough to understand that intellectual worth has nothing to do with adhesion to any one aesthetic formula" [2:
427]); Charlus, who cannot read "d'une manière sérieuse et approfondie" (2:
856) ("in a serious and thorough manner" [3: 778]); Bloch, who defends the
cult of art for art's sake; and Mme de Guermantes, who uses literature only to
impress or offend her entourage. None of these characters realizes that the
good reader must "express a personal, authentic response to the reading"
(Soucy 679).

Among the models provided for the reader is the young Marcel who is able,
when he reads Bergotte, for example (1: 92–95; 1: 129–33), to discover what is
specific and unique about the writer's work while at the same time descending
into himself through personal reflection, both attitudes exemplifying what a
good reading should be.

The Proustian narrator continues to give us a reading lesson not only when
he explains how to read specific authors, such as Balzac and Dostoyevsky, but
also when he describes in detail the many feelings and impressions he experiences when looking at a painting or listening to a piece of music. Regardless of
the form art takes, one can capture its secret only by discovering the unity
behind it, art being nothing but the reflection of the creator's soul. For that reason, the narrator can use literary terms to discuss Elstir's paintings, in which he
discovers metaphors (2: 192; 2: 567). In the same way, Marcel explains to

Albertine that it is possible to find a number of analogies between music and literature:

> "S'il n'était pas si tard, ma petite," lui disais-je, "je vous montrerais cela chez tous les écrivains que vous lisez pendant que je dors, je vous montrerais la même identité que chez Vinteuil. Ces phrases types, que vous commencez à reconnaître comme moi, ma petite Albertine, les mêmes dans la sonate, dans le septuor, dans les autres œuvres, ce serait par exemple, si vous voulez, chez Barbey d'Aurevilly une réalité cachée révélée par une trace matérielle, la rougeur physiologique de l'Ensorcelée, d'Aimée de Spens, de la Clotte, la main du *Rideau cramoisi*. . . . Ce sont encore des phrases-types de Vinteuil que cette géométrie du tailleur de pierre dans les romans de Thomas Hardy."   (3: 877–78)

> "If it were not so late, my sweet", I said to her, "I would show you this quality in all the writers whose works you read while I'm asleep, I would show you the same identity as in Vinteuil. These key-phrases, which you are beginning to recognise as I do, my little Albertine, the same in the sonata, in the septet, in the other works, would be, say for instance in Barbey d'Aurevilly, a hidden reality revealed by a physical sign, the physiological blush of the Bewitched, of Aimée de Spens, of old Clotte, the hand in the *Rideau cramoisi*. . . . Another example of Vinteuil's key-phrases is that stonemason's geometry in the novels of Thomas Hardy."   (5: 506)

But it is in *Le Temps retrouvé* that the narrator clearly reveals the two principles that should characterize the reading of any good book and therefore of his: the good reader must be able to "sortir de [lui-même]" (4: 474) ("emerge from [himself]" [6: 299]) to share the artist's vision of the universe and, paradoxically, to descend into himself or herself to read what lies inside one's self, the book being like an inside "instrument optique que [l'écrivain] offre au lecteur afin de lui permettre de discerner ce que sans ce livre il n'eût peut-être pas vu en soi-même" (4: 490) ("optical instrument which [the writer] offers to the reader to enable him to discern what, without this book, he would perhaps never have perceived in himself" [6: 322]). The narrator's work thus becomes a way for the reader to be "le propre lecteur de soi-même" (4: 489) ("the reader of his own self" [6: 322]) to transform the act of reading into an act of self-discovery.

However, the Proustian reader is expected to go one step further. Stimulated by the narrator's example, prepared by his thoughts and his descent into himself, spurred by the reading that allowed him to experience myriads of sensations and even, as shown by Geneviève Henrot, involuntary memory, the reader must in turn seek his own truth through art (Délits/délivrance). As Vinteuil's music, Elstir's paintings, and Bergotte's novels are a starting point for Marcel's work, the *Recherche* strives to turn the reader into an artist. Indeed, according to the narrator, one of the purposes of art is to encourage other people to create. The artist can only transmit his personal truth; he cannot discover other people's truths for them. At best, he can guide them in their quest. As the narrator remarks:

> Ce que nous n'avons pas eu à déchiffrer, à éclaircir par notre effort personnel, ce qui était clair avant nous, n'est pas à nous. Ne vient de nous-même que ce que nous tirons de l'obscurité qui est en nous et que ne connaissent pas les autres. (4: 459)

> What we have not had to decipher, to elucidate by our own efforts, what was clear before we looked at it, is not ours. From ourselves comes only that which we drag forth from the obscurity which lies within us, that which to others is unknown. (6: 276)

Reading Proust is thus shown to be not only a unique experience that allows students to be introduced to a new world but also a valuable lesson in self-discovery and, ideally, a stepping-stone to an act of creation.

In Search of Hidden Impressions

Geneviève Henrot

The madeleine dipped into a cup of tea must be the most famous small cake in French literature, the most frequently reproduced "morceau choisi" of the whole of *A la recherche du temps perdu*. Present in every anthology, this passage has acquired the status of the model of involuntary memory, and it is frequently invoked, even by people who would be the first to say that Proust was not their cup of tea. For many readers a consideration of involuntary memory in Proust's novel still means jumping straight from the tasty madeleine to the last hours of *Le Temps retrouvé*, to those justly famous pages where the narrator, back in Paris after a long absence, is astonished to see reborn before his eyes the sun-drenched seascapes of Balbec, Venice, and the distant Combray of his childhood.

Those same readers would perhaps be astonished if they were shown that the uneven paving stones, the starched napkin, the spoon striking a plate, and the emergence of George Sand's *François le Champi* from the Guermantes library constitute merely a handful extracted from the large hoard of motifs of memory scattered throughout the novel. Establishing a complete inventory of the theme of involuntary memory involves scrutinizing all the episodes where the hero is troubled by a contingent sensory perception that brings back to his mind distant memories of things that had once moved him but had long since remained in oblivion. An examination of the novel from this perspective reveals a hundred episodes whose common feature could be characterized in the following way: A certain fortuitous sensation reminds me, in spite of myself, of a certain forgotten event and moves me to the depths of my being.

The field of involuntary memory, thus extended and properly surveyed rather than merely sampled, leads us to modify the classic view of the theme of memory—its composition, structure, thematic and narrative significance, and stylistic treatment. Such a survey brings to light certain constants that characterize the theme, certain deep laws that had previously passed unnoticed, and for good reason. I present them here summarily.

1. In agreement with a *profession of aesthetic faith*, which Proust develops elsewhere in his novel, the objects that provoke sensations of memory do not have to be distinguished by their aesthetic quality, because they are original and wholly personal visions of the writer who confers this quality on them by way of analogy or sublimation. Admittedly the dry biscuit of Proust's *Contre Sainte-Beuve* is ennobled by becoming an exquisite little madeleine in the *Recherche*, but the reasons are less aesthetic in the strict sense (its new beauty) or gastronomic (the delicious way it melts) than sensual, as is indicated by the ambiguous comparisons to which the little cake in the form of a shell gives rise from now on. However, the large number of nauseating smells (mildew, car fumes), things rough to the touch (the starchiness of a napkin), and harsh and

aggressive sounds (the whistle of a train, the hoot of a steamer, the hiccup of the heating system) oblige us to admit that the aesthetic value of the object is a matter of indifference, overridden as it is by the effectiveness, the potency, of the sense perception it arouses.

2. Now this perception, if it is to become the object of a memory, must of necessity appear again later on. It follows from one Proustian *law of writing*, exemplified many times in Proust's sketches, that the writer will want to present his memory motifs on at least two occasions. At the beginning of the narrative (for example in Combray or the first stay at Balbec), the first impression carves out for itself what is often a modest place in the flood of descriptions, but the text never fails to record a written trace of such an impression, even if only in a few discreet words. Then, much further on in the narration, when much time—time to forget—lies between the present narrator, the reader, and this original impression, a memory of the first impression comes as a surprise.

3. This law of mimetic composition (which requires that each episode—both impression and memory—be situated in real time inside the story) seems to support a *psychological thesis* concerning the particular way involuntary memory functions. Having described as two separate moments first the impression and then the memory of it, Proust could illustrate in a natural way his psychological law: that memory of this kind is involuntary because it escapes any intention the hero might have to recall events at will. In fact, even if the hero wanted to do so, he would not be able to because the process of forgetting has put certain past experiences beyond the reach of his conscious will. How is this so? A tenacious occultation veils them in his memory: sometimes they are simply obliterated because of the passage of time, or else (more frequently) a sort of repression seems to have brushed aside episodes linked to negative feelings (guilt, lasciviousness, unkindness, cowardice) with which his conscience could not cope.

4. In the wake of the previous point, we can see more clearly the *omnipresence of all-powerful feeling* in this kind of "affective" memory; memory linked to an emotion influences the text at the time of the first impression as much as it does when the impression resurfaces. Such feeling is not confined to the ecstasy experienced on its arrival (as in the episode of the madeleine) and later imperious resurgence (as in the episode of the paving stones), but it is often breathtaking in intensity and shattering in the torment it induces. A *feeling of inscription*, at first, at the moment of impression, may give rise to feelings of euphoria (associated with the holidays at Balbec or the walks at Combray and Venice) or to feelings of dysphoria brought on by mourning or guilt (in the awareness of selfish, lustful, or cowardly feelings manifested toward people who are otherwise greatly loved). Then comes the *awareness of reactivation*, which is often only the awakening to full consciousness of a feeling forgotten or repressed by memory, exaltation as the euphoria is rediscovered and, more frequently, feelings of pain and of being torn apart when the experience of separation or guilt is finally acknowledged.

5. This double play of repression and the return of the repressed to which the first impression and the memory of it are subjected finds its *stylistic equivalent* in textual occultation and illumination. The narration of the first impression (the one that the reader should be in a hurry to forget in the same way the hero does) is camouflaged, whereas the memory of this impression is thrown into relief, as if a spotlight were fixed on the past. The two textual fragments, sometimes composed together, sometimes one in the wake of the other, echo each other: they have to be analyzed through the process of close reading to bring to light the stylistic laws that connect them and those that differentiate them and that lend to each its specific character.

6. One can therefore envision the act of reading involuntary memory in *A la recherche du temps perdu* as involving in equal measure a literary theme, its psychoanalytic basis, and its stylistic implications; that is, there is a solid link between involuntary memory, the unconscious, and style.

MEMORY		UNCONSCIOUS		STYLE
impression		repression		camouflage
————	=	————	=	————
reminiscence		return		revelation

The forgotten impression, entrenched in the hero's unconscious, lies muted in the text, concealing itself in its most secret recesses. The memory, however, spurting forth impromptu from the unconscious by way of the senses, is illuminated by being thrown into relief in an unexpected and surprising way.

The theme of involuntary memory can be explored in a course requiring the active participation of the students through the close reading of short fragments of text illustrating the laws and procedures of involuntary memory. Such an approach would be effective in a course devoted to French literature in which students are already familiar with Proust's work or in an introductory literature course where the close analysis of carefully chosen fragments of the *Recherche* could introduce students to an important aspect of Proust's text. One could, for instance, as I have done, design a course where students focus on the theme of involuntary memory in works by several authors (including Rousseau, Chateaubriand, and Proust).

The modest exercise in textual analysis offered to the students aims to show hands-on how the deep laws of the psychological mechanism of concealment and revelation in involuntary memory can give rise, in their textual expression, to corresponding stylistic laws: camouflaging the first impression and bringing the subsequent memory out into the open. Starting from a minute semantic and stylistic comparison of textual fragments that are fairly easy to handle, we move to observing concretely how involuntary memory unexpectedly and clearly alludes to an impression that the reader does not remember having encountered earlier in the narrative. An attentive reading in reverse will allow the reader nonetheless to discover the original sensation. But at the same time, one will understand why one had not noticed it the first time around: the impression is camouflaged, perhaps concealed, by a choice of words that, although synonymous, sound different; it is perhaps hidden in the multiple folds of a long sentence; or it is perhaps submerged in a swirling description that drowns it in the flow of countless other sensations.

Textual analysis allows us to put a finger on these phenomena of reading and to identify their cause, their procedure, as we confront the passage that describes the original impression with the corresponding passage of involuntary memory, where the same procedure works in reverse, symmetrically. The different procedures employed by Proust, in both cases, operate successively at the levels of lexicon (repetition of words), syntax (exhumation of subordinates), rhetoric (unveiling of the comparison), morphology (identification of the subject), and narrative (dramatization of the event). I focus on the first two, as I set up the principal analytic stages that the students are invited to follow, chosen as much for the logical sequence of the discovery as for the syllogistic effectiveness of the demonstration.

The Identification of a Memory Experience and the Original Impression

We can consider first that each motif of memory necessarily creates a thematic bridge between at least two fragments of the text: the first recounting the original impression and the second the memory that unexpectedly resuscitates it. Now the passage describing a reminiscence always contains clues that send us back to the text where the impression was first recorded. Sometimes it is only by superimposing one on the other that we can understand some of the terms used in the depiction of the memory. For example: It is winter in Paris, so cold you would not let a dog go outside, let alone a young girl. In the gardens of the Champs-Elysées the boy is therefore disappointed that he cannot play with Gilberte, who is not there, when suddenly, against all odds, he hears one of Gilberte's friends call her name:

> "Adieu, Gilberte, je rentre, n'oublie pas que nous venons ce soir chez toi après dîner." Ce nom de Gilberte passa près de moi, évoquant d'autant plus l'existence de celle qu'il désignait qu'il ne la nommait pas seulement comme un absent dont on parle, mais l'interpellait; il passa ainsi près de moi . . . jetant enfin, sur cette herbe pelée, à l'endroit où elle était, *un morceau à la fois de pelouse flétrie et un moment de l'après-midi de la blonde joueuse de volant* (qui ne s'arrêta de le lancer et de le rattraper

que quand une institutrice à plumet bleu l'eut appelée), *une petite bande merveilleuse et couleur d'héliotrope impalpable comme un reflet et super- posée comme un tapis sur lequel je ne pus me lasser de promener mes pas attardés, nostalgiques et profanateurs,* tandis que Françoise me criait. . . .

(1: 387–88; my emphasis)

"Good-bye, Gilberte, I'm going home now; don't forget we're coming to you this evening, after dinner." The name Gilberte passed close by me, evoking all the more forcefully the girl whom it labelled in that it did not merely refer to her, as one speaks of someone in his absence, but was directly addressed to her . . . casting, finally, on that ragged grass, at the spot where it was, at one and the same time a scrap of withered lawn and a moment in the afternoon of the fair battledore player (who continued to launch and retrieve her shuttlecock until a governess with a blue feather in her hat had called her away) a marvellous little band of light, the colour of heliotrope, impalpable as a reflection and superimposed like a carpet on which I could not help but drag my lingering, nostalgic and desecrating feet, while Françoise shouted. . . . (1: 560–62)

The text underlines, without making it explicit, an incongruity in the decor: how is it that "in the place where Gilberte was," the lawn can be simultane- ously "ragged," "withered," and "marvellous," tangible and "impalpable"? And what do we make of the evocation of the "reflection" and the superimposi- tion? Why can the steps of the child be qualified as "lingering, nostalgic and desecrating"? These apparent obscurities of the text invite us to reflect. For the questionable divergence (the text says "at one and the same time") between two states of the setting (a spring lawn, covered in flowers, and a win- ter lawn, bare) and two feelings experienced by the "I" (expectancy and nos- talgia) proves that two stages of his life are present (now, the moment when he is remembering, and then, the moment being remembered) that are con- ⁴ or at least superimposed like a mirage ("reflection") on the mediocre frozen park. The divergence can be explained by the instrusion of ᵉ that the cry of "Gilberte" has awoken in the hero. Thrilled ᴵᴵ (he was convinced that she would not be coming to the diately transported to Combray some years earlier when, Tansonville, one Saturday in early summer, he had heard out in the same way by another feminine voice, that of e's mother:

e laissait voir à l'intérieur du parc une allée bordée de jasmins, de ées et de verveines . . . tandis que sur le gravier un long tuyau d'ᶠ age peint en vert, déroulant ses circuits, dressait, aux points où il ᵉrcé, au-dessus des fleurs dont il imbibait les parfums, l'éventaiˡ cal et prismatique de ses gouttelettes multicolores. . . .

"Allons, Gilberte, viens; qu'est-ce que tu fais," cria d'une perçante et autoritaire voix une dame en blanc que je n'avais pas vue. . . .

Ainsi passa près de moi ce nom de Gilberte, donné comme un talisman qui me permettrait peut-être de retrouver un jour celle dont il venait de faire une personne et qui, l'instant d'avant, n'était qu'une image incertaine. Ainsi passa-t-il, proféré au-dessus des jasmins et des giroflées, aigre et frais comme les gouttes de l'arrosoir vert; imprégnant, irisant la zone d'air pur qu'il avait traversée—et qu'il isolait—du mystère de la vie de celle qu'il désignait pour les êtres heureux qui vivaient, qui voyageaient avec elle; déployant sous l'épinier rose, à la hauteur de mon épaule, la quintessence de leur familiarité, pour moi si douloureuse, avec elle, avec l'inconnu de sa vie où je n'entrerais pas.   (1: 138–40)

The hedge afforded a glimpse, inside the park, of an alley bordered with jasmine, pansies and verbenas . . . while a long green hose, coiling across the gravel, sent up from its sprinkler a vertical and prismatic fan of multicoloured droplets . . .

"Gilberte, come along; what are you doing?" called out in a piercing tone of authority a lady in white whom I had not seen until that moment. . . .

Thus was wafted to my ears the name of Gilberte, bestowed on me like a talisman which might, perhaps, enable me some day to rediscover the girl that its syllables had just endowed with an identity, whereas the moment before she had been merely an uncertain image. So it came to me, uttered across the heads of the stocks and jasmines, pungent and cool as the drops which fell from the green watering-pipe; impregnating and irradiating the zone of pure air through which it had passed—and which it set apart and isolated—with the mystery of the life of her whom its syllables designated to the happy beings who lived and walked and travelled in her company, unfolding beneath the arch of the pink hawthorn, at the height of my shoulder, the quintessence of their familiarity—so exquisitely painful to myself—with her and with the unknown world of her existence into which I should never penetrate. (1: 197–200)

One can easily see that the settings of the two scenes are different: at Combray it is May, and the text describes at length the blossoming of the hawthorns, the flower beds in the park, and the lush grass duly watered by a pierced pipe. What strikes us in the Parisian winter is the rigor of the frost that has stripped the lawn of the public gardens and even frozen the flowing water of the Seine, "an enormous whale, stranded" (1: 565). The incongruities underlined in the Parisian decor are the proof that involuntary memory is producing a (hallucinatory) mental superimposition of two places, two moments, and two states of the "I," indicated discreetly by a few words. By the same reasoning we can explain the adjectives applied to the "little band" of garden: "marvellous" (because its appearance is magical, not real, not rational), "impalpable" (because it is mental), "superimposed" (because it is covering over the real park of the Champs-Elysées with its mirage), whereas the noun "reflection" indicates the visual projection operated by memory. Similarly the words "lingering, nostalgic" take their meaning from the complacent retrospection that reminiscence engenders and "desecrating" from the scorn the narrator still has for the garden of today.

For each motif analyzed, it is therefore important to help the students choose and isolate the coordinates that are peculiar to each of two distinct moments of the narrative that the memory is attempting to superimpose in a way reason sometimes finds strange. What are the spatial, temporal, and personal clues that correspond to the moment of memory? And what are the clues that correspond to the moment of the original impression? The classification of these clues might take the form of the following diptych:

Moment of the Impression   versus   Moment of the Memory

Sensation common to both moments

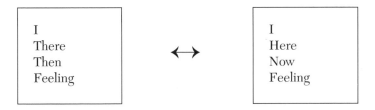

To localize the original impression and its memory and then to distinguish them demands careful attention to the textual clues that allow us to contextualize them in time, space, and the narrative dynamic. Who experiences such a sensation (or such sensations) and such a feeling (or such feelings)? When, where, in what circumstances? Using the example presented above, the two tables will be filled out with the following clues:

Moment of the Impression   versus   Moment of the Memory

Cry of "Gilberte"

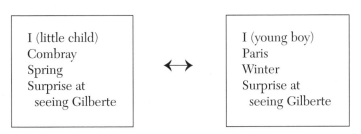

The Assessment of the Relation between Camouflage and Revelation to Which the Sensation in Question Is Subjected

The syntactical procedure   We have already seen the essential elements of involuntary memory: a sudden sensation reproducing by chance an identical but long past and forgotten sensation, a deep emotion opening the floodgates of a strong feeling, and an unexpected memory, all of which escape the will of the hero, who is controlled by the memory more than he is in control of it. The predominance of the fortuitous sensation in this type of memory is reflected in the style of the novel by the procedures employed to present the facts. The most essential and perhaps the most efficacious of these procedures consists in lodging the sensation when it is remembered in a privileged syntactical part of the sentence, such as the subject or object in the main clause. However, because in the passage quoted above this sensation at the moment of the original impression is eclipsed by the child's distraction, it is buried deep in the text and hidden from the eyes of the reader, occupying a secondary place in the sentence as an apparently optional circumstantial complement or as a subordinate clause of the second, third, or fourth level.

Leo Spitzer asserted that the Proustian period is the linguistic equivalent of the act of seeing. The syntactical ordering of the complements and clauses reflects the importance that the character in the scene gives to the constituent elements of the picture: the sentence, once having cleared the privileged situation of the main clause, with its subject and object, allows the acuity of the reader's observation to diminish gradually, and by its very length the sentence ends up exhausting one's attention. Thus a sensation tucked away in a subordinate clause of the third or fourth degree risks being hardly noticed, never mind retained, by the reader. Its subordinate position represents at the same time the degree of inattention that the hero has accorded it: the dampening of the sensation is paralleled by the marginalization of the reading.

Here is an example of the modulating role allotted to syntax. In *Le Temps retrouvé* the narrator reflects on the capricious mechanism of memory. For him, the memory of a book depends less on the fine pages it contains than on the sensations that accompanied his reading so long ago, sensations mysteriously held captive in the leather cover or retained in the smell or the grain of the paper:

> Il en est un de Bergotte . . . lu jadis un jour d'hiver où je ne pouvais voir Gilberte, et où je ne peux réussir à retrouver les phrases que j'aimais tant. . . . Mais du volume lui-même *la neige qui* couvrait les Champs-Elysées le jour où je le lus n'a pas été enlevée, je *la* vois toujours.
>
> (4: 464–65; my emphasis)

> There is, for instance, a book by Bergotte . . . which I read years ago one winter day when I was unable to see Gilberte and which I now search in

vain for the phrases which I then thought wonderful. . . . But the volume itself still glistens with the snow that covered the Champs-Elysées on the day when I first read it—I open its pages and the scene is before my eyes.
(6: 286)

In the French text, the sensory object of the memory, the snow, occupies in this sentence the privileged place of subject (in both the main clause and in the relative "qui couvrait") and is then repeated as a direct object ("la"); the logic of the sentence puts it in the brightest possible light. However, in the narration of these impressions of long ago, the snow and the sentiment it provokes (melancholy) are buried in subordinate clauses as we descend toward the dark dungeons of the sentence. At the end of winter, the snow covers the whole of Paris, and the lawn, white as ermine, saddens the little boy who fears that he will not see Gilberte at the Champs-Elysées:

> Le premier de ces jours—auxquels la neige, image des puissances qui pouvaient me priver de voir Gilberte, donnait la tristesse d'un jour de séparation et jusqu'à l'aspect d'un jour de départ parce qu'il changeait la figure et empêchait presque l'usage du lieu habituel de nos seules entre-vues maintenant changé, tout enveloppé de housses—ce jour fit pourtant faire un progrès à mon amour, car il fut comme un premier chagrin qu'elle eût partagé avec moi.   (1: 391)

> The first of these days—to which the snow, a symbol of the powers that could deprive me of the sight of Gilberte, imparted the sadness of a day of separation, almost the aspect of a day of departure, because it changed the outward form and almost forbade the use of the customary scene of our only encounters, now altered, covered, as it were, in dust-sheets—that day, none the less, marked a stage in the progress of my love, for it was like a first sorrow that we shared together.   (1: 566–67)

The admission of the suffering inflicted by the snow ("could deprive me of the sight of Gilberte") is, in the French version, hidden in two infinitive subordinate clauses of the third and fourth degree (*priver, voir*), whereas the object that stimulates the sensation is in the first relative subordinate clause ("to which the snow"), in a construction imprisoned between dashes. The syntactic position of the snow and its impression, making them apparently secondary, increases the likelihood that they will pass unnoticed.

le 1er de ces jours (the first of these days)
    auxquels la *neige,* image des puissances (to which the snow, a symbol of the powers)
        qui pouvaient (that could)
            me priver (deprive me)
                de voir Gilberte (of the sight of Gilberte)

The lexical procedure   Another reason the reader has difficulty immediately restoring the original impression of this or that involuntary memory is that Proust does not describe the two incidents with the same words. Consequently the impression and the reminiscence sound different to the ear and appear to mislead the reader. Unable to rely on the simple repetition of a single term (seeking out key words would therefore be totally arbitrary and the results would be disappointing), the reader is obliged to scrutinize the global sense of the text, paying scrupulous attention to synonymy, paraphrase, and variation. What counts is less the presence of the same key word occurring in both the impression and reminiscence (such as, e.g., "madeleine" or "paving stones") as the occurrence of a similar isotopy with the same number of semes.

An example makes it easier to understand this bafflement brought about by the lexicon, to which Proust entrusts the task of camouflaging—but not obliterating—the original impression. The first impression of the sea at Balbec inspires the young hero on holiday, who has just settled in at the Grand Hotel, to perform an Alpine reading of the contours of the waves. He contemplates, in a state of profound delight, the maritime scene framed by his window, like a Switzerland that has the color of a peacock's tail, while his routine of washing and dressing does not engage his attention. However, the first memory of this vivid visual impression is prompted by the scent of soap (while the second will be lodged in the stiffening of a napkin): "rien qu'à sentir pour la première fois depuis longtemps, en me lavant les mains, cette odeur spéciale des savons trop parfumés du Grand-Hôtel" (3: 161) ("merely upon smelling for the first time after so long an interval, as I washed my hands, that peculiar odour of the over-scented soap of the Grand Hotel" [4: 222]). The soap, clearly named and qualified in the text of the memory, passed unnoticed in the description of the original impression because it was not even named, and for good reason: the hero had paid it no attention. Nevertheless, now that the sensitive memory has exhumed it from distraction and forgetfulness, it is not difficult to find it (again) on condition that we do not expect to find the word "soap" there, because the object is camouflaged in the temporal subordinate clause "as I washed my hands":

> Mais le lendemain matin!—après qu'un domestique fut venu m'éveiller et m'apporter de l'eau chaude, et *pendant que je faisais ma toilette* et essayais vainement de trouver les affaires dont j'avais besoin dans ma malle d'où je ne tirais, pêle-mêle, que celles qui ne pouvaient me servir à rien, quelle joie, pensant déjà au plaisir du déjeuner et de la promenade. . . .
>
> (2: 33; my emphasis)

> But next morning!—after a servant had come to call me and to bring me hot water, and while I was washing and dressing myself and trying in vain to find the things that I needed in my trunk, from which I extracted, pell-mell, only a lot of things that were of no use whatever, what a joy it was to me, thinking already of the pleasure of lunch and a walk. . . .   (2: 341)

Many other cases of involuntary memory, set alongside the original impression, would reveal these lexical and syntactical procedures, which alternate camouflaging and throwing into relief. Other procedures aim at the same effect, whether morphological or rhetorical. Teachers interested in designing such a method of textual analysis may find the following references useful: Geneviève Henrot, *Délits/délivrance: thématique de la mémoire proustienne* and "Le Fléau de la balance: poétique de la réminiscence." I have conducted a classroom experiment according to this model with students whose first language was not French and found that tackling Proust's novel through small, well-paired fragments is a good means of access. It acquaints students with a work whose uniqueness and complexity they can thus grasp—without too much initial effort—through well-chosen passages. This may encourage them to further explore such a challenging text.

Proust's Esther

Emily Eells

The Book of Esther, which figures prominently in Proust's cultural heritage, provides a profitable approach to teaching Proust. Esther was a standard reference used by Proust's family, who owned a painting by the Flemish artist Francken the Younger (1581–1642) depicting the main episodes of her story (see *Corr.* 6: 327, 336; Le Pichon 216). The family members were known to punctuate their conversation with quotations from the Racine tragedy based on Esther, as Proust relates in one of the autobiographical sections of *Contre Sainte-Beuve.* On one occasion Proust played the role of the despot in bed, while his Jewish mother recited Esther's lines from the Racinian tragedy, accompanied by the chorus part set to music and played on the piano by his friend Reynaldo Hahn (Contre Sainte-Beuve, ed. Fallois 146–48). Given Proust's familiarity with the story of Esther, it is hardly surprising that Proust made it a leitmotiv of *A la recherche du temps perdu,* orchestrating its themes and transposing the artistic renderings of it he knew into his own prose.

Knowledge of the Book of Esther is a prerequisite to understanding Francken the Younger's painting. One of the shortest books of the Bible, it can be easily summarized: The Persian king Ahasuerus, rebuffed by his proud wife's defiance, announces that he is looking for a new wife. He asks his head eunuch to organize a kind of beauty competition so that he can make his choice. Exiled in the palace of Susa, the Jew Mordecai, who has taken his orphaned cousin Esther into his care, presents her to Ahasuerus, who falls captive to her charms and asks her to marry him. Mordecai advises Esther to keep her Jewish origins a secret from her husband, an Amalekite. Mordecai remains close to Esther in the palace of Susa, informing her of a plot to kill the king, who, as soon as he is apprized of the treachery, has the two conspirators hanged. As a Jew, Mordecai obstinately refuses to kneel to King Ahasuerus's power-hungry adviser, the Amalekite Haman, who is so infuriated that he revengefully asks the king to sign an edict ordering the extermination of the Jewish race. Mordecai begs Esther to seek clemency from the king, which she agrees to do if backed by prayers from the Jews. Wearing her ceremonial vestments, she requests admission to the king's exclusive inner court, to invite him and Haman to dinner on the following evening. Unable to sleep that night, the king requests that the chronicles of his reign be read to him, from which he learns that he owes his life to Mordecai. When Ahasuerus asks how he can honor a person to whom he is deeply indebted, Haman believes he is the man in question, so he suggests that the man should be decked out in a crown and sumptuous robes and paraded on horseback through the streets. Ahasuerus dutifully organizes these extravagant celebrations, enraging Haman when he sees that the tributes are meant for his enemy, Mordecai. During her dinner party, Esther reveals her Jewish identity and entreats the king to save her peo-

ple. She exposes Haman's perfidy, which prompts the king to put him under arrest and to punish him by hanging. Esther admits that she is related to Mordecai and asks the king to revoke Haman's bloodthirsty edict and to sign another one to protect the Jews. The Jews celebrate their freedom by shedding the blood of Haman's family and the Amalekite race.

Francken the Younger's *Esther et Assuérus* can be used as a visual aid to teaching Proust. The Jewish theme, with its associated questions of social status and religious identity, serves as a foundation for both works. The biblical story finds a counterpart in the Dreyfus affair, a contemporary political issue that Proust used to reveal his characters' religious affiliations and sympathies.

Francken's painting—like Proust's novel—is a striking representation of time, which depicts the different episodes of Esther's story simultaneously, as a composite whole. This painted narrative is a pictorial equivalent to the temporal layering of Proust's work, in which remembrance of the past and anticipation of the future are superimposed onto present experience. Each scene is placed in its own architectural frame, in the same way that Proust's novel is structured to frame the different stages in the narrator's life.

The central scene takes place in throne room of the palace of Susa. It shows Esther on her knees at the foot of the throne, asking for an audience from the king. He extends his royal scepter toward her as a sign of consent and listens to her, tilting his head with affection. Esther is accompanied by her ladies-in-waiting, who clasp their hands in prayer that her request will be granted. Their prayers are echoed by the pious figure of Mordecai, who is on the right-hand side of the painting, isolated from the numerous attendants and counselors gathered around the king. Behind this scene, other scenes, set in architectural structures, extend backward in receding succession. The foremost scene shows Esther entertaining her two guests at dinner. She is leaning toward the king, who can be seen in his majestically flowing robes. Opposite him is Haman, dressed in foppish, billowing leggings and oriental headdress mounted with a large protruding feather. The figure standing behind the king in the main scene wears the same headdress and can thus be identified as Haman. The next scene back is set in an ogive-shaped window. In the middle, the regal figure clad in scarlet seated underneath a canopy is probably Esther, who is issuing commands to her husband, the king, who can be seen on the left with scepter in hand. In the window on the floor above them, Mordecai is fervently praying for the king's consent to Esther's requests. The third scene is hard to make out, although its sense of chaos and violence suggests that it portrays the arrest of Haman. The last scene back shows the high gallows and the silhouette of Haman hanging. This series of four receding tableaux is joined at the base by the depiction of a procession that makes its way through the different frames. At the center of the procession, a man in noble dress and magnificent turban mounted on a horse attracts the admiration and compliments of the crowd. His thick moustache and long pointed beard identify him as Mordecai, to whom the king is belatedly paying tribute after learning that Mordecai had saved him from assassination.

Francken the Younger's painting presents the events in Esther's story as theatrical scenes, a technique that Proust uses in his narration. Esther poses with respect for the monarch, who responds with a ritual gesture of the scepter. He is seated on his throne, which is on a raised stage, framed by an open curtain and surrounded by his courtiers, who act as spectators. The painter has left the foreground of the painting open, as if this were a stage production. Mordecai appeals to the audience's sympathy with his pleaful look, just as the lady-in-waiting who is holding up the train of Esther's cloak gazes imploringly toward the viewer. The three inset scenes echo the theatrical motif of the central scene, staging the subsequent episodes like little puppet shows. The composition of the painting required representing both the throne room inside the palace of Susa and the scenes that take place outside it, which has the effect of blurring the boundary between exterior and interior, as well as between public and private.

Although Proust grew up with this painting and was necessarily influenced by its aesthetic construction, it is never mentioned in his novel, which almost systematically associates Esther with Racine's tragedy. Several of the quotations about Esther in the *Recherche* are from the central scene depicted by Francken the Younger and thus concern Esther's formal request for an audience with her husband and his compliant response.

Proust saw the strict hierarchical rules regulating social relations in the court of King Ahasuerus as a model for depicting the interactions in the society he portrays. He cites Racine in a passage about the protocol followed by the guests of the Grand Hotel in Balbec. After entertaining the marquis de Cambremer and his wife for lunch in the hotel's restaurant, the barrister disingenuously insists that his friends from the lower ranks would have been welcome to join them. He quotes the line Ahasuerus uses to reassure Esther that she is his equal: "Faut-il de mes Etats vous donner la moitié?" (2: 47) ("Of all my Kingdom must I give you half?" [2: 362]; see Racine, *Esther* 2.7.660). Racine is also evoked to convey the difficulty the narrator experiences trying to cross the threshold that separates him from aristocratic society. The narrator draws an analogy between Mordecai's position of exclusion—he is known as the man at the gates of the palace—and his own: though resident in an apartment that belongs to the Hotel de Guermantes, he is excluded from the social gatherings that his neighbors host there. Proust inflates the importance of the much-coveted invitation the narrator finally receives from the duchesse de Guermantes by comparing it with Mordecai's promotion from a neglected, ostracized Jew to a triumphant hero celebrated by the king. Proust has the duchess justify her remissness by quoting the lines in Racine's tragedy that Ahasuerus uses to explain why he has delayed in acknowledging his indebtedness to Mordecai:

> Peut-être parfois, quand, à l'imitation des princes persans qui, au dire du livre d'Esther, se faisaient lire les registres où étaient inscrits les noms de ceux de leurs sujets qui leur avaient témoigné du zèle, Mme de Guermantes, consultait la liste des gens bien intentionnés, elle s'était dit de moi: "Un à qui nous demanderons de venir dîner." Mais d'autres pensées l'avaient distraite
> *(De soins tumultueux un prince environné*
> *Vers de nouveaux objets est sans cesse entraîné.)*
> jusqu'au moment où elle m'avait aperçu seul comme Mardochée à la porte du palais; et ma vue ayant rafraîchi sa mémoire, elle voulait, tel Assuérus, me combler de ses dons.   (2: 673)

> Perhaps from time to time when, following the example of the Persian princes who, according to the Book of Esther, made their scribes read out to them the registers in which were enrolled the names of those of their subjects who had shown zeal in their service, Mme de Guermantes consulted her list of the well-disposed, she had said to herself, on coming to my name: "A man we must ask to dine some day." But other thoughts had distracted her
> (Beset by surging cares, a Prince's mind
> Towards fresh matters ever is inclined)
> until the moment she caught sight of me sitting alone like Mordecai at the palace gate; and, the sight of me having refreshed her memory, she wished, like Ahasuerus, to lavish her gifts upon me.
> (3: 517–18; see *Esther* 2.3.543–44)

The rules laid down by the despotic Ahasuerus, which make no exception for his queen, are cited as a parodic counterpart to the stringent rules the narrator imposes on his captive, Albertine (3: 11–12; 5: 11–12). When Albertine ventures into the narrator's room one morning, she and the narrator use Racine's *Esther* as a script to enact the scene depicted in the Francken the Younger painting (2.7), with Albertine as Esther and the narrator as Ahasuerus:

> J'espère que je n' ai pas eu tort, ajouta-t-elle. Je craignais que vous ne me disiez:
> *Quel mortel insolent vient chercher le trépas?*
> . . . Je lui répondis sur le même ton de plaisanterie:
> *Est-ce pour vous qu'est fait cet ordre si sévère?*
> . . . j'ajoutai, en continuant à jouer avec elle la scène d'*Esther*
> *Je ne trouve qu'en vous je ne sais quelle grâce*
> *Qui me charme toujours et jamais ne me lasse*   (3: 627)

> "I hope I haven't done wrong," she went on. "I was afraid you'd say to me:
> What insolent mortal comes to meet his doom?"
> . . . I replied in the same jesting vein:
> Was it for you this stern decree was made?
> . . . I added, still enacting the scene from *Esther* with her . . . :
> In you alone a certain grace I see
> That always charms and never wearies me
>   (5: 151–52; *Esther* 2.7.632, 638, 669–70)

Albertine remarks in passing that she had studied *Esther* when she was a pupil at a convent, which acts as a subtle reminder that Racine's tragedy was written for the pupils at Mme de Maintenon's all-girls school in Saint-Cyr and that its first performance involved cross-dressing and therefore sexual ambiguity. Casting herself in the role of Ahasuerus, Sarah Bernhardt revived the use of an all-female cast in a production of *Esther* that Proust would have known, since Reynaldo Hahn composed the music for its choric interludes (see Bidou 32–40). He refers to the actress's performance as the Persian king in an article published in 1905 (see Contre Sainte-Beuve, Clarac and Sandre 509). In Racine's conception of the play, concealed religious identity is coupled with concealed sexual identity. Albertine's and the narrator's playful acting is thus an encoded questioning of sexuality, both of the bisexual Albertine and of the narrator, who plays Ahasuerus, a role that was written to be performed by a girl and that we have seen Proust allot to the duchesse de Guermantes. Proust deftly puts Racine to use, equating the various stages involved in the Jewish queen's unveiling with those of a homosexual coming out, as Eve Kosofsky Sedgwick shows in her discussion of Proust and Esther (75–82).

Racine's Old Testament tragedies *Esther* and *Athalie* are cited so frequently in the passages of *Sodome et Gomorrhe* dealing with homosexuality that they form what Antoine Compagnon, in his *Proust entre deux siècles*, has called a "leitmotiv pédérastique" ("pederastic leitmotiv") (66). The first cluster of references can be found during the party at the princesse de Guermantes's at the beginning of *Sodome et Gomorrhe* 2. Charlus reveals the homosexual leanings of some of the guests to Vaugoubert, who is enthralled with the effeminate secretaries of one of the foreign embassies in Paris. The narrator describes Vaugoubert's reaction by quoting to himself the lines Racine gave Elise as she marvels at the beautiful Jewish girls in Esther's suite, who form the chorus (3: 64–65; 4: 87, cf. *Esther* 1.2.122–24). In the same way, when Vaugoubert learns that the ambassador's choice was motivated by his sexuality, Vaugoubert's expression is conveyed by Esther's lines explaining that Mordecai is responsible for offering protection to the daughters of Sion in the palace of Susa (3: 65; 4: 88; cf. *Esther* 1.1.101–06). Vaugoubert's astonishment that King Theodosius—whom he serves as French ambassador—has homosexual tastes is compounded by his apprehension that the king might discover his own sexual persuasion. The narrator translates Vaugoubert's words and looks into Racinian verse, reciting under his breath the lines Esther utters to express her fear that the king might discover her religious identity:

> Le roi jusqu'à ce jour ignore qui je suis,
> Et ce secret toujours tient ma langue enchaînée.   (3: 66)

> The King unto this day knows not who I am, and this secret keeps my tongue still enchained.   (4: 89; see *Esther* 1.1.90 and 92)

The chorus from Racine's *Esther* also figures in scenes at the Grand Hotel in Balbec, which is compared to a theater in which the spectator (or client of the hotel) takes part in the action, like the courtiers in Francken the Younger's painting (3: 171; 4: 235). When Proust has Charlus cite *Esther* in *Sodome et Gomorrhe,* he points out that Charlus is applying a wholly different meaning to the Racinian verses than that intended by the playwright (3: 376; 4: 525), though the analogy the verses suggest between Judaism and homosexuality is inspired by Racine's use of an all-female cast. Charlus makes his way through the "peuple florissant" (3: 171) ("flourishing race" [4: 235]; cf. *Esther* 2.9.790) of effeminate page boys, addressing them with Elise's exhortation to the Israelite chorus: "Prospérez, cher espoir d'une nation sainte" (3: 376) ("Thrive then, dear hope, of a sacred nation" [4: 524]; cf. *Esther* 1.2.125). The narrator highlights the boys' effeminacy by mentally addressing them with Esther's beckoning words: "Venez, venez, mes filles" (3: 376) ("Come, then, my daughters" [4: 525]; cf. *Esther* 1.1.112).

The pair of tapestries Proust hangs in the Combray church are the novel's first representation of Esther. They illustrate how Proust makes her story into a motif composed of the twisted strands of social intercourse, veiled identity, and literary pursuit (1: 60; 1: 82). The tapestries depict Esther's coronation, a scene that is situated chronologically before the scenes depicted by Francken the Younger and dramatized by Racine. They boldly mix reality and fiction, historical and legendary time, as Ahasuerus and Esther are said to be portraits of a French king and an ancestor of Proust's Guermantes family. Like Proust's novel, the faded colors and blurred outlines of the Esther tapestries record the passing of time and celebrate the triumphant moment when a Jew in exile was crowned queen.

Intertextual Pedagogy: Proust and Flaubert

Mireille Naturel

Intertextuality is, first and foremost, a research activity rather than a pedagogical one. Teaching intertextuality to nonnative readers of French is especially challenging because it presumes a degree of linguistic mastery that is always difficult to achieve in a language that is not one's own. Recognizing intertextuality relies on the reader's cooperation or collaborative input, and even when intertextuality is taught in one's native language it belongs more to the realm of hypothesis than to that of certainty. Citations must be identified and allusions uncovered. Even writers may not be entirely aware of the cultural knowledge that their memory stores up almost despite—or at least independently of—them.

Nevertheless, intertextuality is a good pedagogical objective, not only because it rests on a relatively recent theory of literature (Kristeva, Genette, Riffaterre) that has given rise to a fertile field of research but also because it is itself a source of richness: its heuristic dimension makes it possible to connect certain texts and sensitizes readers to the process of literary creation. How does one write? Why does one write? The writer is no longer the enlightened individual who sees himself or herself as a solitary literary sage. Nor is the writer the mere mouthpiece of the muses, a person simply plying the crafts of the phrase or word, or the pseudoscientist conducting an experiment. Has the author become just an imitator building a work out of fragments borrowed from predecessors? The process is more complex: writing incorporates its own mise en scène.

Working on Proust and Flaubert together, both giants of French literature, may seem ambitious. But the enterprise is in fact supported by the existence of a collection of texts. In a letter to Louis d'Albufera, dated 5 or 6 May 1908 (*Corr.* 8: 112; *Letters* 2: 370–71), Proust announces that he has the following projects under way:

une étude sur la noblesse	a study on the nobility
un roman parisien	a Parisian novel
un essai sur Sainte-Beuve et Flaubert	an essay on Sainte-Beuve and Flaubert
un essai sur les Femmes	an essay on Women
un essai sur la Pédérastie (pas facile à publier)	an essay on Pederasty (not easy to publish)
une étude sur les vitraux	a study on stained-glass windows
une étude sur les pierres tombales	a study on tombstones
une étude sur le roman	a study on the novel

This list is interesting for three reasons: it shows the importance of Flaubert to Proust, it announces what Proust was planning in 1908, and it enables us to compare these plans with his future works.

The first phase of an intertextual approach—which for the researcher entails tracking down information, making painstaking observations, and identifying hypotexts—is an ideal activity for an audience of nonspecialists or, at least, of nonnative speakers. The teacher selects a corpus of texts and distributes them to the students. This corpus comprises the following texts:

> "A ajouter à Flaubert" (Contre Sainte-Beuve 299–302) ("To Be Added to Flaubert" [Against Sainte-Beuve 89–91]): the three pages (or in any case the first page)
>
> "A propos du 'style' de Flaubert" (Contre Sainte-Beuve 586–600) ("On Flaubert's Style" [Against Sainte-Beuve 261–73]): the first two pages
>
> "L'Affaire Lemoine par Gustave Flaubert" (Contre Sainte-Beuve 12–15): the first page
>
> Letter to Francis Chevassu [11 Mar. 1908] (Corr. 8: 57–59): "Mes pastiches . . . un peu éminente," page 58
>
> "Un Cœur simple" ("A Simple Heart"): the entire text (Flaubert, Trois contes)
>
> L'Education sentimentale (A Sentimental Education [Flaubert]): the meeting with Louise, "Frédéric n'entendait plus . . . et de légitimer son enfant" (122) ("Frédéric wasn't listening . . . and made her legitimate" [100])
>
> Du côté de chez Swann (Swann's Way): the meeting with Gilberte, "Tout à coup, je m'arrêtai . . . de ses yeux bleus" (1: 139) ("Suddenly I stood still . . . of their imagined blue" [1: 197–98])

In Proust's work, pastiche and literary criticism are intimately linked. We have two theoretical texts on the subject of Flaubert: the well-known article "A propos du 'style' de Flaubert," published in the Nouvelle Revue Française of 1 January 1920, and an unpublished fragment, "A ajouter à Flaubert," written in 1909–10, which, although embryonic, is close to the 1920 article. Although both of these were written after the pastiches, it seems more pertinent to begin with the literary criticism, which sheds light on what Proust was targeting in the pastiches. The study of the 1910 fragment, in its incompleteness, can also serve as an introduction to genetic criticism, a facsimile of the first page (which can easily be obtained from the Bibliothèque Nationale in France) should be distributed.

The Critical Essays

Proust's choice of Flaubert's works in the 1920 and 1910 essays can clearly be identified. In the fragment "A ajouter à Flaubert," Proust alludes to Madame

Bovary and two stories from *Trois contes:* "Un Cœur simple" and "Hérodias." In "A propos du 'style' de Flaubert," the pertinent texts are *L'Education sentimentale* and the second story in *Trois contes*, "La Légende de saint Julien l'hospitalier." The works cited may be presented in class through concise *exposés*. The class can then turn to the main task: discovering Proust's focus and general arguments.

In "A ajouter à Flaubert," the principal idea is emphatically affirmed: "son immense nouveauté" ("his immense novelty"), "un génie grammatical" ("a grammatical genius"), "son originalité immense, durable" ("his immense, lasting originality"), "une originalité grammaticale" ("a grammatical originality"), "la révolution de vision, de représentation du monde qui découle" ("the revolutionary vision and the ensuing revolutionary representation of the world" Contre Sainte-Beuve 299; Against Sainte-Beuve 89). This revolution accomplished by Flaubert is apparent in his syntax: he makes particular uses of the definite past, pronouns, and the present participle. Through such innovations Flaubert expresses a vision of the world (as Proust himself will demonstrate). Human transcendence is abolished; things acquire as much autonomy as beings. Yet one weakness remains: the images are not yet sufficiently "absorbées dans la prose" (300) ("absorbed into the prose" [90]). Flaubert's taste for "symétries des substantifs et adjectifs opposés" (301) ("symmetries of contrasting nouns and adjectives" [91]) is, Proust finds, the object of pale imitations by rhetoricians and politicians.

Although "A propos du 'style' de Flaubert" begins by recalling the principal facts stated in the 1909–10 fragment—namely, Flaubert's particular use of verb tenses and the comparison with the revolution carried out by Kant—it soon focuses on the use of images and more particularly on metaphors, which allows Proust to assert, indirectly, his superiority over his predecessor.

A student can present the 1920 text in an *exposé* covering the whole article. The point is not only to summarize its principal ideas—which should be related to those of the unpublished fragment, namely, permanence and evolution—but also to identify the connections between Flaubert and Proust.

The study may conclude with a reflection on writing: How did Flaubert conceive of writing? And what does it mean to write well? Proust repeatedly emphasizes what Flaubert in his correspondence called "les affres de l'art" (Flaubert, *Correspondance* 234) ("the agony of creation"; my trans.). It is apparent that in 1909–10 Proust was still wrestling with aesthetic questions (he had just abandoned his writing of *Contre Sainte-Beuve* and was preoccupied with the realist novel, which his reference to Guy de Maupassant's *Boule de Suif* confirms [Contre Sainte-Beuve 300; Against Sainte-Beuve 90]). In 1920, more focused on his own work and its reception, Proust was attuned to those aspects of Flaubert that directly touched his practice: stylistic success (evident, for instance, in the close attention Proust paid to the depiction of Frédéric's search for a vocation and his discovery of love in *L'Education sentimentale*).

The Pastiche: *"L'Affaire Lemoine par Gustave Flaubert"*

> Pasticher, ce n'est pas déformer un texte précis, mais imiter un style: le
> choix du sujet est donc indifférent à la réalisation de cette imitation.
> (Piégay-Gros 65)

> A pastiche is not the deformation of a particular text but the imitation of
> a style: the choice of subject is therefore immaterial to the realization of
> this imitation.   (my trans.)

The series of pastiches known as "L'Affaire Lemoine," first published in *Le
Figaro*, dates from 1908, the year of the important projects announced in the
letter to Louis d'Albufera cited above and of Carnet 1, the first notebook to
which Proust consigned various notes that would serve as material for *Contre
Sainte-Beuve*, an essay of literary criticism in narrative form. The Lemoine
affair had erupted at the beginning of the year: the engineer Lemoine had sold
what purported to be the secret to manufacturing diamonds, and his fraud had
just been discovered.   This news item inspired Proust to write his pastiches.
The pastiche of Flaubert was one of a pair, the second of which was devoted to
Charles-Augustin Sainte-Beuve's criticism of Flaubert in his column in the
Constitutionnel. Ideally, both pastiches should be studied, but the second one
seems to pose difficulties for nonnative readers of French.

To understand the first pastiche, students will therefore have to have read
the story that the pastiche alludes to, Flaubert's "Un Cœur simple." The story,
which is short and simple, should be assigned in its entirety and without any
specific instructions. The edition that seems particularly suited to nonnative
readers of French, because of its judiciously conceived notes, is prepared by a
Flaubert specialist, Pierre-Marc de Biasi (see *Trois contes*). The short story is
a genre that is easy to study, but the meaning of the documentation, the technical precision, and the "effet de réel" ("reality effect") that is characteristic of
the realist (and naturalist) writers may make it difficult for an audience of nonnative readers of French without such background information.

Proust's letter to his *Figaro* correspondent Francis Chevassu provides the
students with additional interesting information and introduces them to a sample from Proust's voluminous correspondence, edited by Philip Kolb. The letter shows an author who is deeply concerned with the fate of his writings,
which is evident in Proust's mention of the desired regrouping of three pastiches, the clear link between the pastiche of Flaubert and that of Sainte-
Beuve, and Proust's wish to appear on the front page of the newspaper.

In an initial phase of discovery, the students are asked to find examples illustrating how Proust applied his aesthetic insights, voiced in his articles of literary
criticism, to his pastiche "L'Affaire Lemoine." The first sentence is particularly
significant: "La chaleur devenait étouffante, une cloche tinta, des tourterelles
s'envolèrent, et, les fenêtres ayant été fermées sur l'ordre du président, une

odeur de poussière se répandit" (Contre Sainte-Beuve 12–13) ("The heat was becoming oppressive, a bell chimed, some turtledoves took flight, and, the windows having been closed on the orders of the magistrate, the scent of dust wafted about"; my trans.). Students should pay attention to the use of tenses (imperfect, simple past, present participle in the passive voice), to parataxis (the lack of hierarchization of elements, of any causal link), and to the importance given to things, which become subjects of sentences and seem endowed with autonomy. The sentence presupposes a certain familiarity with Flaubert because it conveys the importance of the senses and sensations at the expense of action: heat, ringing sounds, scents. It depicts a scene filled with sensory notations and seemingly lacking in any human presence. The window is a symbolic element and leitmotiv in *Madame Bovary*: a demarcation between the pale, disappointing here and the idealized elsewhere, it makes possible a reading of the world. The turtledoves can be seen as prefiguring the parrot of "Un Cœur simple."

In a second phase, the students have to identify, on the first page of the pastiche, the allusions to Flaubert's story. A list of corresponding phrases would include the following examples, with Proust's text cited first, followed by my translations:

"une cloche tinta" (12) ("a bell rang"); "la cloche tinta" (32) ("the bell rang")

"des tourterelles" (12) ("some turtledoves"); "les colombes à cause du Saint-Esprit" (31) ("the pigeons because of the Holy Ghost")

"des prétentions à l'esprit" (13) ("pretentions to wit"); "des prétentions au latin" (20) ("pretentions to Latin")

"En tirant de sa poche une orange, un nègre s'acquit de la considération" (13) ("Pulling an orange from his pocket, a negro became the object of admiration"); "une dame enleva son chapeau. Un perroquet le surmontait" (13) ("a lady removed her hat. A parrot perched on it"); "elles [les filles du sous-préfet] possédaient un nègre et un perroquet" (50) ("they [the daughters of the subprefect] owned a negro and a parrot")

These borrowings should be closely analyzed and discussed: What use did Proust make of them? How did he transform them, and what effect did he achieve in doing so?

The students are then directed to reflect on the following points, which have been treated in the articles of literary criticism: the use of verb tenses and their combinations, the function of indirect speech and of speech in general, symmetrical constructions (adjectives and nouns) in writing, and the nature and function of images.

Style is, of course, of capital importance to Flaubert—and Proust has produced a good imitation of Flaubert's style—but, more important, through Flaubert's stylistic innovation the representation of the world is brought into play. "Un Cœur simple" is above all a realist tale, and it is therefore indispensable to study how Flaubert's universe is described through two traditional components of fiction: the decor (the elements that constitute it) and the characters (who they are, how they speak, and how they are described).

The final phase of study focuses on the success of the pastiche. It is useful to tease out those elements that belong to the news item (in the end, only a name, Lemoine, and a location, a courtroom scene) and those that refer to Flaubert's universe (a closed universe, an art of empty rhetoric, characters who are puppets, a caricatured view of society, a comic world described with humor). As a closing assignment, the students may be asked to write a pastiche starting from the same principle: a news item told in multiple ways (as Queneau did, in his own way, in *Exercices de style*).

The *Recherche* and *L'Education sentimentale*: Portraits of Women

In "A propos du 'style' de Flaubert," Proust refers to the *Trois contes* and to *L'Education sentimentale*, which was Proust's favorite among Flaubert's works. As an example of intertextuality I focus on two portraits of women: that of Louise in *L'Education sentimentale* and that of Gilberte in *Du côté de chez Swann*. Each forms a unit that can be studied out of context. The intertextual relation is based on imitation and transposition. Both portraits are inscribed within the framework of a love encounter, a literary commonplace that comprises a certain number of traditional components: characters—Frédéric, in Flaubert (third-person novel, impersonal) and "je" ("I") in Proust (an anonymous, falsely autobiographical self); a young girl (not named because she is unknown to the protagonist); descriptive attributes (clothing, colors, physical traits); objects; and ways of seeing (which, with Flaubert, pose the problem of point of view).

Although the two scenes begin with the startling effect of fascination—expressed through gestures in the Flaubert passage and through an exchange of looks in Proust—the latter ends with an aesthetic reflection from the narrator's point of view. This reflection takes on as much importance as the description of the encounter itself. The narrator retains and fixes his attention on an impression (the bright sparkle in the young girl's eyes) and not on the observation (he remembers black eyes, whereas they were actually blue). The stakes are therefore no longer the same; an aspect of memory is foregrounded and aesthetic analysis is superimposed on the description. We thus find in tandem the two essential components of Proust's novel.

This study could be complemented by considering the first encounter of Charles Bovary and Emma in *Madame Bovary* or that of Frédéric Moreau and Mme Arnoux in *L'Education sentimentale*. The second encounter is particularly interesting because Frédéric meets a type of woman that is new to him: married, inaccessible, and given to idealized love. He will, moreover, experience yet another kind of relationship with Rosanette, the kept woman who has many points in common with Odette, Gilberte Swann's mother. Likewise, the hero-narrator of the *Recherche* will come to know three kinds of love through Gilberte (young love), the duchesse de Guermantes (idealized love), and Albertine (carnal love).

This intertextual journey has enabled us to realize how much the literary text relies on the meticulous workings of language. The pastiche, which is primariliy defined as a stylistic imitation, turns out to be "literary criticism in action"; my trans.) ("de la critique littéraire en action" *Corr.* 8: 59). Through borrowings from Flaubert, acknowledged or not, Proust defines his own aesthetic; in doing so, he extends and surpasses his predecessor's work.

Homosexuality in the *Recherche*

Lawrence R. Schehr

Read the whole *Recherche* twice if you want to understand the way in which homosexuality occurs at various levels in Proust's work. This recommendation would be the most intellectually and pedagogically sound one a professor could make to students trying to understand the complexity of the novel. Although this position is valid, it is, of course, a utopian ideal, "Had we but world enough, and time" (Marvell, line 1). Students (whether they are undergraduates or graduates) are unlikely to read the thousands of pages twice, and indeed even a reading of the whole *Recherche* once during the course of a semester seems to be pushing the envelope. We recognize the difficulty of the reading, the dislike of reading that often characterizes students' attitudes today, and the sheer length of the project.

Traditionally, Proust has been taught in parts: perhaps a choice of "Combray" and "Un Amour de Swann." At best, a professor might choose to cover one of the volumes (the first) and then, with judicious filling-in of information, plunge directly toward the concluding pages and teach *Le Temps retrouvé* as a counterweight to the first volume. Though so much is omitted, this possibility does allow for certain explorations: a reading of Proustian psychology, thematics, and aesthetics. Students get a sense of the author's style, interests, and obsessions, as well as a sense of the way in which Proust constructs his universe through sinuous prose, layers accreted one on top of another, and the various modulations of time, tense, reflection, and retrospection.

Unfortunately, reading the *Recherche* in parts does not work when it comes to teaching the ways in which homosexuality functions in the novel. With the possible exception of "Un Amour de Swann," the parts of the *Recherche* are not freestanding. Given the circularity of much of the work, involved as it is in a "coming to writing," it is arguable that even the beginning of the book— everything before the madeleine episode—does not make sense until the narrator has become a writer and the exhausted reader has finished the last page of *Le Temps retrouvé*. Moreover, homosexuality is not contained in one section, as if it were the theme of part of the book, soon to be replaced by another. Rather, it is spread throughout the novel, though not evenly. Male homosexuality is barely present in *Du côté de chez Swann*, though the very theatrical performance of Mlle Vinteuil and her friend gives visibility both to lesbianism and to a kind of sadomasochism (1: 158–63; 1: 225–33), both of which will come back over and over. The student who reads only this volume will have no idea that male homosexuality will come to occupy such an important role in the later volumes, especially as Charlus emerges as an episodically appearing protagonist in his own right. The cruising scenes in *A l'ombre des jeunes filles en fleurs* (2: 110–26; 2: 452–73) and the initial pages of *Sodome et Gomorrhe* (3: 3–33; 4: 1–44) bring male homosexuality to the fore by the middle of the

Recherche. If homosexuality is not featured in the Albertine episodes, it certainly remains important because it is featured in the revelations about the homosexuality of various characters, including Saint-Loup; in the relationship between Charlus and Morel; and in the scene set in a gay brothel in which Charlus is whipped (4: 388–412; 6: 173–207).

The pedagogical imperatives, then, put us on the horns of a dilemma. On the one hand, there are the practical considerations: we should not expect too much from the students. On the other, we want the students to have a reasonably representative knowledge of the novel, which means presenting them with some aspects of male homosexuality. Indeed the subject has recently come up with the placement of *Sodome et Gomorrhe* on the reading list for the qualifying exams of the *agrégation*. In the first line of a new manual on *Sodome et Gomorrhe*, Françoise Leriche and Catherine Rannoux point to the revolutionary event that is the raison d'être for their book: "C'est la première fois que *Sodome et Gomorrhe* est au programme de l'agrégation" (12). ("It is the first time that *Sodome et Gomorrhe* is on the reading list for the *agrégation*"; my trans.). Putting this work on the list shows a changing attitude at the heart of the French academy, a change corresponding to various other changes in French society. It means that homosexuality, which is central to that volume, is no longer a taboo.

Let us consider two possible ways of proceeding. To make sense of the part of the book whose ostensible subject is homosexuality, Leriche and Rannoux provide a guide to the uninformed reader by listing the essential episodes that the reader has to know before tackling *Sodome et Gomorrhe*. These essential episodes are the good-night kiss, in "Combray," the spectacle of the relations between Mlle Vinteuil and her friend, the first part of "Un amour de Swann," the first stay at Balbec, and *La Prisonnière*. Other recommended readings include the whole beginning of the book up to "Combray," the grandmother's illness and death, Albertine's visits, and the relations of the hero and Charlus in *Le Côté de Guermantes*. The recommended choices seem wise, but each of those episodes in turn calls others to the fore, until finally the hapless reader has to read the whole *Recherche*.

What other preliminary choices do there seem to be? In the interest of space I would suggest just one, short of asking the undergraduate to read the whole *Recherche* twice. By judicious choice the teacher can organize the Proust part of a course (if the whole course is not on Proust) or the queer reading of Proust (if the course is on multiple approaches to the novel) around one character: Charlus. By making Charlus the focus of the teaching initiative, we can develop coherence in the approach to homosexuality that is dependent not on a choice of episodes but on the integrity of the representation of an individual character. However, I have reservations. First, presenting one character instead of an array of characters seats the homosexual firmly within an individual psychology as opposed to a collective, a representational system, a discursive field, a habitus, or the like. Because the character is presumed a reasonably coherent representation (not without his or her contradictions at various levels), it might seem to the reader that the representation of homosexuality is the same as the representation of a homosexual individual. Second, the study of one male homosexual character does not allow students to consider the interplay between male and female homosexualities or even between different kinds of homosexuality and heterosexuality. The single-character focus sets aside a certain number of facts about the novel, including the theatricalization of sexual performance by the lesbian couple of Mlle Vinteuil and her anonymous friend (the only important character in the novel, aside from the narrator, who remains nameless except for two lapses). Focusing on one homosexual character also forgets the interplay between homosexuality and the narrator's construction of jealousy within a heterosexual relationship that relies both on Albertine's hidden lesbianism and on the narrative model for jealousy in "Un Amour de Swann." Third, this approach cannot contrast homosexualities. We cannot play Saint-Loup against his uncle, nor can we get a full understanding of Charlus's opinions, behaviors, and dicta without a sense of the other homosexual characters in the novel. Fourth, focusing on Charlus could be perceived as an aesthetic perversion that reduces the narrator (or Marcel or the hero) to secondary status in his own novel. In understanding Charlus, the reader may not come to understand the artistic mission of the novel, the coming to being of the writer as writer.

But it is the fifth reservation that is the most problematic: a sea change in the novel happens in the beginning of *Sodome et Gomorrhe* that allows for the perception that the theme of *Sodome et Gomorrhe* is indeed homosexuality, even if calling homosexuality a theme is limiting and reductive. For insofar as the first three parts of the novel are concerned, the seeds of homosexuality are firmly planted. In *Le Côté de Guermantes*, which in many ways represents an alternative to the models of childhood, Proust constructs a constellation of textualities on which the beginning of *Sodome et Gomorrhe* will be predicated. I have already alluded to the role of theatricalized desire in the scene at Montjouvain. I would argue that the critical scenes in Balbec posit an impossible position or a taboo: the narrator might be gay or be perceived as gay.

The sea change, however, is this: during the opening pages of *Sodome et Gomorrhe*, the famous and often decried pages on the "race des tantes" ("race of queens"), homosexuality becomes what we would today call the operating system of the novel. These pages include both the narrator's recognition that Charlus and Jupien are cruising each other and having sex and the establishment of a poetics of homosexuality. In what way does homosexuality become an operating system? In the first half of the novel, while homosexuality is not absent and while the world is homosexualized in a slow process, the norm (without any necessary implication of normality) is heterosexuality. It is figured in the form of the family novel and in the archetypal heterosexual relationship between Charlus and Odette.

For today's students, far more familiar with the language of the computer than the discourses of literature, the analogy to an operating system is, I think, the best way of explaining that homosexuality is not just one theme among others in the *Recherche*. Before examining the consequences of categorizing the novel as one with a homosexual operating system, it is useful to summarize what an operating system might be in a literary context. First, the system provides the basic discourses or discursive formations, almost like a Chomskian grammar, that establish the norms for any utterances, analyses, or even narrative feints. Like a grammar or a foreign language, the operating system does not take another system of representation as its ultimate referent. The genius of Proust's approach here is the introduction of homosexuality as being its own universe, not one dependent on heterosexuality for acceptance. Second, like any system, homosexuality has its own language, rhetoric, and codes (behavioral, linguistic, aesthetic, among others). And third, like any other narrative logic, the system is a meeting between the individual discourse and the collective discourse. So the operating system formulates the inscriptions of desire and makes feasible a whole host of possibilities for that desire.

The entire *Recherche* after the opening of *Sodome et Gomorrhe* is essentially a conflict between two operating systems—like, say, the conflict between Windows and Mac—that the narrator is both discovering and controlling. It is important, therefore, to recognize, as I have suggested, that already in *A l'ombre des jeunes filles en fleurs*, there is a hint at the homosexualization of his position (2: 110–26; 2: 452–73). And by the time Charlus and Jupien have their first encounter (3: 3–33; 4: 1–44), which is overheard by the hero-narrator, who is surrealistically displaced to a position where he does not see but just knows they are lovers, Marcel is fully immersed in homosexuality (without, of course, having become homosexual or had a homosexual encounter): he has become bilingual. The remainder of the novel will be devoted to a struggle between the two operating systems, through the introduction or conversion of so many gay characters; through the display of their secret lives, as in the case of Saint-Loup; or through the focus on their relationships, such as that between Albertine and the narrator. The result, of course, is that the aestheticization of the universe, the creation of the novel as novel, the decrypting of life and hieroglyphics to perform art (the Vinteuil septet) are the means of making both operating systems coexist within the same space. Indeed, if Julia Kristeva is right to suggest that the novel as a genre is the locus in which narrative contradictions are contained, then Proust's novel illustrates this in perhaps its most overarching yet simple form. Through its transformational aesthetics, the *Recherche* contains both operating systems of homosexuality and heterosexuality, finds an instant translator (narrative itself, the narrator as Leibnitzian God) to interpret the two, and queers both in the process.

Indeed, queering is the necessary word. Another way to say it would be deconstructing, if one were to use an older and straighter vocabulary. The queering of heterosexuality and homosexuality is a way of destabilizing the received knowledge about both. Heterosexuality is deprived of its presumption of being both original and originary. It does not found the systems of the world or even provide an absolute referent for narrative. It is part social construction and part fiction. Even if what heterosexuality purports to represent in its most basic aspect, desire before language, that desire is always framed by a changing discourse depending on social class and historical, aesthetic, and cultural constructs. Thus even in the world of this novel, the construction of heterosexual desire is time related, "Combray" is constructed in terms of the family novel, and the family is perceived as being an original structure. The basic heterosexual love affair is constructed as a sociocultural phenomenon founded in the world and discourses of the aristocratic classes of the Second Empire, the classes to which Swann, Odette, the Verdurins, and others belong. Even the narrator's heterosexual love is mimetic in the Girardian sense for both Gilberte and Odette and structural for Albertine. By structural I mean his love is not directly mimetic but, rather, repetitive of other examples of love, such as Swann's love for Odette. Homosexuality too is constructed, both as an individual psychology and as a collective discourse.

Much critical focus has been placed on the initial pages of *Sodome et Gomorrhe* (3: 1–33; 4: 1–44), in which the narrator offers numerous analyses of the "race des tantes" while discovering the truth about Charlus (and about his encounter with Jupien). As gender studies found its voice in the past twenty years, the opening pages became a common focus for criticism and specifically for demonstrating internalized homophobia. Proust, the argument goes, just doesn't like other gay men. André Gide becomes the hero and Proust the straw man, because of the way each writes and lives his life: one is open, the other closeted; one is not homophobic, the other is.

Here, I would offer the following remarks. First, terms like *closet* and *internalized homophobia* are culturally, academically, and institutionally coded. In a simple oppositional way, the French and American contexts are not the same. Culturally, the two perspectives have different senses of what is private and what is public, a different concept of identity politics (because of different conceptions of the self), and different senses of a confessional culture. Second, the opening thirty-two pages of *Sodome et Gomorrhe* are both a poetics and a queering of homosexuality: a massively complicated, interweaving series of intricate metaphors that once again relate to one another but that also relate to previous parts of the novel. Following the chains and the rhetoric of the metaphors is an important pedagogical tool, both for demonstrating the complexities and ambiguities of Proust's discourses and for deconstructing any simple concept of thematics or homophobia. As a queering of homosexuality (and of heterosexuality as well), these pages undo received knowledge by destabilizing it, by putting categories into question, and by introducing discourse only to deconstruct it through rhetoric.

What then does the professor do? Short of asking the undergraduates to read the *Recherche* twice, risking professoricide in the process, he or she has to choose. I would return to the comments and reservations made above: perhaps the class could focus on the character of Charlus from the beginning to the end of the *Recherche* and interweave that with a close reading of the thirty-two-page section of *Sodome et Gomorrhe*. A class that focuses on Charlus, however, leaves major pieces missing and naturalizes homosexuality too much instead of queers it, as the operational-system mode does. Yet by alternating between a narrative, character-oriented reading and a discursive analysis—even including explications de texte—we might just begin to get a pedagogical handle on the revolutionary sense of narrative and discursive aspects of Proust's novel. And in so doing, we might convince the students to read the *Recherche* once or even twice.

Proust and the Cinema

Rebecca Graves

Studying film adaptations of *A la recherche du temps perdu* in the context of a literature course presents certain difficulties: students must be equipped with a new vocabulary, introduced to the fundamental techniques of cinema, and challenged to approach film in a critical and analytic fashion. A good point of departure is Walter Benjamin's essay "The Work of Art in the Age of Its Mechanical Reproduction," which engages with the ontological status of film and how film organizes reality. Other texts that introduce students to film analysis are Sergei Eisenstein's "Beyond the Shot: The Cinematographic Principle and the Ideogram"; Vsevolod Pudovkin's "On Editing"; Siegfried Kracauer's "Basic Concepts"; Christian Metz's "Some Points in the Semiotics of the Cinema"; and, finally, Laura Mulvey's seminal essay on the cinematic gaze, "Visual Pleasure and Narrative Cinema." All these essays can be found in Leo Braudy and Marshall Cohen's anthology *Film Theory and Criticism: Introductory Readings*. Students must, moreover, be made to realize that in film adaptations, fidelity replaces mimesis as the dominant trope of analysis. Yet, as with mimesis, in assessing fidelity students need to consider the peculiarities of the semiotic system—here film—into which the world or text has been translated. As Dudley Andrew has noted in his chapter "Adaptation," on a basic level film adaptation presents students with a delimited and therefore possibly more accessible representational model in which the filmmaker stands in relation to a given narrative as its author stands in relation to the world. As the text engages with and translates the reality it represents, so the film engages with and rewrites the text it represents, which makes for a complex reading that can best be accounted for by a dialogic model of adaptation. Such a model is pertinent not only to a study of film adaptation but also to a more general consideration of representation itself.

A Dialogic Model of Adaptation

Three film adaptations of the *Recherche* have been made to date: Volker Schlöndorff's 1984 *Un Amour de Swann* (*Swann in Love*); Raoul Ruiz's 1999 *Le Temps retrouvé* (*Time Regained*); and Chantal Akerman's *La Captive* (*The Captive*), which saw wide release in 2000. I focus on the films of Ruiz and Akerman. Ruiz provides an interesting example of translation between semiotic systems whereas Akerman attempts to distance herself from the text and thus engages with the concept of fidelity. Yet before discussing the individual films, I would like to briefly outline a dialogic model of film adaptation.

On both sides of the Atlantic, contemporary theories of adaptation invariably invoke André Bazin, whose principal writings on film are collected in *Qu'est-ce que le cinéma?* ("What Is Cinema?") (see also "Pour un cinéma" and "Adaptation"), as both influence and foil. Writing in defense of adaptation, Bazin discards the question of fidelity and privileges a model of adaptation that equates cinematic techniques or visual images with stylistic or thematic aspects of the adapted text. Bazin's insistence on moving beyond a literal notion of fidelity is the point of departure for all subsequent investigations of cinematographic adaptation. Yet he recuperates the concept of fidelity by arguing that a literary text has an essential meaning that transcends language and can be conveyed by nonlinguistic media. Recent theories proposed by Robert Stam and Marie-Claire Ropars-Wuilleumier use this aspect of Bazin's model of adaptation as a foil. Stam's definition of a dialogic model of film adaptation is in explicit opposition to Bazin's: for Stam, a dialogic model must focus not on ontological essence but on diacritical specificity (59). For Ropars-Wuilleumier, whose model is informed by the work of Maurice Blanchot, the dialogic relation between film and text provides a unique chance to theorize the tension between making and unmaking that lies at the center of both literary and filmic texts (*Ecraniques* 164–70). Stam calls into service Gérard Genette's taxonomy of transtextuality (see *Palimpsestes*), proposing that the relation between hypotext (the novel) and hypertext (the adaptation) be viewed as dynamic rather than imitative. In accordance with the specific capacities and needs of film, the adaptation in effect translates the novel. The final result is not simply a transposition of the original work into another medium but a new work that is nonetheless defined by its dialogic relation to the novel (64). Finally, Stam insists that the historical moment and material conditions of the production and dissemination of both text and film constitute integral aspects of the dialogics of adaptation. An appreciation of the multifarious facets (formal, political, ideological, aesthetic) of any given work and its adaptations necessitates an engagement with its particular situation, in the broadest sense of the term.

Should Proust Have Made a Film?

In the December 1946 issue of *La Revue du cinéma*, Jacques Bourgeois suggests that *A la recherche du temps perdu* is in fact "un appel désespéré de la littérature au cinéma" (28) ("literature's despairing appeal to cinema"; my trans.). He argues that Proust strives to endow words with sensory rather than intellectual value. As this is in Bourgeois's eyes impossible, it is his view that for the evocation of sensation film is a far more efficacious medium than language because it is composed of visual and aural images rather than words (20).

Bourgeois's argument is an interesting means of introducing students to the question of translation from one semiotic system to another. Founded on the fundamental difference between language and the filmic image, his polemical stance invites students to analyze their difference and familiarizes them with the concept of cinematic montage, the filmic equivalent of syntax.

Ruiz integrates some of Bourgeois's suggestions in his adaptation of *Le Temps retrouvé*. Ruiz's choice of the last volume underscores where his interests in the *Recherche* lie: the complicated achronology of memory is another example of what Bourgeois finds to be cinematic in the work. Using the illusionist capabilities of film to represent the associative chronology of the last volume of the *Recherche*, Ruiz juxtaposes, rather than transitions between, sequences involving different characters from the novel. The sequences play off one another and create a resonance that resists the classic narrative pattern of conflict and resolution. Ruiz also employs to great effect the various technical devices available to him: roses fade into birds in the wallpaper of the narrator's room; the furniture moves around, as if to suggest the passage of time, or grows to fill the room, suggesting a change of perspective; as he reads a letter from Gilberte, the narrator's chair rises to the top of a crowded café as the child version of himself projects footage of the First World War on the wall; and, finally, a series of montages evoke the all-important moments of involuntary memory experienced by the narrator as he waits for admittance to the matinee at the home of the princesse de Guermantes.

As Jonathan Rosenbaum demonstrates in his review of the film, a comparison of the opening lines of *Le Temps retrouvé* and the opening sequence of Ruiz's film is an effective means of appreciating both Ruiz's effort to remain close to the text and the distance that necessarily separates language from visual image. Another possible point of comparison between text and film is the episode of the oeil-de-boeuf, in which the narrator observes a young ruffian beating the baron de Charlus in Jupien's brothel (4: 394; 6: 181–82). The film sequence departs from the fairly straightforward textual account and thus demonstrates the dialogic model of film adaptation. Rather than seek out the isolated room at the top of the stairs, which the narrator does in the novel, in the film he hears the muffled cries while resting in his own room. He listens at his door rather than at the door of Charlus's room, a simplification that does indeed affect the significance of the sequence, since the narrator takes a less active role in seeking out the source of the disturbing noise. Furthermore, before the chained Charlus is revealed to the narrator and the spectator, the camera, trained on the hallway outside Charlus's room, remains static in a long take as the narrator fetches one chair and, unsatisfied, puts it back in its place, finally returning to his room and coming back with a different chair. This delay serves a dual purpose: to create suspense and to illustrate the fastidious character of the narrator.

Marcel at last climbs onto the chair, and the spectator watches him cringe at the spectacle revealed to him through the round window. The camera lingers for several moments before satisfying the spectator's curiosity, as if to emphasize the narrator's voyeuristic pleasure, in which the spectator is implicitly participating. A rapid series of shots follows the extended shot of the hallway: we see a whip hitting a scarred back; Charlus's face pressed into his pillow and framed by chains; a close-up of an eye, which we assume to be the narrator's; Charlus laughing; the backlit figure of the boy; another close-up of the eye, this time rolling back into the head. In the final two shots, a viscous red liquid drips down the camera lens, and we hear the sound of children at play. The red liquid, reminiscent of low-budget horror movies, playfully undermines the iconic status of the Proustian text. Furthermore, the soundtrack of children laughing and playing that accompanies the sadomasochistic display recalls an earlier sequence in which the young Marcel is playing with Gilberte, linking Charlus's adult sex games with the games the narrator played as a child. This association suggests to the spectator that there was a sexual dimension to these childish games with Gilberte, a suggestion that also exists in the text, as the narrator and Gilberte's wrestling match in the Luxembourg Gardens attests (1: 484–85; 2: 90).

On another level, this sequence makes an important point about the narrator's position vis-à-vis the spectacle he is recounting; the second close-up of the eye, in which it rolls back into the head as if at the height of sexual ecstasy, creates a metonymic link between Charlus and the narrator, a link underscored by the soundtrack. The film sequence thus accomplishes many things: it connects the narrator's voyeurism with the voyeurism of cinema; collapses the distance between low and high culture by using a B-movie technique; and evokes the important, if occulted, link between Charlus and the narrator. The film is engaging the text, the iconic status of the text, and cinematic convention, a range of operations that can be accounted for only by a dialogic model of adaptation.

Being Unfaithful

Close comparative analysis of text and film, as we have seen above, ineluctably problematizes the concept of fidelity, exposing its inadequacies; Ruiz's re-visioning of the oeil-de-boeuf episode is not faithful to its textual equivalent in the strict sense of the term. In an even more radical engagement with the trope of fidelity, Akerman's *La Captive* aggressively distances itself from the volume of the *Recherche* that inspired it, *La Prisonnière (The Captive)*. Akerman positions herself at a much greater remove from Proust's novel than does Ruiz: she introduces elements from other volumes, especially from *Albertine disparue (The Fugitive)*; Marcel and Albertine become Simon and Ariane because the former names are, in Akerman's words, "too mythic"; and, although the decor and the costumes are stylized, they are not of the period in which Proust's novel takes place (Akerman, "Proust"). Moreover, there is no voice-over, no echo of Proustian narrator. These strategies of distanciation are crucial; Akerman is preoccupied with evoking a central Proustian theme, namely, the impossibility of achieving complete harmony with and understanding of the object of one's love. Her directorial decisions in a sense mirror that theme; one cannot hope to re-create or even represent the novel in another medium. Akerman is engaging directly with film's putative fidelity to reality and calling it into question, even by the directorial strategy that precedes any actual filming.

Both Ruiz's and Akerman's films, albeit to different degrees, are implicitly addressing not only Proust's text but also spectatorial expectations about the synesthetic—and therefore more efficacious, Bourgeois would say—nature of film. Akerman's choice of the Albertine topos is a way of thematically engaging with the impossibility of ever having total possession or knowledge of the beloved other and with the impossibility of finding truth or reality in film. Moreover, Akerman is bringing to light an important aspect of spectatorship: What are we really looking for on film? Are we as spectators inevitably in the position of the jealous Proustian narrator, hoping to surprise the truth that is manifest on the screen before us? In its very first sequence *La Captive* alludes to the innate opacity of film. Simon is watching a Super 8 film of a group of young girls playing in the waves (the "jeunes filles en fleurs" of the novel's second volume). The camera eventually singles out Ariane and then cuts to a shot of Ariane and Andrée sitting together on the sand, staring straight into the camera lens. Ariane says something, and Simon replays the film until he can make out her words. She says "Je vous aime bien" ("I like you"), but it is impossible to know whether she is speaking to the camera (and thus perhaps to Simon) or to Andrée. Since there is no sound to the home movie, it is impossible to know whether Ariane expected her words to be deciphered by the person filming them. Simon moves out from behind the camera and approaches the screen, bending down and caressing Ariane's image in a *mise en abyme* of the spectator's relation to film. We, the spectators, are the jealous lover with the epistemological obsession; we are looking to film to learn something not only about the others on the screen but also about the text that inspired the film. What we do learn, and what film adaptations of Proust have to offer students of the text, is insight into the diacritical specificity of particular semiotic systems, thereby providing a heuristic model that, by problematizing the concept of fidelity in the limited context of film adaptation, problematizes mimesis. Moreover, studying the relation between two artifacts facilitates an investigation of the historical, political, and ideological dimensions of cultural production.

Teaching the *Recherche* through Explication de Texte: Proust's Time-Outs

Roger Shattuck

Some parks—the Bois de Boulogne in Paris, Central Park in New York, the English Garden in Munich—are so extensive and so varied that one can never exhaust all their attractions. Their formal gardens yield to footpaths meandering through woods and meadows. Along certain walkways, one will come upon a zoo or a museum, a carousel or a lake. And if one pushes too far in an unfamiliar direction, it is possible to get lost.

Reading Proust and keeping the several volumes of his novel on your shelf is much like living next to such a park. As you gradually explore *A la recherche du temps perdu,* you will discover the layout of the paths and ponds and vistas. From the other sources you may learn how carefully Proust planned the structure of his autobiographical novel, to the point of writing a draft of the final pages at approximately the same time as he wrote the opening. In 1913, when he found a publisher for the first volume, he envisioned a two-volume novel. After the four-year interval of the First World War and after new developments in his personal and literary life, Proust's careful planning combined increasingly with intervals of variation and even improvisation. The book took on a vigorous life of its own. By his death in 1922, it had grown to seven volumes and a total of three thousand pages.

I believe that the most helpful way to describe the shape of this immense narrative is the phrase lost and found. Marcel, the young protagonist, only reluctantly ventures forth from his extended and sensation-filled childhood. Hesitantly yet persistently, he tries out the paths of love, social climbing, and art. They all turn out to be false scents and lead to disappointment. After 2,800 pages, the narrative breaks off in the middle of a sentence (4: 433; 6: 237). At this point Marcel, who has reached a tentative maturity, collapses completely. When he wakes up again several years later, like the prodigal son or Rip van Winkle, he finds his way home and lives to tell the tale.

For readers with the patience to explore its many vistas, Proust's sprawling park of a novel reveals a remarkably simple and sturdy structure. And the scale on which he records the narrative does not detract from the vividness and subtlety of the sections and scenes that compose the book. There is a crude yet often revealing procedure available for judging a novel: Can you open it at random and find a prose style and a movement of thought and action that will catch your attention within a few lines? Proust will pass this test most of the time for his admirers. Others are rebuffed by his writing.

A more refined and accepted test modifies the previous one to substitute selection for randomness. The French call it explication de texte and have elaborated it into a ritual of reading that is intended to bring out the most significant features of a short passage. Those features include the individual sounds and rhythms of the prose; the function of the passage in the narrative structure; and its psychological, social, philosophical, and spiritual significance. Usually Proust's writing is called difficult. I shall not try to demonstrate the opposite. Instead, I shall examine the way he achieves the effects for which he is best known—psychological probing, comic effect, and the precise rendering of sensation.

A simpler term for my project is close reading. Any passage chosen for close reading, or explication de texte, will, after many readings aloud and comparison with other passages, suggest the terms and the order of events for its own analysis. One should not begin with a system or an approach already decided on from other sources. The first step is to allow the passage to make itself heard, not to impose one's preconceptions about literature or about the author.

The passage I have selected lies in the middle section of the novel where Marcel is taking his first awkward steps out into the world of aristocratic receptions and dinner parties. The knowing and haughty behavior of these noble personages puzzles him more than it dazzles him. In the midst of these social scenes, Marcel's beloved grandmother falls ill, is misdiagnosed, and has a mild but unmistakable heart attack while walking with Marcel in the Champs-Elysées gardens. The following thirty-two pages form one of the most convincing and moving deathbed scenes in all literature. Barely out of his teens, Marcel watches in fascination the social, medical, and personal rituals surrounding death in an advanced civilization. After two weeks of slow decline, the grandmother must endure the application of leeches to her face and head, a medical treatment that transforms her into a Medusa figure. Meanwhile Françoise, the family servant, becomes preoccupied with fittings for her new mourning dress. Then, without transition, comes this self-contained episode:

> Quelques jours plus tard, comme je dormais, ma mère vint m'appeler
> au milieu de la nuit. Avec les douces attentions que, dans les grandes cir-

constances, les gens qu'une profonde douleur accable témoignent fût-ce aux petits ennuis des autres:

"Pardonne-moi de venir troubler ton sommeil," me dit-elle.

"Je ne dormais pas," répondis-je en m'éveillant.

Je le disais de bonne foi. La grande modification qu'amène en nous le réveil est moins de nous introduire dans la vie claire de la conscience que de nous faire perdre le souvenir de la lumière un peu plus tamisée où reposait notre intelligence, comme au fond opalin des eaux. Les pensées à demi voilées sur lesquelles nous voguions il y a un instant encore, entraînaient en nous un mouvement parfaitement suffisant pour que nous ayons pu les désigner sous le nom de veille. Mais les réveils trouvent alors une interférence de mémoire. Peu après, nous les qualifions sommeil parce que nous ne nous les rappelons plus. Et quand luit cette brillante étoile qui, à l'instant du réveil, éclaire derrière le dormeur son sommeil tout entier, elle lui fait croire pendant quelques secondes que c'était non du sommeil, mais de la veille; étoile filante à vrai dire, qui emporte avec sa lumière l'existence mensongère, mais les aspects aussi du songe, et permet seulement à celui qui s'éveille de se dire: "J'ai dormi."

D'une voix si douce qu'elle semblait craindre de me faire mal, ma mère me demanda si cela ne me fatiguerait pas trop de me lever, et me caressant les mains:

"Mon pauvre petit, ce n'est plus maintenant que sur ton papa et sur ta maman que tu pourras compter."   (2: 631)

A few days later, while I was asleep in bed, my mother came to call me in the early hours of the morning. With the tender concern which in the gravest circumstances people who are overwhelmed by grief show for the comfort and convenience of others, "Forgive me for disturbing your sleep," she said to me.

"I wasn't asleep," I answered as I awoke.

I said this in good faith. The great modification which the act of awakening effects in us is not so much that of ushering us into the clear life of consciousness, as that of making us lose all memory of the slightly more diffused light in which our mind had been resting, as in the opaline depth of the sea. The tide of thought, half veiled from our perception, on which we were still drifting a moment ago, kept us in a state of motion perfectly sufficient to enable us to refer to it by the name of wakefulness. But then our actual awakenings produce an interruption of memory. A little later we describe these states as sleep because we no longer remember them. And when that bright star shines which at the moment of waking lights up behind the sleeper the whole expanse of his sleep, it makes him imagine for a few moments that it was not a sleeping but a waking state; a shooting star indeed, which blots out with the fading of its light not only

the illusory existence but every aspect of our dream, and merely enables
him who has awoken to say to himself : "I was asleep."

In a voice so gentle that it seemed to be afraid of hurting me, my
mother asked whether it would tire me too much to get up, and, stroking
my hands, went on:

"My poor child, you have only your Papa and Mamma to rely on now."

(3: 456–57)

In the middle of a dramatic, intensely moving, and sometimes almost surrealist description of the death of a loved one, Proust inserts this half-page
digression on mental states of sleep and waking. It reads like a mistake, a sudden pothole in the road, a lurch in another direction. What is going on? Can
this carefully framed, self-contained passage serve any purpose except to dis-
tract us, even to annoy us as readers? With infinite considerateness the mother
comes to wake her son. He responds with such a transparent and contradictory
untruth that we nearly laugh at him.

When the narrator undertakes to explain the inconsistency of Marcel's
response, "I wasn't sleeping," the prose shifts into a measured expository
rhythm that contrasts with the animated narrative of entrances and exits and
unexpected developments in the stricken household. The six sentences in the
central passage are comparatively brief and uncomplicated for Proust and ask
to be taken seriously. Marcel's dream life benefits from lighting so convincingly
real that he truly believes, before the afterglow has faded, that "I wasn't sleeping." He has just emerged from a prolonged descent into the submarine depths
of himself and for a few lingering moments doesn't register that he has come
back to the real world.

The key word, at the start of this passage, is *modification*, which is explained
by the short declaration, "Mais les réveils trouvent alors une interférence de
mémoire" ("But then our actual awakenings produce an interruption of memory"). The narrator is reconnecting us to earlier and later awakenings of Marcel in Balbec, in Doncières, in Paris. And the dream motif strongly evokes the
opening pages of the novel, which float on the ambivalent frontier between
sleeping and waking, outside time and place.

For, despite its confusions, this border zone of waking up, *le réveil,* enjoys a
privileged status in the novel. It affords us a glimpse of our deepest recesses in
dream and holds in clear association the many real places where we have awakened during our lives. Thus here, just before he will have to face the last searing
moments of his grandmother's life, Marcel is carried back to earliest childhood,
and we readers are carried back to the opening pages of the novel. The filtered,
pearly, underwater dream sequences are introduced to contrast with the unchal-
lengeable realities of the death of a loved one. This brief return to beginnings,
to the netherworld of sleep, recalls the way we wake up every morning to the
task of resuming our identity, name, and social being. We need a moment of rest
and renewal to survive our daily death and to resurrect ourselves.

The passage also plays a role in the larger action of the book. As the mother's words try ever so softly to suggest, the grandmother's death marks the loss of Marcel's childhood and his rite of passage into maturity. From here on, the father simply disappears, and the mother retreats into a shadowy background. For a time, Marcel seems to have little response to the death of his grandmother and, with her, of his secure childhood. He makes further groping advances in his pursuit of Albertine and in his social acceptance by the snobbish Guermantes clan. It is only in the following volume, four-hundred pages and almost a year later, that Marcel registers the full shock of his loss. Proust gives to those pages the title "Intermittences du cœur" ("The Intermittencies of the Heart"), a term that closely echoes "interruption" from the passage we are analyzing. During the later episode in Balbec, Marcel's grandmother is almost restored to him first in the form of a vivid apparitional memory and then in the form of apple trees that he had seen the previous August with her and that are now dazzlingly in bloom. The death of the grandmother, like many other significant events in Proust's novel, occurs in the form of a double take. Full apprehension of an occasion comes later, takes time, sinks in slowly.

The half-page passage on sleep and memory, framed by the mother's tender words to her son, represents a brief side step, a hesitation enclosing a short prayer and pep talk to Marcel's timorous faculties, before the narrative moves forward again into death, grief, and the new responsibilities of maturity. And if you have explored Proust's park for long enough to know the terrain, you will recognize the pattern. This is how the paths have been laid out—with little sidings near key intersections where we can pull over for a moment to see where we are and where things are going. This double-take sequence is also Proust's unconventional form of suspense.

Many other passages emphasize the comic side of these hesitations. When Albertine's succulent pronunciation in response to Marcel's frank proposition signals that she is ready to be kissed, Proust spends several minutes, and a full page of prose, stopping the action to get all the multiple and contradictory images of the girl lined up properly in Marcel's sights so that he can kiss her completely—body and soul. Both Marcel and Proust need the time-outs to know exactly how to plan their moves.

In the following volume (*Sodome et Gomorrhe*), Marcel receives an invitation to the most desirable of aristocratic receptions at the princesse de Guermantes's house; he suspects it is counterfeit and a trick. Nevertheless, he goes to the occasion in great trepidation, and when he enters the salon full of elegant people, the footman trumpets Marcel's name to the assembled throng as protocol demands. What will happen now? We have to read a half-page aside in the form of an absurd story about T. H. Huxley while Marcel waits in dread of being hustled out as an uninvited guest and imposter. Proust prolongs the suspense to the point of comic grotesquerie before the hostess comes forth to welcome Marcel and the narrative machinery can start turning again.

In the final sequence of the novel, when Marcel attends the huge reception at the Guermantes' townhouse, he is shunted into the library to await the end of the concert. This time, extended by a series of involuntary memories and urgent reflections on Marcel's vocation as a writer, the interruption stretches out over some twenty minutes and fifty pages (4: 446–96; 6: 257–332) of Proust's most intense writing on memory, suffering, and literature. The time-out threatens to usurp the game itself. But once again, the performance, the real game, recommences, and Marcel ventures out among all the aged and caricatured personages who have composed his life.

The original passage I discuss, framed within the grandmother's death sequence, is the most modest and least emphatic of all these scenes of intermission and digression. Its return to the world of sleep and uncertain memories and its insistent imagery of light and shadow signal to us the importance of the events that surround it. We are prompted to remember that the opening pages are balanced precariously on the same frontier between sleep and waking. This passage may well mark the continental divide in the novel's action, the point after which all events will testify not to the lingering of childhood but to an encroaching maturity of solitude, disillusionment, and suffering. It also grants us, in the middle of an astonishing sequence of social antics and medical rituals, a momentary respite in which to look around and regain our balance.

What looks like a digression—perhaps just one of those butterfly slips of manuscript that Proust pinned into his immense draft of the novel—turns out to be a characteristic feature of his narrative rhythm. This particular time-out, called toward the end of a major episode, provides what I read as a form of narrative syncopation. The initial effect of such time-outs disconcerts and even annoys us. We don't like to have the story line interrupted. The second effect is comic—mischievous delay at a moment of evident expectation. In this particular example, one sentence is a blatant laugh line: "'I wasn't sleeping,' I said, waking up." But I believe that the principal effect of the time-outs serves the purpose of cross-ventilation and internal communication. The major motifs of Marcel's gradual discovery of human experience are kept circulating through incidents of dramatic action. This connecting impulse appears most powerfully in the last fifty-page time-out. That great philosophical and psychological recapitulation brings all the previous pages into view and prepares us for the immense disillusionment and triumph of the final scene.

Thus there is a place left for the reader who is trying to keep up. At intervals, with little flourish and with great skill, Proust pulls his whole act together while offering us a brief rest. Some would call it being reader-friendly. I prefer to call it narrative mastery.

Teaching Proust through "Morceaux Choisis": Peddling Proust

Michèle Magill

For several years in my career I did not have the opportunity to teach a literature course, much less a class on Proust. For a long time my colleagues and I hoped that one day our department would be able to offer at least a master's degree in French to our majors. Now, because of the declining enrollment in French studies in American universities, I must either abandon the idea of ever teaching Proust or, like the narrator's grandmother in *A la recherche du temps perdu* who adds "several layers of art" (my trans.) "plusieurs épaisseurs d'art" (1: 40) to her gifts to Marcel, try to inject a healthy dose of Proust in all my courses, at every opportunity. Proust wrote in a letter to his friend Mme Straus, "pour ce second ouvrage, qui sera certainement le dernier (sauf des recueils d'articles, des études critiques) il me plaisait de m'adresser à un public plus vaste, aux gens qui prennent le train et achètent avant de monter dans le wagon un volume mal imprimé" (*Corr.* 11: 292); ("for this second work, which will certainly be the last [except for collected articles and critical studies] I was eager to address a larger audience, people who take the train and buy a poorly bound volume before getting on board"; my trans.). Introducing Proust's work, making his name well known, both familiar and intriguing, to every college student taking one of my classes is therefore not betraying the writer's wish.

Recently, in France, major authors, Proust in particular, have been popularized in videos, comic strips, photo books, and mystery novels (see Heuet; Bouchart and Dezon-Jones; Monbrun). Proust has become a household name to the average French person. Though Proust's presence in American popular culture has also become more prominent, students, even those studying French, may graduate knowing hardly anything about Proust. In general, they are so intimidated by the famous length and complexity of *A la recherche du temps perdu* that they dismiss the idea of reading it, even just parts of it. Teachers must thus explain that, as Proust once said, it is not his work that is complicated but life itself.

Students at any level can be given the opportunity of knowing something about Proust. Some may then become curious enough to begin reading his work (even as a comic strip) or to watch a video about it (see *Marcel Proust: A Writer's Life*). Curiosity might lead to a taste for Proust; perhaps this taste will develop into the desire to study *A la recherche du temps perdu* in depth.

There is always a way to peddle Proust, even in beginning French courses. Grammatical examples using his name or the qualities of his work allow me to reveal right away my interest in Proust. Students quickly get the message: our professor teaches us French 101, but she is above all a fan of Proust. After a few weeks the name of Proust becomes an inside reference for the whole class: they start using his name in examples, skits, presentations, and papers as a way to wink at their classmates while poking fun at, as well as honoring, my passion for Proust.

I frequently have the opportunity to see some of my first-year students again in their fourth semester, a turning point since they have to decide then whether to drop French or pursue it as a minor or major. Proust's name, which they have not forgotten, immediately re-creates complicity between us. They do not mind sharing it with newcomers, and it becomes a shortcut to get to know one another. Though in their first year I had stressed the difficulty of the *Recherche*, the length of sentences and of the book itself, defying them to ever have the courage to read it, I now use another technique. I suggest to them that maybe they could, and definitely should, try to read the *Recherche*. I mention that Proust is not the idol of eccentric French professors only; millions of fans throughout the world also revere his work. Then I quote writers familiar to them—Virginia Woolf, William Faulkner, Shelby Foote, Albert Camus, John Updike—who have praised the genius of Proust. I tell them about the wealth of Proustian criticism and the number of books and articles on *A la recherche du temps perdu* that appear every year; it becomes clear to them that Proust is a very big deal indeed. By now a few students are considering reading some excerpts in translation. I then unabashedly make my next strategic move: reverse psychology. I tell them not to read the whole work. I make an analogy to a rich chocolate: they can't eat the whole thing all at once; they have to take little bites and savor each to the fullest.

I encourage my students simply to open the book—anywhere—choose a page, and tell me if they found at least one sentence that was worth reading. As Paul Valéry said in his *Hommage à Marcel Proust* about *A la recherche du temps perdu*: "L'intérêt de ses ouvrages réside dans chaque fragment. On peut ouvrir le livre où on veut" (772) ("The interest of the book lies in each fragment. We can open the book wherever we choose"; my trans.). This way they do not feel pressured. One page, one sentence—surely they can handle such small doses. By that time my students have become no more intimidated by Proust than they are by English-language writers such as Shakespeare or James Joyce. If they stop studying French after the fourth semester, they might quickly forget the grammar and vocabulary, but they are prepared to approach Proust's work if they so choose later in their life.

If students decide to pursue their French studies, most will take an advanced conversation class. This is a really easy course in which to peddle Proust; whatever the topic, chances are Proust wrote about it. Love, jealousy, life and death, aging and sickness, the arts, literature, time and space, society, psychology, philosophy, medicine, memory, politics—Proust has reflected on each of these subjects. You can quote him about almost anything. Alain de Botton's book *How Proust Can Change Your Life* shows how reading Proust can make a difference in one's life, and students who read Botton in turn have to reflect on how Proust has indeed already enriched their own.

Students who pursue French as a major or minor take a civilization course, which does not allow much time for Proust but does provide the opportunity, for a week or so, to place Proust in the historical, sociological, and artistic context of his time and to mention his influence on twentieth-century writers. Proust discusses the Dreyfus affair, the belle époque, music and visual arts, and fashion at length in *A la recherche du temps perdu*, and his novel can be used for research papers on these topics. If the students want to capture a glimpse of the society, costumes, and decors of this era, they can watch the movies *Céleste*, directed by Percy Adlon; *Un amour de Swann*, directed by Volker Schlöndorlff; or *Le Temps retrouvé*, directed by Raoul Ruiz, but they should be made aware that these movies are not always faithful to Proust's work. I stress the *Recherche*'s artistic wealth as Proust shows masterfully how trends come and go and come around again. The many writers, painters, and musicians who appear in the *Recherche* also make it an excellent reference work for a student's cultural knowledge.

In translation courses, I usually create a syllabus à la carte according to the composition and interests of the class. They work in groups and we devote half our time to translating recent articles on various and current topics and the other half to translating literature. No author is better suited for this task than Proust. The course starts with authors whose style is easier than Proust's to tackle: Annie Ernaux, Marguerite Duras, Camus, Julien Gracq, Sylvie Germain, Colette, and Guy de Maupassant. Then, when it is time to study Proust, students can compare their translations of Proust with Proust's French text. Students are encouraged to question one another's translation choices and to make suggestions for improvements or corrections. The class first ponders the translation of the title for the *Recherche*; this generates many interpretations and discussions concerning the principles of translation. We also translate the excerpt on the names of the villages of Brittany and Normandy in "Noms de pays: le nom" (1: 379) ("Place-Names: The Name" [1: 549]). Here the students can observe how words signify not only by what they mean but also by the way they look, sound, and feel in one's mouth when pronounced. They start to understand that language can be a sensual experience, which makes it all the more difficult to render in translation.

The course sequence for majors and minors includes a literature survey course where we can approach Proust's text in French. In the first part of the course, students examine Montaigne's *Essais* and Rousseau's *Confessions*. Later they will be able to compare *A la recherche du temps perdu* with these works. In the second part, we study Chateaubriand, Balzac, Stendhal, Flaubert, and Zola. When we get to Proust, students read his comments about these writers and then study his own style. Since time for studying Proust is limited to about ten days, two or three sessions can be dedicated to his literary criticism and the rest to his theories about the creative process.

The next course in the sequence focuses on masterpieces of the twentieth century, where we can spend three weeks on Proust. If students have been well prepared, they are eager to start reading *A la recherche du temps perdu*. They feel that, after being driven around for so long, they are finally at the wheel. However, time allocated to Proust is limited, and I warn them not to be gluttons; three weeks is not that much time. They still have to take small bites and chew them well. I tell them not to read more than the first hundred pages of *Du côté de chez Swann*, and I wait for the inevitable objections. They soon claim that they fall asleep after ten pages and some complain, just as some of Proust's first critics did, that the author spends too many pages on his sleeping habits. I remind them that in Kafka's *Metamorphosis*, several pages dwell on the character waking up and that even a tale as full of action as Melville's *Moby-Dick* contains lengthy chapters on whaling customs and whales' physiology. I tell them that this is not an action movie—no need to hurry or to find out what is happening next. Instead, we study in depth the following excerpts from the *Recherche*: the good-night kiss (1: 27–37), the madeleine (1: 43–47), the steeples of Martinville (1: 174–77), the hawthorn lane (1: 134–37), and Vinteuil's *petite phrase* (1: 202–25). For the careful stylistic analysis of these passages, I rely on Jean Milly's *La Poétique des textes*, which introduces critical terminology and techniques, as well as on his *Proust et le style* and *La Phrase de Proust*.

Finally, every few years, when I do teach the senior seminar on Proust, I no longer have any need to peddle Proust: I can actually teach *A la recherche du temps perdu* in French (or at least *Du côté de chez Swann*, *La Prisonnière*, and *Le Temps retrouvé*). Most students who follow the curriculum have had a good introduction to the originality of Proust by the time they graduate. Students can start their graduate studies with a solid cultural and literary background. My efforts may not be quantifiable and certainly they cannot be compared to directing a dissertation. But one has to do one's best for French studies in these lean times. I remain convinced that for both students and teachers, some Proust is better than no Proust.

Introducing Proust:
The Segmentation of "Combray"

Julie Solomon

When undergraduates begin to read "Combray," they often bring to the text preconceptions that reading Proust will be hard work. And, indeed, many will experience an initial difficulty in seeing how the story is structured. This difficulty can confirm Proust's reputation as dense and laborious, if not downright boring. One way to stave off this kind of reaction is to show that although the *Recherche* might give the impression of flowing along and avoiding distinct breaks, it is not in fact an amorphous stream of consciousness. This essay presents a segmentation of "Combray" (1: 3–184; 1:1–264) and an analysis of the story's organizing principles: the temporal, spatial, and logical relations among the different segments. It also highlights the kinds of phrases Proust uses to signal a new section and the discourse strategies he uses to encourage the reader to move from one segment to the next without being clearly aware that a new section has begun.

Traditionally, a narrative text is understood as being organized in terms of chronology. While "Combray" certainly does not recount a simple story, temporal relations do govern its global structure:

> Intermediate subject—waking at night (3–9; 1–9)
> Marcel—"Combray" 1 (9–43; 9–58)
> Intermediate subject—the madeleine (43–47; 58–64)
> Marcel—"Combray" 2 (47–183; 65–262)
> Intermediate subject—conclusion (183–84; 262–64)

In the first section, the narrator describes his adult self from a few years before. This subject may be termed the "intermediate subject," who is chronologically different from both the older narrator and the boy of "Combray." It is this intermediate subject who is unable to sleep at night, passes the nights thinking back over his life (see Muller, ch. 2). The second section is a flashback in which the narrator recounts what the intermediate subject used to remember of Combray. This memory was limited to a single incident—the *drame du coucher* (good-night kiss). In the third section, the intermediate subject experiences the revelation of the *petite madeleine*, which permits him to remember more completely his childhood vacations in Combray. Since the narrator is able to look back over his entire life, he is not obliged to relate events in the order he experienced them. He can mention the things that he did not understand as a boy and can frame the childhood memories by recounting the intermediate subject's different acts of remembering. Classroom discussion of why Proust might have adopted this narrative structure leads to a consideration of his modernist conception of the subject and of his ideas about memory and time.

Only isolated sections of "Combray" are narrated in a traditional, chronological way, what Genette terms "singulative" narration. An example is the end of "Combray" 1 (23–43; 30–58), which relates a single and unique occurrence. The dominant narrative mode of "Combray" is the "iterative," where habitual, repetitive events are recounted primarily in the imperfect tense (Genette, *Narrative Discourse* 113–16). Iterative narration overrides the sequential nature of events by positing an identity among a series of similar occurrences. Again, it is the privilege of the older narrator to look back on his past and perform this synthesis.

Chronological criteria are often insufficient for reading Proust. Because of his frequent use of parentheses and digressions, the logical relation between one segment and the next is often of primary importance. The temporal is not always indicated in any specific way, although it may be suggested. Parentheses fulfill a variety of functions in Proust. They are used to provide background about a character, to pause for a traditional description (although this is in fact rare for Proust, who usually narrativizes his descriptions), to announce or subtly prepare important episodes that will occur later in the novel, and to develop different kinds of generalizations (philosophical, aesthetic, social). Parentheses often serve important "associative functions," drawing together "seemingly incommunicable parts of the novel" (Suleiman 467).

In "Combray" 1, the drama of the good-night kiss is complicated by parentheses on the grandmother and her passion for the open air and on Swann's elegant social life, unsuspected by the family. The passage in which the hero's unhappy situation—waiting with little hope for his mother to answer his note—is compared with Swann's past experiences begins: "cette joie trompeuse que nous donne quelque ami, quelque parent de la femme que nous aimons" (30) ("that false joy which a friend or relative of the woman we love can give us" [40]). The story about "nous" ("us") and an unnamed woman not only links Swann's past and Marcel's future but also suggests that the reader might have lived through a similar experience. These *romans abstraits* ("abstract novels") are a common type of parenthesis in the *Recherche* (Muller 76–77). The following is an outline of "Combray" 1, showing how the iterative narration of Marcel's bedtime anguish leads into a transitional section and, finally, into the singulative narration of one particular evening. Also included in this table are indications of the major parentheses in the passage.

"Combray" 1: The Bedtime Drama (1: 9–43; 1: 9–58)

Iterative Section (9–13; 9–15)
  The magic lantern (9–10; 9–12)
  The hero is obliged to leave his mother (10–13; 12–15)
    (includes parenthesis on the grandmother in the garden on
    rainy nights) (10–13; 12–15)
  Nights when mother comes up to kiss Marcel goodnight (13; 15)

Transition from iterative to singulative (13–23; 15–30)
  Nights when there are visitors; The arrival of Swann (13–23; 15–30)
    (includes parenthesis on the family's ignorance of his brilliant
    social situation) (15–23; 18–30)

Singulative Section (23–41; 30–55)
  Marcel sent to bed waiting for the goodnight kiss (23–33; 30–38)
    (includes parenthesis on Françoise's code) (28–29; 32–33)
  His mother accepts to stay with him that night (33–43; 38–58) ·
    (includes parenthesis on the grandmother's criteria for
    choosing his gifts) (39–41; 52–55)

In many sequences—for example, in the section of "Combray" 2 that describes Marcel's afternoons reading—the digressions are longer than the main topic that is under discussion. As the young hero leaves the table after lunch, his mother sends him outside for a few minutes "pour ne pas lire en sortant de table" (71) ("get a little fresh air first; don't start reading immediately after your food" [98]). Spending the afternoon reading thus frames Marcel's visit to the back garden, which becomes a digression leading into the flashback about Uncle Adolphe and the lady in pink (74–79; 102–10)—which, furthermore, contains an internal parenthesis about the theater (72–74; 99–102). The complex parenthetical, indeed telescopic, structure outlined below is related to and indeed occasioned by the iterative nature of the event described. Many of the parentheses recount singulative exceptions or iterative variations in Marcel's Sunday afternoon routine:

Reading (1: 71–99; 1: 98–139)

A few moments in the back garden before going upstairs
to read (71–79; 98–110)
      (includes parenthesis on visiting Uncle Adolphe's sitting
      room in "earlier days") (71–79; 98–110)
      (with internal parenthesis on Adolphe in Paris and the lady
      in pink) (71–79; 98–110)
      (and within the internal parenthesis, another on Marcel's
      love of the theater) (72–74; 100–03)

Marcel reading in his room (79–82; 110–14)
      (with parenthesis on the scullery maid) (79–81; 110–13)

Marcel sent into the garden and reads there for the rest of
the afternoon (82–99; 114–39)
  The four levels of consciousness (83–87; 115–21)
      (Parenthesis. "Sometimes" the soldiers march through
      town) (87–89; 121–23)

Singulative variation: "Once" Swann visits as Marcel
    reads Bergotte (89; 124)
Generalizing digression: remarks about Bloch (89–92; 124–29)
General comments about reading Bergotte (92–96; 129–34)
General comments about Swann's personal acquaintance
    with Bergotte (96–99; 134–39)

Although the reader may be lulled into forgetting the frame as the digressions
develop, the core of the passage is an iterative narration of Marcel's Sunday afternoons in Combray. At its conclusion, the following sequence begins: "Tandis que
je lisais au jardin . . ." (99) ("While I was reading in the garden . . ." [139]).

We have seen that in "Combray" chronology is effaced through extensive
use of the iterative mode and of parentheses and digression. A third principle
that governs the relation between segments is the typically Proustian figure
Gérard Genette names "syllepsis": "we could give the name *syllepses* (the fact
of taking together)—*temporal* or other—to those anachronic groupings gov-
erned by one or another kinship (spatial, temporal, or other)" (*Narrative Discourse* 85). Following John Porter Houston, Genette points out that the last
fifty pages of "Combray" are based on a geographic rather than temporal
structure—the two "côtés" ("ways"), of course. Syllepsis, in this sense, is a
widespread structuring principle in all the *Recherche*, as Genette points out in
Narrative Discourse Revisited (40), noting that the iterative itself is a kind of
syllepsis. "Combray" 2 is organized by two syllepses, the first being "Tante
Léonie" (Aunt Léonie) and the second, the "deux côtés" ("two ways"). In the
first part of "Combray" 2, it is the character Aunt Léonie, in her central,
unmoving position in her bedroom, that commands the other episodes and
variations woven around the description of her life. Since the primary narrative recounts Aunt Léonie's daily routines, the narrator always keeps us
informed of what Aunt Léonie was doing in the meanwhile, when describing
what Marcel or the rest of his family would do when not in her presence. The
church sequence, for example, begins: "Pendant que ma tante devisait ainsi
avec Françoise, j'accompagnais mes parents à la messe" (59) ("While my aunt
was gossiping on in this way with Françoise I accompanied my parents to
mass" [80]) and ends: "Quand, à notre retour ma tante nous faisait demander
si Mme Goupil était arrivée en retard à la messe . . . " (67) ("When, on our
return home, my aunt would send to ask us whether Mme Goupil had indeed
arrived late for mass . . ." [93]).

Although these sylleptic structures are important, chronological structure is
not absent from "Combray." Despite the dominance of the iterative mode, we
are not presented with one unchanging, timeless summer. The Aunt Léonie
section follows a typical Sunday from morning to evening, and the whole of
"Combray" moves through the seasons from Easter to autumn and through the
hero's life from childhood to adolescence. Toward the end of "Combray," his
sexual desires and possible literary talent are awakened during walks on the

"deux côtés," one leading to Swann's property, the other to the Guermantes' château (Houston 38-41).

Given Proust's propensity for veiling transitions, it is useful to study the expressions that do signal a new section in his narrative. First, although Proust disliked the Balzacian *voici pourquoi* ("this is why"), such constructions are not absent from the *Recherche*. That Marcel no longer goes into Uncle Adolphe's room after lunch is explained by the lady-in-pink episode, introduced by the following statement: "ce dernier ne venant plus à Combray à cause d'une brouille qui était survenue . . . dans les circonstances suivantes . . ." (71) ("for he no longer came to Combray on account of a quarrel which had arisen . . . in the following circumstances" [99]). Logical words like *ainsi, pourtant*, and *mais* (*thus, however*, and *but*) often serve to open or close sections. Second, words that mark the passage from iterative to singulative or that introduce variations within an iterative sequence frequently provide chronological bearings (even if somewhat vague) : "*Longtemps* je me suis couché de bonne heure. *Parfois* . . ." (3; my emphasis) ("For a long time I would go to bed early. Sometimes . . ." [1]). Temporal expressions such as *tous les jours, longtemps auparavant*, or *un jour* (*every day, a long time earlier, one day*) can open a new section. There are also deictic temporal indicators like "maman passa *cette nuit-là* dans ma chambre" (37) ("Mamma spent that night in my room" [49]). A particularly important temporal signal in the *Recherche* is *tout à coup* (*suddenly*), as, for example, in the madeleine episode: "Et tout d'un coup le souvenir m'est apparu" (46) ("And suddenly the memory revealed itself" [63]); and on his first encounter with Gilberte: "Tout à coup, je m'arrêtai" (139) ("Suddenly I stood still" [197]).

In the sylleptically organized sequences, it is often an explicit mention of the structuring concept itself that prepares the reader for the new segment. For instance, the first Montjouvain passage is introduced in this way: "C'est du côté de Méséglise, à Montjouvain" (145) ("It was along the Méséglise way, at Montjouvain" [206]). Other sequences, such as the one that follows, also begin with this geographic specification: "Comme la promenade du côté de Méséglise était la moins longue des deux . . ." (148) ("Since the Méséglise way was the shorter of the two" [211]). Simply mentioning Méséglise way signals that a new section of "les deux côtés" is being introduced and reminds the reader that these episodes are linked and recounted together because the places in which they occur are physically located near each other.

Finally, the transition from iterative to singulative may be signaled by a phrase like "un jour, pourtant" ("one day, however") but often passes unheralded and unnoticed. In the "drame du coucher" (good-night kiss) the narrative begins, almost arbitrarily it would seem, using the preterite instead of the imperfect tense. On closer examination, we find that the text moves through a long, ambiguous section in which the iterative gradually becomes what Genette calls the "pseudo-iterative" (*Narrative Discourse* 121). The singulative is only clearly established with: "Nous étions tous au jardin quand *retentirent* les deux coups hésitants de la clochette" (23; my emphasis) ("We were all in the garden when the double tinkle of the visitors' bell sounded shyly" [30]). Phrases like "Pensez à le remercier intelligiblement de son vin" (23) ("See that you thank him intelligibly for the wine" [30]) continue seamlessly from the preceding pseudoiterative pages and thus further blur the border between the general and the particular. The pseudoiterative is not an unusual narrative practice. Readers understand that the detailed event, complete with dialogue and written in the habitual imperfect, is meant to stand as an example of the many similar events that took place. It is Proust's extensive and insistent use of the pseudoiterative that suggests, as Genette claims (*Narrative Discourse* 122–23), that the novelist actually intends us to take such passages literally, as true iteratives.

Apart from the slippage between iterative and singulative episodes, other types of sliding transitions may be noted. As we approach the end of the Aunt Léonie section, the hero's family meets up with Legrandin "au bord de la Vivonne" (128) ("on the banks of the Vivonne" [182]) during an evening stroll. The evening walk is thus introduced into the narrative as we approach the end of the previous section. The narrator begins the second major part of "Combray" 2 by highlighting its sylleptic organizing principle, "les deux côtés"; yet the new section also seems to continue from the meeting with Legrandin by the river: "Nous rentrions toujours de bonne heure de nos promenades" (131) ("We used always to return from our walks in good time . . ." [186]). Further, the first two pages of "les deux côtés" concern Marcel and his family's return home to say good-night to Aunt Léonie, after the walks, including those in the Guermantes direction, which result in their late arrival. Aunt Léonie's day is thus brought to a conclusion and sewn into the fabric of the new section, and the reader is taken through the transition between the two major parts of "Combray" 2 without pause.

Needless to say, I propose this approach not to the exclusion of other readings but as a preliminary step to them. Nor do I dismiss the value and indeed pleasure of becoming lost in the *Recherche*. But all students may not enjoy such disorientation, and may not develop a sufficient sense of the story's shape to pursue their reading meaningfully. The solution is surely to teach how the Proustian text succeeds in getting us deliciously lost while showing that the narrator is not lost at all and will eventually provide the necessary bearings if we learn to read for the signals: "suddenly, like Marcel on his walks in Combray, we discover, at the very moment we thought we were lost, that we are 'back home'" (Suleiman 461; see "Combray," 1: 113–14; 1: 160).

It is not necessary to provide a detailed summary of the text and all its subsections at the outset. If the class has read, for example, "Combray" 1, this section can be used as a basis for discussing the difference between hero and narrator, the use of long parentheses, and the movement between iterative, pseudoiterative, and singulative narration. One may later assign individual students or groups to prepare a segmentation of, for example, "les deux côtés" (1:

131–83; 1: 186–262) or more modestly, the Sunday afternoon readings (1: 71–99; 1: 98–139). Ideally, students will develop an understanding of the overall narrative movement of the text. At the same time, they will have been introduced to concepts that invite further reflection on questions such as the identity of the narrating subject and the treatment of space, time, and memory in "Combray." The suggestions in this essay can thus easily be integrated into various levels and frameworks of teaching Proust.

Proust and Architecture:
Reconstructing the Churches of "Combray"

J. Theodore Johnson, Jr.

Given that "the greatest literary masterpiece is but an alphabet in disorder"
and that, as Proust puts it in *Le Côté de Guermantes,* art "n'est pas plus avancé
qu'au temps d'Homère"(2: 624) ("is not more advanced now than in Homer's
day" [3: 446]), the question of how an original writer generates and sets down
a text seems always relevant in literary studies. In the essays on reading in
Sesame and Lilies, which Proust translated, John Ruskin urges us to examine
words even down to their syllables and letters: "you must get into the habit of
looking intensely at words, and assuring yourself of their meaning, syllable by
syllable—nay, letter by letter" (Ruskin, *Sesame* 15) ("vous devez prendre
l'habitude de regarder aux mots avec intensité en vous assurant de leur signifi-
cation syllabe par syllabe, plus, lettre par lettre" (Proust, *Sésame* 138). Proust's
Ruskin years, during which he considered closely reading medieval architecture and constructing texts, correspond, in a sense, to the years a *compagnon*
(journeyman) spent working in various *chantiers* (building sites) during a *tour
de France* before coming home to produce and submit a masterpiece before
judges. Genetic criticism invites us to peer into manuscript drafts to observe
Proust shaping the textual stones that will form his cathedral-novel. As did the
compagnons of times past, students can learn much by carefully examining the
drafts of certain masterful texts of Proust. Over the years, I have asked students
to write analytic essays dealing with the nine-sentence text "les clochers de
Martinville" (1: 179–80) ("the steeples of Martinville" [1: 255–56]) and the
nine-paragraph text on the village church Saint-Hilaire de Combray (1: 58–66;
1: 80–91), and I have found these assignments extremely helpful in bringing
students to a better understanding of French language, literature, and culture.

At the outset of the twentieth century, Proust began to look deeply into
medieval architecture and iconography through his work translating Ruskin's
The Bible of Amiens (1885) into French as *La Bible d'Amiens* (1904), with the
help of his mother and the erudition of Emile Mâle's *L'Art religieux du XIIIe
siècle en France: étude sur l'iconographie du Moyen Age et sur ses sources d'inspiration* (1898), a work still in print and invaluable as an introduction to
French Gothic architecture and iconography. The general area of Proust and
architecture has been explored by Richard Bales (*Proust*), Kay Bourlier, Luc
Fraisse (who weaves interconnections between elements of ecclesiastical art
and architecture and Proust's literary works ["Les Eglises"; *L'œuvre cathédrale*]), Dominique Jullien, Luzius Keller, Diane Leonard, and Jean-Pierre
Richard ("Proust et la nuit"). My articles "Proust and Giotto," "Proust, Ruskin,"
"Marcel Proust," and "Proust's Referential Strategies" review scholarship and
explore iconography and interpretation. Useful for the genesis, analysis, and

place of the Martinville and Saint-Hilaire texts within the structure of the novel, are the studies of Eliane Boucquey, Bernard Brun ("Une des lois"), William C. Carter ("Proustian Quest"), Linda A. Gordon ("Parallax"; "The Martinville Steeplechase"), P. L. Larcher, Annie Méjean, Thierry Mézaille, P. Michaudon and J. Chabot, Marie Miguet-Ollagnier, Jean Milly (*La Longueur; La Phrase*), Claudine Quémar, and Akio Ushiba. These several thousand pages of drafts, texts, analyses, and commentaries are useful to specialists, but anyone who has enjoyed imaginative literature and who has visited a celebratory structure such as a church will understand architecture and literature more deeply through the two exercises I propose for dealing with the churches of Martinville and Saint-Hilaire de Combray.

The Steeples of Martinville

Toward the end of "Combray," the narrator inserts into his narrative a short text that he composed as a child in the carriage of Dr. Percepied. The text deals with the two sunlit steeples of Martinville and the single steeple of Vieuxvicq, which appear to rise up out of the plain, turn, move along the horizon, and then disappear into the night (1: 179–80; 1: 255–56). The narrator is urged by his father to show the ambassador M. de Norpois the "petit poème en prose" written "with an exaltation" that is intended to be communicated to whomever reads it. The ambassador returns the text without a word (1: 447; 2: 35), but much later it appears as part of the mature narrator's article published in *Le Figaro* (4: 148–52; 5: 766–72) where, "thanks to the miracle of the multiplication of his thought" through print, the narrator envisions it read by everyone.

Over the years, students at the University of Kansas in a fifth semester French course, Intensive Review of French Grammar, have discovered the exaltation of this text, "Les Clochers de Martinville," by writing a five-page paper in French dealing with its grammatical beauty. Toward the end of the course, we set aside our textbook and take a close look at the poetics of grammar, beginning with Proust's wonderful statements in "A propos du 'style' de Flaubert" (Contre Sainte-Beuve 586–600). Proust begins with the extraordinary affirmation that Flaubert

> par l'usage entièrement nouveau et personnel qu'il a fait du passé défini, du passé indéfini, du participe présent, de certains pronoms et de certaines prépositions, a renouvelé presque autant notre vision des choses que Kant, avec ses Catégories, les théories de la Connaissance et de la Réalité du monde extérieur.

> by the entirely new and personal use that he made of the past definite, the past indefinite, the present participle and certain pronouns and prepositions renewed our vision of things almost as much as Kant, with his Categories, renewed our theories of Cognition and of the Reality of the outside world.   (Against Sainte-Beuve 261)

Proust then demonstrates that there is "une beauté grammaticale" ("a grammatical beauty") by examining Flaubert's use of personal pronouns, prepositions, adverbs, conjunctions, and tenses (e.g., "dans le plan incliné et tout en demi-teintes des imparfaits, le présent de l'indicatif opère un redressement" [591]) ("the present indicative brings us upright, on the inclined plan of imperfects, all in half tones" [265]). These remarks by Ruskin and Proust help students as they analyze sentences and then compose their essays.

Proust's brilliant prose poem in the "les Clochers de Martinville" section, running from the letter S to T in 390 words and 9 sentences, deserves to be analyzed repeatedly in the brightest light, thus whatever students discover in it will motivate them to generate original and perceptive essays. At first they may resist, but the assignment engages them, and they are proud when extracts from their essays are read aloud in class. Several English translations of the passage set into relief the grammatical beauty of Proust's style in French. Whereas the English text begins with the two beats of "Alone," the French original begins with an extraordinary monosyllabic word that sounds singular but surprises us when we read it written in the plural: "Seuls."

I encourage students to make multiple copies of "les Clochers de Martinville" on which they highlight certain grammatical, lexical, or philosophical points, such as the tenses, horizontal and vertical movements, or the dynamic interrelations of time and space. By highlighting verbs (also adjectives and nouns based on verbs) and then identifying tenses, students come to appreciate how, within the fabric of the text, Proust weaves the threads of time verbally. The steeples of Martinville thrust themselves up from the plain through a reflexive present participle: "Seuls, s'élevant" ("Alone, rising"), while a masculine plural past participle shows them to be "perdus" ("lost"). These participles create a spatiotemporal grid out of which emerges a conjugated verb in the imperfect tense—"montaient" ("rose")—whose subject (effect before cause) comes into focus at the end of the sentence—"les clochers de Martinville." On one copy of the text students indicate all words dealing with time and space with a "T" for "temps" and "E" for "espace" and indicate with a horizontal line horizontal movement ("du niveau de la plaine"; "from the level of the plain"); with a vertical arrow ascending movement ("Seuls, s'élevant," "montaient vers le ciel"; "Alone, rising, rose towards the sky"); and with a downward arrow descending movement ("comme perdus"; "seemingly lost") (1: 179–80; 1: 255–56). I encourage students to draw sketches of the churches and their steeples as they move along the horizon. During our discussion of their essays, students compare their drawings with the beautiful way the artist Stéphane Heuet has adapted and illustrated the text in his *bande dessinée* of "Combray" (68–70).

On another copy of the text, students highlight adverbs, prepositions, nouns, and adjectives indicating time. By highlighting and analyzing approximately forty pronouns, students discover how Proust uses them to advance his text poetically, such as the wonderful ambiguity in the displacement of the three steeples—"Parfois, l'un s'effaçait pour que les deux autres pussent nous apercevoir" ("Sometimes one would withdraw, so that the other two might watch us"). Highlighting texts reveals the considerable extent to which Proust personifies steeples, sun, carriage, and village or sets into relief themes such as solitude and collectivity, light and color, the natural world, and human beings and their constructions. The first half of the text proceeds positively with ever longer sentences until the carriage jerks to a halt before the church at Martinville with a clatter of terms of negations and monosyllables: "on n'eut que le temps d'arrêter pour ne pas se heurter au porche" ("we had barely time to stop before being dashed against the porch"). In the second half of the text students admire the gradual and elegant disappearance of the steeples in gathering darkness and the resolution of the text in present infinitives: "chercher . . . se serrer . . . glisser . . . ne plus faire sur le ciel encore rose qu'une seule forme noire, charmante et résignée, et s'effacer dans la nuit" (1: 180) ("seeking . . . drawing close to one another . . . gliding . . . forming now against the still rosy sky no more than a single dusky shape, charming and resigned, and so vanishing in the night" [1: 256]).

More advanced students, such as those in a semester-long survey course of twentieth-century French literature that includes "Combray," can examine in more detail the four prosaic paragraphs that set this extraordinary text into relief and the earlier version of the text in "Impressions de route en automobile," published initially in *Le Figaro* in 1907 and later in *Pastiches et mélanges* in 1919 (see Contre Sainte-Beuve 64–65). Analyzing the grammar and vocabulary of this prose poem helps students appreciate Proust's dynamic style, which combines "technique and vision" (4: 474; 6: 299) so that grammar and images whirl kaleidoscopically. A number of students have said that while examining this text deeply, they "felt the earth turn."

Sainte-Hilaire de Combray and Saint-André des Champs

In both an undergraduate survey course of French literature of the twentieth century and a graduate course entirely devoted to *A la recherche du temps perdu*, I have students write a paper on the nine paragraphs that constitute the text on the church Saint-Hilaire de Combray (1: 58–66; 1: 80–91). Each student chooses one of the nine paragraphs, analyzes it thoroughly as in an explication de texte, and then compares it with the notes and *esquisses* (sketches) published in the recent Pléiade edition (1: 728–43; 1129–35; 1445–49). This exercise introduces students to genetic criticism, because they must discuss the changes Proust brings to his text and make critical judgments about how the changes contribute to the quality of the literary text. They are thus better prepared to appreciate the organization and depths of Proustian texts elsewhere in the novel. The next part of the paper situates the paragraph in the context of the nine paragraphs in which Proust constructs the church Saint-Hilaire de Combray. In the conclusion to their essays, students then link the ideas and themes that have emerged through their analysis to the whole of "Combray." Compared with the dynamic nine sentences that make up "les Clochers de Martinville," the nine-paragraph text on the church Saint-Hilaire de Combray seems quite static, which befits an ancient stone church. Here the energy derives from the intellectual (literally "reading in between") associations students establish across time: the concave trace of an absent fossil in stone formed at the bottom of a sea several hundred million years ago, eventually quarried and shaped, becomes part of a sixth-century tomb in the Merovingian crypt of a church constructed during the reign of Théodebert I (504–48) and named to honor the fourth-century Saint Hilaire of Poitiers. Because the church was continuously under construction, sisterly Gothic tracery screens a rude Romanesque brother. In the nave, sunlight pulses through medieval and modern stained-glass windows, projects slowly moving colorful designs across the ancient stone floor where Gothic letters on tombstones flow beyond their boundaries, and gradually fades tapestries where the story of Jewish Esther and the features of a Christian Guermantes blur. Mantles and fingers daily erode the stone of the holy-water font while birds wheel around the bell tower as they have for centuries.

The church Saint-André des Champs, with its references to chthonic people—Saint André (who, with Peter, was one of the first two apostles), Françoise (France), and Théodore (gift of God)—firmly establishes that the real *opus francigenum* ("work of the French people") is not Gothic architecture but the French people themselves (1: 149–50; 1: 212–13). The text, as well as Elstir's analysis of the Balbec church in *A l'ombre des jeunes filles en fleurs* (2: 196–98; 2: 575–76) owes much to Mâle's *L'art religieux du XIIIe siècle en France*. These explicit texts on ecclesiastical architecture prepare students to search out the implicit architecture of the novel, such as the scene between Mlle Vinteuil and her friend at Montjouvain. The Catholic poet Francis Jammes had urged Proust to remove the scene, but Proust saw it as a structurally important column and historiated capital whose removal would bring down a vault on the reader's head several volumes hence (see letters to François Mauriac and Paul Souday in *Corr.* 18: 404; 464).

While graduate students examine a number of primary and secondary sources on reserve in the university library, I invite all students to look for themselves very deeply into the dynamic grammar of "les Clochers de Martinville"; the static, historical allusions that form the church Saint-Hilaire de Combray; and the iconography on the porch of the church Saint-André de Combray. Once students have reconstructed these texts dealing with churches—the biblical and historical cornerstones for the cathedral novel, they are then prepared to analyze the style, structure, and representation of French culture in *A la recherche du temps perdu*.

Proust in a Graduate Seminar:
Structuring the Proustian Experience

Christie McDonald

It has been noted by Roland Barthes, among others, that *A la recherche du temps perdu* is a book to be read and reread and that one of life's great pleasures is skipping different passages with each reading (*Pleasure* 11). One of the daunting tasks in teaching this work is to make a first reading of Proust as meaningful as a rereading. The danger is that, rather than savoring the complexity of the language and its rich evocations of the senses and reflections on art, memory, and love, students may feel more as if they are running in the Kentucky Derby. The challenge for teachers is to find a way to make the temporality of the reading experience both intensive and expansive.

The problem of reading the *Recherche* in a graduate course is linked to understanding the work as an ongoing project or total work. By considering Proust's ideas in 1908–09, the version of the *Recherche* published in 1913, its subsequent expansion into several volumes, as well as new material provided by the recent editions, one can teach the novel both genetically and structurally and thus provide students with a global view of his method of composition.

Proust's early project is totalizing, and the novel unfolds as it produces its own genesis: the novel recounts the discovery of the vocation of the hero-narrator as a writer. It is a project leading to the completion of understanding and meaning in writing—initially a hermeneutic project. However, the subsequent writing of the novel becomes labyrinthine or rhizomatic (in Deleuzian terms) and generates an anxiety of indeterminacy. Thus the two sides of Proust create a cross-current of thought that tends both toward a notion of totality and truth through art and toward the unraveling of meaning in love and jealousy.

One can read the dominant thinking patterns of two centuries in these tendencies, in which fragmentary thought of the nineteenth century is subsumed into totalizing thought and twentieth-century thinking moves toward fragmentation in the infinite referral of interpretation. Proust, in a letter to René Blum (20 Feb. 1913), argued that the overall compositional structure of the *Recherche* was tight, even though it was not evident to his readers in 1913: "Quant à ce livre-ci, c'est au contraire un tout très composé, quoique d'une composition si complexe que je crains que personne ne le perçoive et qu'il apparaisse comme une suite de digressions. C'est tout le contraire" (*Corr.* 12: 82) ("This book . . . is a very structured whole, although the composition is so complex that I fear no one perceives it and that it seems like a series of digressions. It is the very opposite"; my trans.). In another letter to Blum three days later, Proust added, "Il y a beaucoup de personnages; ils sont 'préparés' dès ce premier volume. . . . La composition . . . est si complexe qu'elle n'apparaît que très tardivement quand tous les 'Thèmes' ont commencé à se combiner"

(*Corr.* 12: 92) ("There are many characters; they are prepared from the first volume. . . . The complexity of the composition only appears late when all the themes have begun to combine"; my trans.). Unlike works from the nineteenth century whose unity Proust maintained was imposed late in the writing process, the singularity of the *Recherche* was to be inscribed by the writer from the beginning and recalled through the expression of feeling. In his reflection on the relation between affect and the intellect, Proust elaborated the elements of his secret plan, the structure that would grant a retrospective order to the forthcoming work (see Contre Sainte-Beuve 211–18; Against Sainte-Beuve 3–11). To set up a framework within which the particulars of life and thought could come alive, Proust claimed a firm structure that included both exposition and narrative. Memory provided the basic principle because, as he analogized, like memory the work in his head was always the same, yet perpetually coming into being.

I divide my course roughly into two parts, corresponding to the two sides of Proust's thought. The first half deals primarily with the project of writing the *Recherche*, largely based on the first conception of the work sketched out in 1908–09. The readings include *Du côté de chez Swann* and *Le temps retrouvé*. In a letter to Paul Souday, Proust proclaimed the unity of the first and last sections of the book and pointed to their contemporary creation: "Le dernier chapitre du dernier volume a été écrit 'tout de suite après le premier chapitre du premier volume. Tout l'entre-deux' a été écrit ensuite" (*Corr.* 3: 72) ("The last chapter of the first volume was written right after the first chapter of the first volume. Everything in between was written after that"; my trans.). He sketched the sequence of experiences in involuntary memory that were to furnish the support and inner structure of the total work.

In these passages, Proust juxtaposes the two sequences of involuntary memory: the first flush of joy as memories irrupt into consciousness when he drinks tea and dips toast, feels uneven paving stones, and hears a spoon drop on his plate. Mysteriously calling forth feelings of elation, of "pure life conserved pure" (Contre Sainte-Beuve 211–13; Against Sainte-Beuve 4), these moments frame the novel. In "Combray," the scene of the madeleine summons total recall of childhood remembered only fragmentarily; in *Le Temps retrouvé*, the same such memories repeat and amplify the experience of involuntary memory, preliminaries or rites of passage through Proust's ontology to his aesthetics.

The second part deals with those sections that exceed the project and ultimately question its unity; we circle back and read *A l'ombre des jeunes filles en fleurs*, *Sodome et Gomorrhe*, and *Albertine disparue*. Proust wanted to recreate the evolution of thought in the individual and to make it "live," as he explained in a letter to Jacques Rivière on 6 February 1914 (*Corr.* 13: 98). But he always followed thought in its associative wandering through particulars. Generalities emerge from a pattern of details narrated from a given point of view. In this way Proust created from reminiscence a new kind of epistemological tool grounded in the experience that "Notre âme n'est jamais une" (1:

753, *esquisse* 31) ("Our soul is never one"; my trans.). If the narrator struggles to find a unified conception of art, the experience of change in love and art nevertheless proves to be multiple and evanescent.

Proust puts an image through successive states by an associative process that comes to define the artist's mode of thinking. Repeated throughout the novel, the process allows events to emerge as new experiences and to be relived in memory. For example, love is subjected to an inexorable law of memory and forgetting, no matter how exceptional the experience may feel to the lover. By probing the way in which associations guide thought and by translating the simultaneity of associations into temporal sequences of writing, Proust teased out of individual experience a general quality resembling a scientific law, while still maintaining what was unique about experience. This makes association for Proust the privileged domain of thought and the basis on which he creates literature.

Throughout the course, I ask students to reconstruct with me a sequence of microstories from the novel and to analyze how the narrator passes from the complexity of specific scenes to more general formulations about memory, art, grief, death, and so on. We read in detail well-known scenes—from *le drame du coucher* (the bedtime drama), *la mémoire involontaire* (involuntary memory), and Montjouvain to *la petite phrase de Vinteuil* (Vinteuil's little phrase)—as well as other less-well-studied passages. My approach is to open theoretical questions through close textual readings; it is in these readings that the Proustian idiom emerges. Proust wrote literature to produce the universality and necessity of what is individual and uncertain. He was a master at tracing the way in which accidental events become transformed into past givens.

I have taken the position that all documents, whether private or public, sketch or final draft, have gained the status of text, because, like the sketches and drawings hung in a museum, they present the retrospective showing of the artist. We can now x-ray Proust's work, as it were, as machines might a painting. The infinitely patient work demanded of the editors produces a novel that passes out of their hands into the domain of readers, and students can now benefit from a great deal of new material.

The criticism of *A la recherche du temps perdu* in the twentieth century changed considerably. Three general approaches have dominated: phenomenological criticism in the period before the mid–1960s tended to concentrate on the phenomenology of mind inscribed in the project. During the period of structuralism in literary studies in the 1960s and 1970s, critics focused on the semiological aspects of the work. In the 1980s, genetic criticism developed as critics gained access to variants and previously unavailable material. More recently, there have been a number of broadly popular books and biographies. I believe that one can almost teach a history of twentieth-century criticism through Proust, and in any case it is important for graduate students to make presentations throughout the semester on different approaches (either taken generally or through particular critical readings).

Phenomenological studies dealt with the concept of the object and analyzed consciousness and time in relation to it: Jean-Pierre Richard's *Proust et le monde sensible* provided a hermeneutics of the object, and Georges Poulet's *Espace proustien* (*Proustian Space*) showed the importance of time and memory. Semiological studies opened up levels of linguistic patterning and narrative aspects in the work: through the explicit movement away from rhetoric as traditionally conceived, studies such as Gérard Genette's *Figures* and *Figures 3*, to cite only two of his many texts on Proust, sought to establish a form of systematization that ensured semiotic coherence of the work of art. The genetic approach began largely with work on manuscripts and the preparation of editions (see Hay; Grésillon, *Eléments*). This approach explores the *Recherche* as a work in progress and has brought out problems of uncertainty, similar to those claimed for the finished text in deconstructive criticism. Recent work in psychoanalytic analysis and gay studies often incorporates aspects of the other three currents—hermeneutic, semiotic, and genetic.

Each of these periods of criticism has produced strong critics, although no one approach has proved adequate to describe the model of Proust's project: the phenomenological studies left aside preoccupations of language and the unconscious and semiological studies left aside the problem of the subject, time, and history. Gilles Deleuze writes in *Proust et les signes* that "L'essentiel, dans la *Recherche*, ce n'est pas la mémoire et le temps, mais le signe et la vérité. L'essentiel n'est pas de se souvenir, mais d'apprendre. Car la mémoire ne vaut que comme une faculté capable d'interpréter certains signes, le temps ne vaut que comme la matière ou le type de telle ou telle vérité" (109) ("What is essential in the *Search* is not memory and time, but the sign and truth. What is essential is not to remember, but to learn. For memory is valid only as a faculty capable of interpreting certain signs, time is valid only as the substance of type of this or that truth" [Proust and Signs 89–90]). Deleuze's semiological study brackets memory and displaces the narrator's need to believe in truth. Paul Ricoeur argues rather that apprenticeship of signs requires investigative meandering that substitutes for the epiphany of involuntary memory. The totality of the work comes from both: if one grants that the *Recherche* is a fable about time, it is because involuntary memory must be related to the apprenticeship of signs. Ricoeur believes the discovery of an extratemporal dimension is the final revelation of the novel's hermeneutic key (*Temps et récit II: la configuration* 195). Genetic criticism suggests that the reinsertion of a literary event in its historical context allows the reader to measure the plurality of meanings in a text. Antoine Compagnon's theoretical position goes beyond the external historical reconstruction of manuscripts (*La Troisième République*).

Vincent Descombes distinguishes among historical, aesthetic, and philosophical readings of Proust by critics in the past. If the reading is based on facts, then it is historical. If it relies on interpretation, it is aesthetic (or critical in the sense of literary criticism). If arguments grounded in philosophical reason dominate, then the reading is philosophical. The purpose of philosophical readings is to see if the meaning that one gives to the work is logically clear. In distinguishing the thought of the novelist from that of the theoretician, he shows Proust the novelist to be superior to Proust the theoretician. The theoretician in Proust may balk at a sociological comprehension of human life, but the novelist, who must create characters and dramatic scenes, shows a remarkable flair for sociology. Proust pits the philosophy of the novel against the philosophy of the essay, and the novel triumphs (1–19).

The narrator's quest for the general laws of love and emotion frame—in rational terms—the desire to write. The project of writing, as a philosophical endeavor, forms a coherent whole in the exploration of creativity and the creative subject. Attempting to make sense out of impressions as a writer, Proust's narrator addresses the relation of the singular to the universal in an ongoing struggle between poetry and philosophy, which, when it recognizes contingency, separates individual literary self-creation (see Rorty) from the philosophical endeavor of realizing universality through transcendence.

The phenomenological, rhetorical, and genetic analyses in Proustian studies opens the way for exploration of the ways in which the mechanisms of association—as thought (whether philosophical or artistic)—generate investigations of identity and the self in history. For Proust, the rational notion of totality and the concept of an all-encompassing theory are at some level synonymous. By putting in motion a kind of writing for which there is no adequate speculative theory, Proust's texts raise a key epistemological question about how association in literature redefines thought as neither simply rational nor irrational.

I believe Proust leaves behind the initial structure of the *Recherche* after 1914 by displacing his project of mediating rational thought and a theory of the artistic subject. The novel unfolds in affective movements, which, though not simply irrational, escape the logic of rationality. I ask the students to work on the complexities of this unfolding by following either a character or taking one of the arts to see how they are explored as models for the future writer. I have almost always taught the course in French, and while differing levels of French competency can pose a problem (and are in fact a good reason for limiting the number of students in the class), diversity of background and interest makes for rich discussion. The experience of classroom exchange can be as intense as the experience of reading the work.

Proust in a Gender Studies Course:
What to Do with Montjouvain?

Brigitte Mahuzier

"Combray," whole or in selected passages, is the section of Proust's *A la recherche du temps perdu* that is by far the most often taught. There are many reasons for its classroom popularity, the most obvious being that as the first volume in a long series, it is easier to handle than one of the many middle volumes that would plunge students in medias res. It is short and, better still for classroom purposes, full of set pieces, episodes, and descriptive tableaux lending themselves to close readings as well as to broad generalization. It is quaint, picturesque, and offers students a double cultural *dépaysement* ("displacement") in space (provincial France) and time (the pre–First World War era). In fact, "Combray" contains a highly pedagogical blend of familiar and unfamiliar elements that places it in the Barthesian category of "textes lisibles" ("readable texts"), a category Roland Barthes defines in *S/Z* as accessible or reader-friendly (9–12). The effort required by the act of reducing the unfamiliar to the familiar is then rewarded by a sense of accomplishment and excitement at having mastered an acclaimed work of Western literature, despite its notorious difficulty and tediousness.

"Combray" would be eminently teachable were it not for a short scene toward the end, known as Montjouvain (1: 157–63; 1: 224–33), which seems to fulfill none of the above-mentioned conditions of readability—a scene that, for both structural and thematic reasons, does not quite fit in the picture. The hermeneutic advantages of starting at the beginning, which places students in a similar position to readers in 1913, are compromised by this scene because it does not fully make sense except in the light of passages occurring much later in the novel. The Montjouvain scene, like the many other explicit prolepses that punctuate the *Recherche*, clearly indicates that the reader must wait until later ("on verra plus tard que . . ." [1: 157]) ("we will see, in due course . . ." [1: 224]) to understand the role played by the Montjouvain scene in the narrator's life. Unlike readers in 1913, though, today's students have access to this textual posterity; and unlike Proust, who had to defend the Montjouvain scene to his friends and prospective editors by asking them to wait for the publication of future volumes, today's instructor can choose to fast-forward to these later passages. The teacher of "Combray" has the benefit of subsequent scenes that cast a retrospective light on Montjouvain and explain its presence in "Combray" as well as in the work as a whole.

This capacity to fast-forward and even zap back and forth through the text has its drawbacks and perverse effects, but it offers ways to measure the complexity of the novel's architecture while underlining the third dimension of the text, its temporality (see Genette, *Narrative Discourse*). Reading ahead to make sense of an obscure scene allows students to grasp Proust's theory of *intermit-*

tences du cœur ("intermittencies of the heart"), according to which there is a temporal gap between an experience and its realization. Reading ahead also makes students aware of the textual strategy of a first-person quasi-omniscient narration that generally tells it not like it is but as it appears to be. Finally, proleptic reading emphasizes the text's historical dimension and the crucial role of the reader since each retrospective explanation adds a new layer to the text.

There are many passages in later volumes of the *Recherche* that hark back to Montjouvain, mostly scenes of voyeurism with a sodomite motif, such as the scenes disclosing Charlus's homosexuality in *Sodome et Gomorrhe* 1 (3: 3–13; 4: 1–13) and his masochism in *Le temps retrouvé* (4: 388–412; 6: 173–210). Many passages in earlier works by Proust anticipate Montjouvain: the theme of matricidal guilt showcased in Montjouvain obsessed Proust and can be traced back to his earliest writing (see Ladenson, ch. 4). But the most obvious choice for classroom use is the closing scene of *Sodome et Gomorrhe* 2, known as "Désolation au lever du soleil" ("Desolation at Dawn") in the chapter entitled "Les intermittences du cœur" (3: 497–515; 4: 699–724). In this scene, the protagonist, who has just decided to break up with Albertine because life with her has become too predictable, suddenly decides that he must marry her when she remarks that she knows Mlle Vinteuil and her friend. The words "cette amie, c'est Mlle Vinteuil" (3: 512) ("That friend is Mlle Vinteuil" [4: 720]), like the crumbs of the madeleine, have the powerful effect of bringing back in a flash the Montjouvain scene in which the narrator now imagines Albertine taking the role of Mlle Vinteuil's friend. But, in contrast to the prodigal return of the past brought about by the madeleine, the words make him realize that Albertine will never be in his possession and will always remain an object of suspicion and jealousy. Albertine, as one of the many citizens of Gomorrah, will from this point on incarnate for the narrator the radical unfamiliarity that inhabits even the most familiar places—Freud calls this effect the *unheimliche*, the uncanny. In the words of Emmanuel Levinas, Albertine represents "fundamental strangeness . . . this strangeness which mocks knowledge" (160–65). In short, the dawn that is breaking offers the desolate picture of a landscape after all assumed truths and values have been blown to pieces.

Published in 1922, almost a decade and two thousand pages after readers had read—and possibly forgotten—the Montjouvain scene, "Desolation at Dawn" is usually considered the justification for Montjouvain. "Desolation" not only casts a retrospective light on Montjouvain, fulfilling the promise made by the older narrator to elucidate the scene, it also functions as the turning point for the entire story of Albertine. "Desolation at Dawn" launches the next volumes, *La Prisonnière* and *Albertine disparue*, in which Albertine, "grande déesse du Temps" (3: 888) ("almighty goddess of Time" [5: 520]), functions as the driving force of the narrator's endless erotic and epistemological quest, a sort of *figure de proue* for the *Recherche* itself, "m'invitant, sous une forme pressante, cruelle et sans issue, à la recherche du passé" (3: 888) ("urging me with cruel and fruitless insistence in quest of the past" [5: 520]).

Although it is true that today's reader has the advantage of reading the work retrospectively and that a lot of scenes, like photographic negatives, remain barely perceptible until a later scene, like a chemical developer, makes the pattern visible, a reader can approach Montjouvain without leaving "Combray." An early interpretation of Montjouvain was proposed by Georges Bataille. Analyzing Montjouvain as an imaginary coming-out scene addressed to a maternal figure, Bataille suggests that if the reader switches the gender of Albertine, a portrait of the author emerges. This interpretation, which clearly evokes Proust's own life, might appear convincing to students but reduces the scene to biography. To better assess the complexity of the Montjouvain episode without extrapolating meanings from outside sources, one can read it in conjunction with a first, and usually ignored, Montjouvain episode, taking place some fifty pages earlier (1: 111–12; 1: 156–57) and featuring the narrator's parents on a visit to M. Vinteuil.

All elements of the homoerotic scene are already in place in this first Montjouvain, however here they form a banal family affair: the role of Mlle Vinteuil's friend in the second scene is played by the narrator's mother in the first (paying a friendly visit to M. Vinteuil with her husband); the role of Mlle Vinteuil is played by M. Vinteuil (who receives his guest in his living room); and the prop, in the later scene the portrait of the dead father, is in the first scene Vinteuil's own musical composition. The unchanging element is the audience, in the form of the young protagonist, who in both scenes offers improbable justifications for his presence. The scenario and even the scripted words for the two scenes are also similar: a fake embarrassment at attracting the attention of the visitor to the object displayed and profaned—the music composition and the father's picture.

What is represented, as we read both scenes together, is the guilt produced by the profanation of private, family matters by publication, by making them public. As Jacques Lacan humorously points out when he speaks of "poubellication" (from *poubelle* 'dustbin') to publish is always in some sense to trash, to profane (29). The Montjouvain scenes lay bare the guilt of the writer who makes use of the most intimate family secrets to win notoriety and gain posterity as a writer. By the same token, the scenes also lay bare the hypocrisy of readers as witnesses, their implication in the act of distant and voyeuristic viewing called reading. But the profanation of private familial matters would not be so condemnable were it not for the hypocrisy that consists in denying the effects of profanation of family members.

The root of all evil, as the discourse on sadism in the second Montjouvain scene attempts to show, is found not in cruel acts occasionally performed but rather in indifference, "cette indifférence aux souffrances qu'on cause et qui . . . est la forme terrible et permanente de la cruauté" (1: 163) ("that indifference to the sufferings one causes, which, whatever other names one gives it, is the most terrible and lasting form of cruelty" [1: 233]). Mlle Vinteuil, a "sadist," an "artiste du mal" ("artist of evil"), would not be so good in her roles as sadist and artist if she were not so sensitive and if she did not have such a profound adoration for her father. All "sadists" are "des sensibles pervertis" ("perverted sensitive souls"), Proust explains in a letter to his friend Louis de Robert (cited in Ahlstedt 25), since it takes a sensitive and virtuous person to make a good sadist, a naturally good person to make a "méchant" (1: 162) ("wicked" [1: 231]), a devoted daughter to make a blasphemous one, and so forth. Sadistic perversion, as described in the second Montjouvain, is not unethical, since Proustian sadism is a sign of extreme sensitivity to the suffering of the other. In fact, perversion is an index of sensitivity. The real danger lies in the disappearance of this sensitivity to the other, in moral indifference.

In the end, "Combray" as a whole can be reread in the light of Montjouvain and the discourse that accompanies it. Scenes of cruelty, especially those enacted by Françoise—the benign embodiment of provincial France—and witnessed by the protagonist, take on a new dimension. The picturesque and humorous descriptions of Françoise torturing the kitchen maid or killing the Sunday chicken while blaming the poor hapless victims for their demise can easily turn sinister, especially if one considers the role played by the young protagonist (1: 119–22; 1: 168–70). Aware that cruelty is being enacted, he would rather ignore what is going on in the kitchen to enjoy with unperturbed pleasure the delicate asparagus and the tender chicken. As the narrator reminds us, our apprenticeship of indifference starts at an early age, when we avert our eyes from what is right in front of us. In an episode situated early in "Combray," the young protagonist is described running to his room rather than witness his great aunt torturing his grandmother in front of the whole family, assembled in the garden: "déjà homme par la lâcheté, je faisais ce que nous faisons tous, quand nous sommes grands, quand il y a devant nous des souffrances et des injustices: je ne voulais pas les voir" (1: 12) ("in my cowardice, I became at once a man, and did what all we grown men do when face to face with suffering and injustice: I preferred not to see them" [1: 14]).

As we reread "Combray" through the Montjouvain episodes, we can see, under the picturesque and charming village, with its familial closeness and religious rituals, a projection of a world whose secure values and truths are about to be blown to pieces, a world before "Desolation at Dawn," necessarily unaware of its future. Although Montjouvain represents "evil as a dreadful and thrilling world," that world is not a "apart from us" but within us (Finch 171). Such a world is intimately linked to the very "rouage" ("workings") of the little provincial town—Aunt Léonie's "traintrain" being the best expression of its boring and apparently innocuous nature (see 1: 108; 1: 152)—just as it is an intrinsic part of the *Recherche*.

Montjouvain presents a genuine problem in the classroom because of its sharp incommensurability with the text within which it is embedded. That incommensurability, however, can be an advantage since Montjouvain represents in a nutshell the complexity of the *Recherche* as a whole, a complexity too easily elided in the prelapsarian world of "Combray."

Teaching Proust Comparatively:
Proust, Ruskin, and the Visual Arts

Diane R. Leonard

I teach Proust most frequently in the context of a comparative literature graduate course on the novel. This is a class I have taught for a number of years; it
has evolved into its present form largely because of my research interests in the
role played by John Ruskin's writings in the development of Proust's
Recherche. Many of Proust's central aesthetic concepts derive from Ruskin, a
nineteenth-century British writer on the visual arts most widely known for his
efforts to revive and preserve the Gothic style of architecture and for his
defense of the paintings of J. M. W. Turner. Proust translated two volumes of
Ruskin's writings (*The Bible of Amiens* and *Sesame and Lilies*), read widely in
Ruskin's work, and wrote various articles about Ruskin during the years preceding his composition of *A la recherche du temps perdu*.

Over many semesters of teaching Proust, I have become convinced that the
best way to approach the essential features of his narrative is through Ruskin.
So I begin my course with two Ruskin volumes on the visual arts—*The Elements of Drawing* and *The Seven Lamps of Architecture*—representing the
two major concerns of Ruskin's thought, impressionism and architecture. After
going on to explore the Ruskinian elements in Proust's narrative, I conclude
the semester with a consideration of Virginia Woolf's *To the Lighthouse* to show
the extension of these elements under the influence of postimpressionism. For
the purposes of this volume, however, I highlight only the central Ruskinian
aspects of the course.

Ruskin's Writings on the Arts

The Elements of Drawing is a small volume of exercises Ruskin wrote for his
drawing students, which I use to set up the impressionistic elements in his
thought. The brief introduction by Lawrence Campbell gives an interesting
account of the influence of this work on French impressionism, citing a remark
by Monet that "ninety per cent of the theory of Impressionist painting" is contained in it (viii). In the preface, Ruskin argues that "the excellence of an artist
. . . depends wholly on refinement of perception" (12), and he devotes the rest
of the volume to helping his students learn to see. In letter 1, "On First Practice," he opposes the teaching of art through rules, insisting in a famous foot-
note that "the whole technical power of painting depends on our recovery of
what may be called the *innocence of the eye* . . . a sort of childish perception of
these flat stains of colour, merely as such, without consciousness of what they
signify,—as a blind man would see them if suddenly gifted with sight" (27).
Ruskin gives his students a series of exercises aimed at achieving this state of
innocence in which the artist learns to abandon himself or herself to the

"instinct of the eye," letting go of rules and logic and learning to see the complex gradations of tint that compose even the most apparently uniform color.

The next sections of *Elements* provide an introduction to Ruskin's use of typology or figuralism. In letter 2, "Sketching from Nature," he gives an important lesson on the "visible objects of Nature as a type of the human nature" (120), and in letter 3, "On Composition," he shows how trees serve as types or figures of essential truths (186–87). I use these passages as the basis for a discussion of Ruskin's use of typology in reading the visible, drawing on various excerpts from *Modern Painters* in which he explains his aesthetic theory. Ruskin believed that the artist must remain entirely open to the impressions of nature, not distorting them in any way, because those impressions are made by God's writing in types and figures in the book of nature, which it is the artist's duty to translate. I find that this is the most difficult part of teaching Ruskin today—helping students understand the typological or figural foundations of his view of nature and art, a tradition about which most of them have little or no knowledge. To give them some background in this mode of medieval exegesis, I draw on E. R. Curtius's chapter "The Book of Nature" (*European Literature* 319–26) and on Erich Auerbach's rich essay "Figura."

To amplify this discussion, we next turn our attention to a chapter from the fourth volume of *Modern Painters*, "On Turnerian Topography," in which Ruskin explains the "sacredness of the truth of Impression" in Turner's drawing of the pass of Faido in the Swiss Alps (*Works* 6: 36). Ruskin shows how Turner drew this scene in "an act of dream vision," passively obedient to the impression the pass had made on him (*Works* 6: 41). Then Ruskin illustrates why Turner's sketch is superior to the kind of truth found in a mere topographical drawing based on scientific fact (of which Ruskin himself provides an example). I ask the students to analyze the differences between Turner's impressionistic and Ruskin's scientific drawings, and we also examine slides of the oil painting Turner made from his sketch of the pass of Faido. We then discuss a series of slides of his major paintings, which I present chronologically to reveal the evolution of Turner's work from its roots in the neoclassical landscapes of Claude Lorrain (Claude Gelée) and Nicolas Poussin, through its break with rules and conventions, and into its liberation in a kind of poetry of light. Throughout this discussion our focus is on the increasing dominance of the impression—of optical effects of light and color—over the representation of the object.

We move from impressionism to architectural concepts with *The Seven Lamps of Architecture*, a book Proust claimed to know "par cœur" ("by heart") (*Corr.* 2: 387; *Letters* 1: 213). We discuss the typological elements of Ruskin's discussion of architecture—in particular, the opening passage in "The Lamp of Power," where Ruskin presents human memory as a geologic landscape composed of deposits of impressions sedimented in memory and worn away by time (70– 71), and a well-known passage from "The Lamp of Life" in which he uses a brittle growth on a tree as a type of the false life as opposed to the true life of human beings (149–50). We also examine Ruskin's concept of the continuum of realization and abstraction in architectural design (131–36) and note how a cathedral, for instance, mediates between the two poles, since it must be designed for both distant and close-up viewing. I elaborate on this concept using passages about ornamentation in architecture from Ruskin's *The Stones of Venice*. We then move to "The Lamp of Memory" and Ruskin's discussion of how the "golden stain of time" on a building serves as a kind of public memory, connecting "forgotten and following ages with each other" (187). We close with a moving passage from "The Lamp of Life" that will serve as a bridge to Proust: Ruskin's description of a small stone figure carved on the portal of Rouen Cathedral, illustrated by his own engraving of it (172–73).

Ruskinian Pilgrimages

We use "The Lamp of Life" as a transition to the essays on Ruskin that Proust wrote in 1900, the year of Ruskin's death. We begin with the essay, "John Ruskin" and the story of the pilgrimage to Rouen Proust made to seek out the little figure in commemoration of Ruskin at the time of his death (*On Reading Ruskin* 44–48; Contre Sainte-Beuve 124–28). We discuss the way in which Proust recontextualizes this figure, removing it from the art-historical context in which Ruskin had placed it and reinscribing it in a matrix of images associated with Ruskin's death and afterlife. During this discussion I show slides of Rouen Cathedral, the portal of the booksellers, and the little figure seen from different viewpoints (slides I made myself to re-create the experience of Proust's pilgrimage). We focus on Proust's description of the survival of the expression of the little figure despite the wearing away of the stone in which it is carved and on how this expression permits the figure (along with Ruskin's soul) to be resurrected from the death of oblivion under Proust's gaze.

We then move on to Proust's essay "Notre-Dame d'Amiens according to Ruskin" (*On Reading Ruskin* 9–28; Contre Sainte-Beuve 69–105). I show a series of slides I've made of Amiens, reproducing Ruskin's and Proust's directions for approaching the cathedral, ending with the statue of the gilded Virgin on the south portal (*On Reading Ruskin* 13–17; Contre Sainte-Beuve 83–86). We explore the long text by Proust on this statue and focus on the temporal dimension of the Virgin, the crumbling of her stone and its weathering by the winds over the centuries. Yet at the same time we observe the persistence of her individuality not only through many years in the mind of the aging Ruskin but also through many centuries. We discuss the theme of the cathedral as a book written in a picture language of types and figures and follow Proust as he imitates Ruskin's lessons in how to read the cathedral (in *The Bible of Amiens*). We focus on how Proust reinscribes Ruskin's description of the gilded Virgin in the context of his own preoccupations with the survival of Ruskin's thought and how he narrativizes the statue, making it a character in a story. Here again, we see the statue become representative of both the survival of the artist's soul through time and the resurrective power of memory.

Finally, we discuss the postscript that Proust appended to his essays on Ruskin in 1903, when he prepared them to serve as the preface to his translation of Ruskin's *The Bible of Amiens*. In particular, we examine the scene in which Proust portrays himself reading Ruskin's *The Stones of Venice* inside Saint Mark's Church (*On Reading Ruskin* 53–54; Contre Sainte-Beuve 133) in the context of another Ruskinian pilgrimage. Proust compares Ruskin's text to the church mosaics, which are identified by Byzantine inscriptions bearing their names and their legends, and he accuses Ruskin of idolatry, by which he appears to mean that Ruskin sacrificed his artistic "innocence of the eye" to his erudition in interpreting the types and figures of religious architecture (*On Reading Ruskin* 50–55; Contre Sainte-Beuve 129–34). This accusation marks a turning point in Proust's aesthetic: no longer will he follow in Ruskin's footsteps, reading his texts to see through his eyes. Rather, Proust will give himself over to his own "truth of impression" (*On Reading Ruskin* 324), which he will try to represent in figures that project meanings through their visual form, qua images, without didactic commentary.

Reading the Figures of the Recherche

Now we have arrived at the portal of *A la recherche du temps perdu* itself. I ask the class to provide an open sesame by identifying traces of the little figure in "Combray" 1, and usually some of the students point to the madeleine-and-tea scene. We then discuss this scene in terms of the theme of involuntary memory and the resurrection of the souls of the past, comparing the treatment of these themes in the *Recherche* with their presentation in the Ruskin essay. At the end of our discussion we eat madeleines and sip lime-blossom tea while looking at slides I've made of a pilgrimage through Illiers-Combray. We then explore how characters or events can be outside time by existing in two disparate moments simultaneously and how the past interpenetrates the present throughout the opening section of the narrative—in Françoise, in the language of George Sand, in the magic-lantern illuminations, and so forth. We note the dislocation of the narrator (and hence the reader) from the normal parameters of time and space through the breaking of syntactic and narrational codes in the opening pages, where the narrator is whirled through space and time in a kind of time machine à la H. G. Wells. We explore the narrator's tricks of hurling us forward and backward in time, thus making the temporal dimension of the text reversible.

At this point we examine the text on the church of Combray, described as a time machine moving across the centuries in the fourth dimension (1: 58–61; 1: 80–84). We discuss the marks of time on the church and note that its destructive force has distorted the Latin inscriptions on the tombstones, rendering them illegible, thus leaving the church to speak through its images alone—its sculptures, its tapestries, and especially the figures in the stained-glass windows whose illuminations lie across the tombstones like the projections of the magic lantern on the wall of the narrator's bedroom. We relate this text to the passage on reading inside Saint Mark's Church where Proust deplores the effects of the Byzantine inscriptions that divert our attention from the beauty of the figures themselves, thus destroying the truth of impression. In passing, we note the impression made in the "Merovingian night" (1:61; 1:81) of the church's crypt by the lamp that embedded itself in the rock, leaving a shape very like the shell-like figure of the madeleine—suggesting how impressions are struck in our subconscious during our early years.

We then explore the church of Combray as a type or figure of the *Recherche* itself. I present several passages from Proust's correspondence in which he reveals that his narrative is constructed in the form of a cathedral and insists on its architectural integrity, despite its apparently random sequence of materials. We discuss the problems that are inherent in constructing a narrative of impressions and that underlay Proust's decision to adopt an architectural structure to hold the whole together. We look at the opposition of opacity (stone) and transparency (stained-glass windows) in the church, which is reflected in the narrative as a contrast between habit and the truth of impression. Then we trace various elements in "Combray" that point to the cathedral-like nature of the text, such as the comparison of Aunt Léonie and Françoise to stone statues in their niches or the resemblance of the statues on the porch of Saint-André des Champs to the local peasant girls.

Now we explore some other impressions that the narrative stamps in the reader's consciousness, focusing on three successive figures of flowers. In the opening pages of "Combray" 2 (1: 50–51; 1: 69–70), we examine the dried lime blossoms from which Aunt Léonie makes her tisane and note how they serve as a figure for the simultaneity of different ages (much like the church of Combray itself). Then we examine the famous hawthorn passage (1: 136–38; 1: 193–97), in which we see a figural relation of promise and fulfillment—the white hawthorns are a promise of which the pink are a fulfillment (just as a sketch is fulfilled by an oil painting or a melody by a full orchestral arrangement). Finally, we look closely at the water-lily text (1: 166–68; 1: 237–40), another promise-fulfillment relation in two parts: first there is the single "nénuphar," chained to its place by its stalk and condemned to perpetually repeating its back-and-forth movement, like a figure in Dante's *Inferno*; then there are the "nymphéas," cut loose from the linear flow of the current to float free in a fourth-dimensional kaleidoscope of color.

This text invites a figural reading because of its reference to Dante, who stated explicitly that he wrote his *Divine Comedy* to be read on four levels (literal, figural, moral, anagogical) in imitation of God's way of writing in types and figures. Yet if Proust has given us Dante in the first section of this painting, he has given us Monet in the second, so we look at slides of Monet's *nymphéas* cycle and discuss it in relation to Proust's text. We experiment with giving

Proust's water lilies a figural reading: the contrast between the two sections suggests that not only may we move from imprisonment by the linear flow of time and habit to the freedom of free-floating impressions—but we also may be liberated by this text from our habits of reading. Narrative thus becomes poetry and all times one, the linearity of the text (that is, its one-way direction and temporal flow) being overcome by a simultaneous patterning that, like the colors of the pond, is always changing yet harmonious.

To continue our discussion of the reading of the *Recherche*, a reading different from one that we give to a normal narrative since it places certain special demands on its readers, we turn to another Ruskinian figure in "Combray," the kitchen maid who is compared to Charity in Giotto's fresco, and to another cathedral-book structure, the Arena Chapel in Padua (1: 79–80; 1: 110–11). I present some materials from Ruskin's *Giotto and His Works in Padua* and then show slides of the Arena frescoes, including the narrative sequences on Mary and Jesus and the representations of the vices and virtues. We end with Giotto's fresco of Charity and discuss its description in "Combray," which gives us an opportunity to explore the differences between realistic and figural representation. We then look at several texts on the narrator's reading experiences and note their relation to some of the passages in Proust's Ruskin essays.

Here we switch from reading to writing and conclude our discussion of "Combray" with the passage on the steeples of Martinville. The passage is based on a Turneresque description of Caen seen from a speeding automobile that Proust wrote in a 1907 account of one of his last Ruskinian pilgrimages— to see the porch of the cathedral of Lisieux that Ruskin had described in *The Seven Lamps*. Proust rewrites the description, deleting the visit to Lisieux and changing the automobile to a horse-drawn carriage. But he retains the poetry of speed that cuts the steeples loose from their rootedness in actuality and allows them to dance freely in the sky, liberated from the axes of history and geography to become pure impression. This impression gives birth to the narrator's passage on the steeples (1: 177–80; 1: 254–56), described with the innocence of the eye that no longer seeks to identify or explain but simply allows the steeples to blossom in the fullness of their metaphorical unfolding—into pivots; birds; flowers; and, finally, maidens lost and alone, groping their way in the dusk.

Again, we look at the two panels of this text as a promise-fulfillment sequence: the impression of the steeples on the horizon promises the writing of the narrator's fragment. But there is a larger promise-fulfillment relation here: the steeple of Saint Hilaire that opens "Combray" 2, seen by the narrator from the train approaching the town, prefigures not only the town of Combray but also the steeples of Martinville that are to come, unfolded out of the steeple of Saint Hilaire to inscribe in the sky the narrator's first literary work. They will be folded back into a single steeple in the last pages of the final volume of the narrative, when the aging narrator at the princesse de Guermantes's reception discovers he has become taller than a church steeple in the dimension of time and, at the same moment, discovers the secret of his literary vocation. We end our study of Proust with a discussion of this last section of *Le Temps retrouvé*, noting to what extent Proust's aesthetic treatise on the reading and writing of his narrative rests on the two Ruskinian concepts of the truth of impression and the interpretation of figures, combined with the resurrective power of memory. Moreover, we examine how the elderly characters of his text have metamorphosed into crumbling stone statues, thus bringing to the fore the cathedral-like elements of the narrative, allowing it to be read like the cathedral of Amiens.

As we watch the steeple of Proust's cathedral-novel fading into the distance, we move back to England to consider another narrative of impression and architecture: Virginia Woolf's *To the Lighthouse*. It too makes use of types and figures, of distance and close-up perception, of architectural structures, though in a more schematic fashion, showing the impact of Paul Cézanne (through Roger Fry) and his belief that all of nature could be assimilated to simple geometric shapes. But that is a story for another essay.

Proust in an Interdisciplinary Context: Literature and Music

Jean-Louis Pautrot

A unit on Marcel Proust and music may be integrated into a course on *A La Recherche du temps perdu* or into a course on music and French literature in the twentieth century. In the latter course, time might not allow for reading the whole novel, and excerpts would have to be chosen. Even with limited time and well-chosen excerpts, several class meetings may still be necessary to explore adequately the subject of Proust and music.

For students to understand the impact of music on Proust's art, it is important to consider music's historical, biographical, and literary aspects. Thus, after a survey of the musical context and of the influence of music on literature in Proust's time, instructors may find it rewarding to proceed to an analysis of the author's musical tastes and to an exploration of the role played by music in the narrator's quest for and discovery of the artistic redemption of life.

The central musical figure of the late nineteenth century is undoubtedly Richard Wagner, whose endeavors are linked to a wider movement of making music serve a predetermined, external narrative (*musique à programme*). Wagner's growing prestige in France, and the shadow thereby cast on French music, elicited artistic responses from French composers, from César Franck to Ernest Chausson and Emmanuel Chabrier to Claude Debussy. By the end of the century, musical impressionism and a taste for Far Eastern music, such as Debussy's pentatonic and whole-tone scales, had also established themselves. Proust mentions all these musical developments in the *Recherche*, and many are incorporated into the novel through musical descriptions.

Writers of the time developed what one would call a Wagner complex. Some poets' national pride was hurt by the Wagnerian *Gesamtkunstwerk*, or total work of art, which incorporated theater, music, dance, architecture, poetry, myth, and metaphysics and which embodied what some poets had been searching for: "un moderne équivalent de la tragédie, c'est-à-dire un art proprement religieux" (Lacoue-Labarthe 11) ("a modern equivalent of antique tragedy, in other words a thoroughly religious art"; my trans.). Charles Baudelaire secretly perceived Wagner's achievements as an intrusion of music into the realm of literature (Lacoue-Labarthe 38). Stéphane Mallarmé felt challenged by Wagner because he "usurpe[d]" the duties of poets (qtd. by Lacoue-Labarthe 96).

Wagner had dedicated followers in France. Edouard Schuré wrote *Le Drame musical* in support of Wagnerian drama, and Edouard Dujardin launched *La Revue wagnérienne* in 1885. In the novel *Les Lauriers sont coupés* (*The Boys are Sere*) (1888), Dujardin invented the *monologue intérieur*, or stream-of-consciousness narrative, conceived as a literary transposition of the Wagnerian leitmotiv. Proust will expand on this technique.

Wagner's fame also reached the general public by the end of the century. *A la recherche du temps perdu* is evidence both of the composer's imprint on French society and of the competition that Wagner inspired in Proust, who in his own way rose to the challenge with a cyclical story of gigantic proportions describing a modern quest for the grail. The *Recherche* establishes interrelations with Wagner: it contains numerous references to operas and characters, such as *Tristan und Isolde*, and its various themes have been compared to recurring leitmotiv in Wagnerian opera (see Nattiez for an analysis of the Wagnerian dimensions of the *Recherche*, for *Parsifal* as a "redemptive model for the redemptive work" [12–33], and for "music as redemptive model for literature" [34–77]).

At the dawn of the new century, attempts to integrate the arts, and music in particular, into the novel became more frequent. Writers felt the need to move beyond limitations in style, size, and scope because of the aforementioned Wagner complex, while they were calling into question realistic representation. Romain Rolland coined the expression roman-fleuve for his novel *Jean-Christophe*, whose main character is a musician (8). After the First World War, writers continued to experiment with expansive novels, reaching for a totalization of fragmented experience (Rabaté 14).

Through the 1880s and 1890s and into the new century, one can observe disaffection with realism and with the novelistic forms and techniques associated with it. Authors were looking for new means of representation that were less descriptive and more imaginative. They searched for poetic narrative styles, which would become prevalent in novels of the 1920s. Some, following Mallarmé, questioned the referentiality and transparence of language itself. Causality, with its deterministic implications, was also being questioned. The very pillars of conventional representation were demolished, as Sigmund Freud rendered void traditional modes of psychological analysis and as Henri Bergson questioned conventional, objective notions of time. Both proposed a self that was multiple. Humanistic culture was crumbling under the realization that human experience is fragmentary and not easily recaptured into a complete representation.

A la recherche du temps perdu seems to stand at the intersection of past and future trends. It reflects and sometimes anticipates new concerns and changes; theorizes associative, involuntary memory, which resembles the Freudian unconscious; and explores subjective time, which recalls Bergson. At the same time, the novel retains the sociological analysis characteristic of realism.

For many twentieth-century novelists, music represented a tempting stylistic alternative to the logical and abstract order of analytical speech, which Proust called "l'oblique discours intérieur (qui va s'éloignant de plus en plus de l'impression première et centrale)" (4: 469) ("an oblique interior discourse [which deviates gradually more and more from the first and central impression]" 6: 291). Music was a metaphysical and formal challenge to narratives and a better voice for the inner, emotional self. Proust uses all these perceived aspects of music, thereby foreshadowing modernist, Anglo-Saxon writers, such as James Joyce and Virginia Woolf, and the nouveau roman authors, who, later in the century, will be fascinated by musical strategies of repetition and variation. (See Milly, *La Phrase*, for a study of Proustian style; Costil; Matoré and Mecz for studies of musical narrative structures in the *Recherche*).

Proust developed an appreciation for music at an early age, thanks to his mother, who often played piano and who was particularly fond of Beethoven's sonatas (Piroué 15). Later, as a regular of the Parisian salons, Proust expanded his musical knowledge by listening to performances of works by Wagner, Robert Schumann, Ludwig van Beethoven, and also by Jules Massenet, Johannes Brahms, Camille Saint-Saëns, and Gabriel Fauré. He was a perceptive listener. Lucien Capet, the famous founder of the Capet String Quartet, recalling a conversation with Proust after a performance, mentioned with delight that he had never come across such a deep appreciation as Proust displayed of Beethoven's genius or of the talent and soul that Capet brought to the execution of the piece (Piroué 20).

Proust was also well acquainted with some musicians. He knew Saint-Saëns, on whom he wrote two articles, "Camille Saint-Saëns, pianiste" and "Figures parisiennes: Camille Saint-Saëns" (Contre Sainte-Beuve 382–84; 385–86), and whom he describes playing in another article, "Un Dimanche au conservatoire," which is included in *Contre Sainte-Beuve*. Proust also knew Fauré, whom he often invited to play in salons. However, Proust was probably introduced to Wagnerism not by a musician but by a music lover, Robert de Montesquiou (Piroué 24), who served as a model for the Charlus character. Proust's intimate relationship with Reynaldo Hahn, himself a remarkable pianist and composer, also contributed to Proust's musical erudition (Piroué 30).

During his voluntary seclusion at the Boulevard Haussmann apartment, Proust was not totally cut off from music. He owned a pianola, or player piano. He subscribed to the *théâtrophone*, which allowed him to listen to opera performances on the telephone. It was in this manner that, in 1911, he listened to the *Meistersinger* and other works by Wagner and to Debussy's *Pelléas et Mélisande*. His interest in some pieces of music was so acute that he did not hesitate to wake up musicians in the middle of the night and hire them for private performances of various string quartets by Debussy, Franck, and Fauré (Piroué 32, 33).

Even during the 1914–18 war, when anti-German sentiment was exacerbated in France, Proust remained truthful in his admiration of Wagner, whose works were banned by then. During that period, Proust also became thoroughly familiar with Beethoven's late quartets, which are central to the meditation on posterity in the *Recherche* (1: 522; 2: 148–49).

Composers mentioned in the *Recherche*, especially those who inspire Marcel in his meditations on art and bring him closer to his final revelation, are a direct echo of Proust's personal tastes. Wagner's name is mentioned twenty-four times (not including the numerous references and allusions to his works).

Beethoven's name appears seventeen times; Debussy's, ten; Bach, Fauré, Franck, and Saint-Saëns follow. This personal pantheon of favorite composers steadily serves a purpose throughout the hermeneutical quest in the *Recherche*. One function of music is to allow the narration to distinguish among those who pretend to understand, such as Mme Verdurin; the true amateurs, the first of which is Swann; and the true artist, Marcel, who will be the only one to finally elucidate the musical mystery. Music is, from this point of view, a judgment of God and brings about an aesthetic as well as a metaphysical revelation, as shown by Georges Piroué (45–93) and Claude-Henri Joubert (39–59).

The main musical scenes in the *Recherche* illustrate this progress toward revelation. At first, Swann is confronted with music in the following scenes: memories of the first execution and andante of the Vinteuil sonata at the Verdurins (1: 205–09; 1: 294–99); other performances at the Verdurins (1: 215–16; 1: 308–10); Odette plays the sonata on the piano (1: 233–35; 1: 335–39); the sonata is performed on piano solo at the Verdurins (1: 260; 1: 374–75); the sonata is performed on piano and violin at the soirée Ste-Euverte (1: 339–47; 1: 490–501). Marcel then resumes the quest abandoned by Swann in these scenes: the transmission by Odette of the sonata to the narrator (1: 520–25; 2: 146–54); Marcel, playing piano, compares Vinteuil to Wagner (3: 664–68; 5: 204–10); Marcel's audition of Vinteuil's "Septuor" (3: 753–69; 5: 331–53); Albertine's pianola sessions (3: 873–87; 5: 501–19); Marcel's meditation on the work of art and affirmation of his literary vocation (4: 446–96; 6: 257–332).

A sonata is also mentioned in an episode of *Jean Santeuil*, but the composer is Saint-Saëns ("La sonate" 3: 222–27). Time should be devoted to studying Proust's change from a real composer in *Jean Santeuil* to the fictional character Vinteuil in the *Recherche* and to the parallel change from a real composition to fictional constructs such as Vinteuil's sonata and *Septuor*. Such a process of fictionalization is the essence of Proust's evolution as a writer. The obscure, humble Vinteuil, an unknown genius whose meaningless existence is transcended into art and posterity, functions as a role model for Marcel. Vinteuil therefore had to be virtualized, just as the book that Marcel plans to write at the end remains a virtuality. In the context of an interdisciplinary class, this *mythe du compositeur* can be shown to have echoes in later writers, such as Jean-Paul Sartre, André Hodeir, and Pascal Quignard.

Vinteuil belongs to the group of fictional artists of the novel to which Bergotte, the writer, and Elstir, the painter belong. The art of these characters borrows traits from various real artists. Vinteuil's art is fictional but supported by reality. Proust's strategy to make Vinteuil's music tangible to the reader is to keep it close to real musical impressions through textual associations with works by musicians with which the reader is or could be familiar.

Fictional and real music are superimposed in various manners. For example, one measure of the sonata reminds Marcel of a phrase in *Tristan* (3: 664–65; 5: 204–05). To describe Wagner's themes, the narrator then uses almost exactly the same words with which he will later describe the "Septuor" (3: 764; 5: 350). Also, descriptions of Vinteuil's compositions contain specific allusions to real works, mostly by Wagner, Franck, Debussy, and Beethoven (see Fraisse, "Vinteuil"; Souza, "L'Importance," "Pourquoi"; Yoshikawa, "Vinteuil").

Proust is unique in his systematic technique of making fragmentary echoes between reality and fiction, which triggers processes of involuntary musical memory during reading, thereby making his prose powerfully evocative. The following musical works could be listened to and compared with Proust's descriptions of Vinteuil's music: Beethoven, Quartets nos. 14 and 15. Concerning Vinteuil's sonata specifically: Saint-Saëns, Sonata no. 1 and Fauré, Violin Sonata no. 1. Regarding Vinteuil's "Septuor": Franck, Piano Quintet in F Minor; Debussy, String Quartet; Debussy, *La Mer* 3, "Dialogue du vent et de la mer"; *Images* 2 for piano, "Cloches à travers les feuilles," "Et la lune descend sur le temple qui fût," and "Poissons d'or: animé." More generally: Debussy, Arabesque no. 1 and Sonata for Flute, Viola, and Harp.

A unit on Proust and music might be fruitfully completed with an examination of the philosophical and psychoanalytic implications of music. In *Proust and Signs*, Gilles Deleuze argues that signs of arts, which stand at the core of the novel's philosophical system, are platonic essences, the ultimate step in interpreting reality and in the quest for truth. This essentialist approach could be challenged with a psychoanalytic study of musical descriptions that lend themselves to rediscovering the mother figure at the heart of musical experience (Pautrot 132–89), in the same manner as studies by Vincent Descombes, Gérard Genette (*Figures* 3), and Maurice Merleau-Ponty have discovered metonymy at the heart of the Proustian metaphor. Proust's system could then be appreciated as a fragmented construct, characteristic of modernity, and his musical aesthetics deconstructed to show his debt, beyond Wagner to Arthur Schopenhauer, using Samuel Beckett's essay on Proust and works by Anne Henry (*Proust*; *Schopenhauer*) and Jean-Jacques Nattiez (78–87).

Finally, instructors may encourage further reflection by emphasizing what remains a fascinating aspect of the Proustian project: a self-reflexive, introspective narrative that oscillates between past and present, which progresses through echoes and reminiscences, linear and cyclical at once—the ultimate meaning of which is deferred until the end. Such a narrative could truly be called musical.

Proust in a Humanities Course:
A Place for the Madeleine

Susan Rava

The madeleine scene as emblematic of Proust's work belongs in humanities courses in the undergraduate curriculum. This article explores my journey to develop a pedagogy for Proust and to find a place for the madeleine in courses for nonliterature, nonlanguage students.

Over the past several years, I have found that place for the madeleine in a course called Voyages and Discoveries. It focuses on eight French chefs d'œuvre but is taught in English with all readings in English. Its audience consists of students who are fulfilling a humanities distribution requirement and who are seldom students in literature of any sort. Many are junior or senior science or social sciences majors who come reluctantly to unfamiliar and daunting texts by Voltaire, Balzac, and Gide, among others. I had never ventured to try Proust except for an occasional foray into a few paragraphs of the madeleine scene. Yet my academic trajectory from Proust scholar to language teacher to pedagogy scholar and back to Proust scholar would not let me abandon the idea of adding a more substantial section of Proust to the course's constellation of masterpieces.

Convinced that this course, which focuses on young people's voyages—both literal and figurative—should include a voyage into memory, I asked myself how to make a segment of Proust's work come alive in such a setting. My working premise was that because of the nonliterature audience and the demanding text, I would consider approaching the madeleine section of "Combray" as if it were as foreign as a work in a foreign language. Even in English, the text poses problems of syntactical and lexical complexity; it transpires in a culture, a society, and an era unfamiliar to most undergraduates; its intellectual and aesthetic wealth challenges all. As both a pedagogy and a literature specialist, I hypothesized that the use of recent second language acquisition and pedagogy theory might render a portion of "Combray" accessible, enjoyable, and intellectually productive for a nonliterature and nonlanguage public.

I decided to use selected second language acquisition, reading, and pedagogical research to develop a pedagogy for Proust in translation. In so doing, I diverged from second language acquisition and pedagogy research by emphasizing the literariness of the text rather than treating it as a linguistic or cultural sample. I also hoped to address a need noted by Claire Kramsch and Olivier Kramsch. The two find that despite an expansion of second language acquisition research and concomitant pedagogies, little material has emerged as a pedagogy of literature qua literature (567).

The approach to "Combray" echoed my course goals: to foster an appreciation of and insight into several major works of fiction from three centuries of French literature; to explore the characters, structure, style, and role of voyage and discovery in each work; to exchange ideas in the interest of developing an intellectual classroom community; and to develop oral and written expression of critical ideas. These goals reflect my belief that students should be responsible and involved in their own learning and willing to take interpretive risks in a nonjudgmental but rigorous environment. For the Proust unit, I chose the opening sixty-four pages, including the madeleine scene, from Enright's edition (1: 1–64; 1: 3–47). I have also used the cattleya portion of *Un Amour de Swann* (*Swann in Love*) (1: 224–37; 1: 322–41) in a continuing education course for adult learners. (I would note that Proust's is the only work that the class does not read in toto.)

My theoretical position in this course was to replace the transmission model in which the teacher as authority transmits an expert understanding and interpretation of a text to the student. Instead, adapting recent theory, I emphasized student interpretation of the literary work and interaction with one another as cointerpreters. I drew inspiration from the work of scholars who have conducted research on the development of reading skills through literature, although, as mentioned above, most use literature merely as a representative cultural or linguistic sample (Fecteau; Lee; Lee and VanPatten; Saito, Horwitz, and Garza; Turner and Cowell).

Approaches to second-language reading frequently divide the teaching process into three phases: prereading; during reading; and postreading. June K. Phillips suggests five: "Preteaching / Preparation Stage; Skimming / Scanning Stages; Decoding / Intensive Reading Stage; Comprehension Stage; Transferable / Integrating Skills" (qtd. in Omaggio Hadley 207-08). These demarcated stages are useful for teaching Proust in translation. The prereading phase combines brief informational input and extensive exploration of students' background knowledge. (Although input and input processing are theoretical terms central to current second language acquisition studies, input here means comprehensible informational content, that is, content that both activates knowledge already familiar to students and that adds new and unfamiliar material.) The during-reading phase of this Proust pedagogy examines the cast of characters; stylistic elements such as sentence structure; and narrative traits, including point of view, themes, and humor. The postreading phase asks students to synthesize and expand their commentary on the text.

My approach follows the view of scholars who stress the importance of the prereading phase. Schema theory is the basis for many activities of this first phase. James F. Lee and Bill VanPatten quote D. E. Rumelhart's definition: "All knowledge is packaged into units. Those units are the schemata. Embedded in these packages of knowledge is, in addition to the knowledge itself, information about how this knowledge is to be used. A schema, then, is a data structure for representing the generic concepts stored in memory" (190). Because of the potential foreignness of "Combray," accessing the "packages of knowledge" or schemata that students already have about childhood memories, their families in the past, and so forth is crucial. Monique L. Fecteau, for instance, emphasizes the entry into a second language text through schemata activation for "successful or thorough comprehension" (489). Moreover, Claire Kramsch divides the background knowledge that students bring to bear on literature into "content" and "genre" schemata (*Context* 141). Thus my pedagogy utilizes a variety of tasks to activate students' schemata before students begin to read. The preparation phase allows students to undertake their assignments with curiosity and motivation and to acquire sufficient tools that will allow them to read with understanding.

Early in the prereading phase, I hold what I call a Proust bazaar. The bazaar includes a brief segment of the videocassette *Marcel Proust: A Writer's Life*, a five-minute minilecture about Proust in relation to other writers studied in my Voyages and Discoveries course, a display of photos and news articles with Proustiana, several transparencies such as Alain de Botton's spiral diagram of a Proust sentence (31–32), a selection of recent books like William C. Carter's biography (*Marcel Proust*) and Roger Shattuck's *Proust's Way*, and a challenge to students to bring in pop-culture references to Proust. Students are invited to circulate and browse. This tangible exposure demystifies Proust and inspires students to tackle the celebrated writer.

Prereading activities explore students' background knowledge, reminding them that they already have a framework for grasping a novel based on memory. An initial activity asks students to consider how they would shape a memory into the opening of a written work and what genre of written work it would be—memoir, novel, or poem. Students are then advised to jot down that memory. Pairs compare and contrast their choices and then discuss them with the whole class. Discussion accomplishes several of the course goals as well as Virginia M. Scott's objective of building "a community with a common interest" (542). This multistepped memory activity helps activate students' specific literary knowledge as well as their general informational schemata.

A vocabulary exercise serves both as a reminder of what students already know and as a predictor of the story ahead. Kramsch proposes group brainstorming before reading to collect "necessary vocabulary" and "to gather . . . the resources of the group" ("Literary Texts" 359). I would add that vocabulary-predicting activities, even in the first language, reinforce the idea that a collaborative effort may enhance reading comprehension. Such activities also provide students with a lexical and conceptual touchstone in the often overwhelming first encounter with a new novel. Anticipating vocabulary has proved to be a valuable tool for the opening pages of "Combray" in translation. For example, when students are asked to suggest words or expressions about falling asleep as youngsters, they readily volunteer "drifting," "fading," "frightening noises" or "sights" that foreshadow "les craquements organiques des boiseries" or "le kaléidoscope de l'obscurité" (1: 4) ("the regular squeaking of the wainscot" or "the shifting kaleidoscope of the darkness" [1: 2]).

Teachers can read the first two pages aloud to students with dramatic attention to potentially difficult formal and thematic elements. This can be an appropriate send-off for students poised to commence reading the *Recherche*.

This send-off in class demystifies the text and aids students as they begin reading assignments at home. For introducing the *Recherche* in class, students can also be given a handout or view a transparency of the opening passage. They can then assess how their predicted vocabulary and expressions compare with the Proustian text. They may be given true or false or multiple-choice questions to verify their initial comprehension of the passage. Finally, students can share answers to elucidate any stumbling blocks.

Prereading activities are especially effective preparation for what Kramsch and Kramsch call the "literariness" of a text, "the representational nature of language, the poetics of language use, and the role that [students] play . . . in the symbolic construction of foreign literature texts" (569). By opening avenues to comprehension, these activities aim to create the pleasure that Marcel himself finds reading in his garden on a summer afternoon. He describes the experience: "Ce qu'il y avait d'abord en moi, de plus intime . . . c'était ma croyance en la richesse philosophique, en la beauté du livre que je lisais, et mon désir de me les approprier, quel que fût le livre" (1: 83) ("My primary, my innermost impulse . . . was my belief in the philosophic richness and beauty of the book I was reading, and my desire to appropriate them for myself . . ." [1: 115]).

In Voyages and Discoveries, students read assignments after I have signaled features, tasks, or questions to consider during each reading. As I prepare the syllabus for "Combray" in translation, I arrange assignments as follows with the pages due to be read before the class indicated.

Day 1: Introduction to Proust. Proust bazaar. Prereading activities.
Day 2: Pages 1–9 (Enright, vol. 1). Memories of falling asleep and waking up.
Day 3: Pages 9–39 (Enright, vol. 1). Bedtime rituals and Swann's visit.
Day 4: Pages 39–64 (Enright, vol. 1). The good-night kiss and the madeleine.
Day 5: Student wrap-up of Proust. Quiz.

Throughout this unit, each class opens with input, often a playful look at Proust. For example, commentary from Botton's *How Proust Can Change Your Life* resonates with undergraduates. The Monty Python sketch of a contest to summarize Proust, a brief scene from the film *Un Amour de Swann*, a reading of a passage to illustrate Proust's humor such as the comical account of Aunt Léonie's talking to herself (1: 50; 1: 68–69)—all these expand and enrich students' exposure to Proust, encouraging them to read on.

In the during-reading phase, classroom activities lead students to engage the text while developing analytic and critical skills. One such activity is creating titles. Small groups title one assigned paragraph of the ten between pages 1 and 9 and present the title with an explanation to the class. The titling activity requires a grasp of literal detail and contextual importance and provides a comprehension check. Inventing a title also promotes cognitive and sociopsy-chological skills such as negotiation, explication, and justification. A similar activity requests that students extract key words, and thus main ideas, from paragraphs. Both activities are effective reading aids that I repeat as an at-home assignment for the next passage.

On day 3, the focus is on Swann: a whole class discussion considers who knows what about Swann, when they know it, and why the Swann sequence is funny. Next, small groups use a modified explication-de-texte format previ-ously learned to perform a close reading of the passage beginning "Et il me fal-lut partir sans viatique . . ." (1: 27) ("And so I must set forth without viaticum . . ." [1: 36]). Each group develops just one step of the explication that the class pools for a collective analysis. The explication exposes students to classical French literary analysis techniques and highlights compositional and stylistic elements. An analysis performed by small groups further reinforces the value of shared literary study. The theme of the passage circles back to bedtime rit-ual and announces the final day's class.

A myriad of other during-reading activities combines approaches from lan-guage and literature analysis. Betsy Keller suggests worksheets at home and frequent in-class writing projects (62, 64) while Kramsch proposes brain-storming and role-playing ("Literary Texts" 360–62). Kramsch also maps out exercises that vary elements of the text such as point of view or text time (Con-text 147–53). The first three days progress, then, from activating students' background knowledge and schemata to constructing a new framework or schemata for comprehension. The program incorporates during-reading activ-ities that highlight thematic and stylistic aspects of "Combray." In contrast, the final class is more open-ended and focuses on the meaning of the good-night-kiss episode. This is the day for students to take risks and to volunteer their own interpretations. Working together, they discuss why the kiss might be transgressive and dangerous. I ask them to consider the humor in the episode; invariably they cite Mamma's choice to omit the love scenes from her reading (1: 41; 1: 56). Students recap how Swann relates to the good-night-kiss episode and finally examine the unifying elements of the passage.

As for the madeleine scene, students read it aloud in pairs or small groups and dissect it in segments. Their commentary underscores the madeleine's power to generate a whole world of memory. A discussion of students' own remembrances of privileged childhood moments reconnects the text to the personal realm. Tea and madeleines accompany their recollection of the unex-pected stimuli for their own most vivid memories. Students conclude with a brief writing exercise, a similar remembrance, thus appropriating Proust's text as their own intellectual and inspirational property. On day 5, the postreading activity is a graded explication of a passage not previously analyzed in class.

The "Combray" unit contains a pedagogical model for teaching other Prous-tian texts. The model is grounded in second language acquisition studies such as the schema and input theories. It embraces student-centered learning as it transfers the responsibility for engaging the text and extracting its meaning to the students as active and critical readers. Second language acquisition and pedagogical studies promise more innovative possibilities for a pedagogy of literary texts in translation like Proust's that pose comprehension problems often similar to those of second-language works. Indeed my hypothesis that reading the emblematic madeleine segment could and should be a great pleasure and source of intellectual pride for students is well founded. At the end of the course students asked that the university offer a nonspecialists', lower-level humanities course in English on Proust alone.

NOTES ON CONTRIBUTORS

Joseph Brami is professor of French at the University of Maryland, College Park. He is the author of *Les Troubles de l'invention: essai sur le doute poétique de Joe Bousquet* (1987). He and Michèle Sarde coedited *Marguerite Yourcenar: lettres à ses amis et quelques autres* (1995). He has also published *Mademoiselle de Maupin* (1993) and articles on Alain Chartier, Jean Paulhan, Roger Caillois, and Jacques Borel. He is currently working on an essay on Proust and Jewish identity.

Bernard Brun is chargé de recherches at the Centre National de la Recherche Scientifique and the editor in chief of the *Bulletin d'informations Proustiennes*. In collaboration with Henri Bonnet, he edited Proust's *Matinée chez la Princesse de Guermantes* (1982). He is also the editor of *Du côté de chez Swann* (1986), *Le Temps retrouvé* (1986), and *Le Côté de Guermantes* (1992). He has published articles on the genesis of *A la recherche du temps perdu* and is currently working on the transcription of Proust's manuscripts at the Institut des Textes et des Manuscrits Modernes in Paris.

William C. Carter is professor of French at the University of Alabama, Birmingham. He is the author of *The Proustian Quest* (1992) and *Marcel Proust: A Life* (2000). He also coproduced the documentary film *Marcel Proust: A Writer's Life* (1993). He serves on the editorial board of the *Bulletin Marcel Proust* and is a permanent correspondent of the Centre de Recherches Proustiennes (Paris III, Sorbonne nouvelle). He is working on a book tentatively entitled "Americans in Paris."

Mary Ann Caws is distinguished professor of English, French, and comparative literature at the Graduate Center, City University of New York, and has written widely on movements in art and literature. Her most recent books are *The Surrealist Look: An Erotics of Encounter* (1997), *Picasso's Weeping Woman: The Life and Art of Dora Maar* (2000), and *Virginia Woolf* in the Overlook Illustrated Lives series. Her recent anthologies include *Manifesto: A Century of Isms* (2000), *Surrealist Painters and Poets* (2001), *Mallarmé in Prose* (2001), and *Vita Sackville-West: Selected Writings* (2002). She is also a translator of poetry and the editor of "The Yale Book of Twentieth-Century French Poetry" (forthcoming 2004).

Elyane Dezon-Jones is professor of French at Washington University, Saint Louis. She is the author of *Proust et l'Amérique* (1982) and *Marie de Gournay: fragments d'un discours féminin* (1987). She has edited Proust's *Le Côté de Guermantes* (1987), *Du côté de chez Swann* (1992), and Marguerite Yourcenar's *Sources 2* (2000). The former editor in chief of *Bulletin Marcel Proust*, she has published articles on Proust, Yourcenar, and French women writers. She is currently working on a critical edition of Yourcenar's letters.

Emily Eells is maître de conférences in English at the University of Paris X, Nanterre. She edited Proust's *Sodome et Gomorrhe* for Flammarion in 1987 and has written articles on Proust concerning intertextuality and the visual arts. Her book entitled *Proust's Cup of Tea: Homoeroticism and Victorian Culture* was published in 2002.

Rebecca Graves is director of studies at Rockefeller College, Princeton University. She is currently working on a book tentatively titled "Writing Machines: Language, Gender, and Technology in Modern France."

Margaret E. Gray is associate professor of French at Indiana University, Bloomington. She is the author of *Postmodern Proust* (1992) and of essays on Proust, George Sand, Samuel Beckett, Albert Camus, and the Belgian writer Jean-Philippe Toussaint. Her current book manuscript is entitled "Stolen Limelight: Display, Excess, and the Feminine in Modern French and Francophone Narrative."

Virginie Greene is associate professor of medieval French at Harvard University. She is the author of *Le Sujet et la mort dans* La Mort Artu. She was Philip Kolb's assistant from 1989 to 1992 and is a founding member of the Kolb-Proust Archive for Research. She has compiled *Dictionnaire bibliographique des correspondants de Proust* and is currently working on the notion of ambivalence in courtly literature.

Geneviève Henrot teaches French language and literature at the University of Padua. She is the author of *Délits/Délivrance* (1991), *L'Usage de la forme: essai sur* Les Fruits d'or *de Nathalie Sarraute* (2000), and *Le Vertige du seuil* (2003). She has written numerous articles on Proust, Gaston Compère, Georges Simenon, Albert Camus, and Rémy de Gourmont. She is currently working on the questions of dialogue and memory in *A la recherche du temps perdu*.

Edward J. Hughes is professor of modern French literature at Royal Holloway, University of London. He is the author of *Marcel Proust: A Study in the Quality of Awareness* (1983), *Albert Camus:* Le Premier Homme / La Peste (1995), and *Writing Marginality in Modern French Literature* (2001). He has edited, with Peter Dunwoodie, *Constructing Memories: Camus: Algeria and* Le Premier Homme (1998). He is a contributor to the forthcoming *Dictionnaire Marcel Proust* and is currently working on a new study of Proust.

Pascal A. Ifri is associate professor of French at Washington University. He is the author of *Proust et son narrataire* (1983), *Céline et Proust: correspondances proustiennes dans l'œuvre de L. F. Céline* (1996) and Les Deux Étendards *de Lucien Rebatet: dossier d'un chef d'œuvre maudit* (2001). He has also written articles on Proust, Louis-Ferdinand Céline, Lucien Rebátet, André Gide, Stendhal, and Alfred de Musset. He has been the editor of the *Bulletin Marcel Proust* since 1995. He is currently working on a book tentatively titled "Proust au cinéma."

J. Theodore Johnson, Jr., is professor emeritus of French at the University of Kansas, Lawrence. He is founding editor of the *Proust Research Association Newsletter* (1969–86), and his numerous publications as well as current research deal primarily with Proust and the visual arts.

Diane R. Leonard is associate professor of comparative literature at the University of North Carolina, Chapel Hill. She has published articles on Proust, Ruskin, and modern narrative, has completed a volume of translations of Proust's essays on Ruskin, and is working on a critical study of Proust's reinscription of Ruskin in the *Recherche*. She is a contributor to the forthcoming *Dictionnaire Marcel Proust*, to be published in 2004 by Honoré Champion.

Françoise Leriche is maître de conférences at the Université Stendhal, Grenoble. A specialist in textual studies, she has edited Proust's *Sodome et Gomorrhe* (1993) and published articles on Proust and the arts. She is the coauthor of Sodome et Gomorrhe *de Proust* (2000), and her *Anthologie de la correspondance de Proust* is to be published by Plon in 2004.

Michèle Magill is associate professor of French in the Department of Foreign Languages and Literatures at North Carolina State University. She is the author of *Répertoire des arts et de la littérature dans* A la recherche du temps perdu (1991) and has written articles on Proust and Sylvie Germain. Her latest book is "Dit des femmes," in collaboration with Katherine Stephenson, forthcoming in 2003. She is currently working on a book on Proust and Germain.

Brigitte Mahuzier is associate professor of French at Bryn Mawr College. She is the author of essays on Stendhal, Honoré de Balzac, Charles Baudelaire, Colette, Auguste Rodin, and Proust. She edited a special issue of *Littérature* on Proust's new editions (1992) and coedited the *Yale French Studies* special issue *Same Text / Different Sex* (1996). She is currently finishing a book entitled "Proust and the Great War."

Nathalie Mauriac Dyer is a researcher at the Institut des Textes et Manuscrits Modernes, Centre National de la Recherche Scientifique, Paris. She has published the last revised version of *Albertine disparue* (1987) and editions of *Sodome et Gomorrhe* 3 and *La Fugitive:* Cahiers d'*Albertine disparue,* which challenged the editorial canon in 1993. Her recent contributions include *Les Années perdues de la* Recherche (1999) and articles on the aesthetics of the unfinished and medical intertextuality in *A la recherche du temps perdu.*

Christie McDonald is Smith Professor of French Language and Literature and chair of the Department of Romance Languages and Literatures at Harvard. She has written *The Proustian Fabric* (1991) and numerous articles on Proust.

Mireille Naturel is maître de conférences at Paris III, Sorbonne Nouvelle. She is the author of *Pour la littérature* (1995) and *Proust et Flaubert: un secret d'écriture* (1999). A specialist in textual studies, she has edited *Un Amour de Swann* (2002). She is the coeditor of *Bulletin Marcel Proust* and secrétaire générale of the Société des Amis de Marcel Proust.

Eugène Nicole is professor of French literature at New York University. He collaborated on the 1987–89 Pléiade edition of *A la recherche du temps perdu* and was the editor of *A l'ombre des jeunes filles en fleurs* and *Le Temps retrouvé* for the Livre de poche classique edition. A specialist in Proustian onomastics, he has also written articles on twentieth-century poets and novelists and has published three novels: *L'Œuvres des mers* (1990), *Les Larmes de pierre* (1991), and *Le Caillou de l'enfant perdu* (1996).

Jean-Louis Pautrot is professor of French at Saint Louis University, where he teaches contemporary literature, culture, and film. He is the author of a psychoanalytic study of music in Jean-Paul Sartre, Proust, Boris Vian, and Marguerite Duras entitled *La Musique oubliée* (1994) and of articles on Alain Robbe-Grillet, André Hodeir, Patrick Modiano, Louis Malle, Pascal Quignard, Vian, and Jacques Tati. He is currently completing a monograph entitled "Pascal Quignard, ou l'écriture du fonds du monde."

Susan Rava is senior lecturer emerita in French at Washington University. She is the author of articles on Proust, Marguerite Duras, language pedagogy and language curriculum, and teacher development. Her work has appeared in the *ADFL Bulletin, Foreign Language Annals*, and the *French Review*. She has also published op-ed pieces, short stories, and reviews. She has served as a program and curriculum consultant in secondary and higher education.

Lawrence R. Schehr is professor of French, comparative literature, and gender and women's studies at the University of Illinois. He is the author of *Flaubert and Sons* (1995), *The Shock of Men* (1995), *Alcibiades at the Door* (1995), *Rendering French Realism* (1997), *Parts of an Andrology* (1997), and *Figures of Alterity: French Narrative and Its Others* (2003). He is the coeditor of *Articulations of Difference: Gender Studies and Writing in French* (1997), *French Food: On the Table, on the Page, and in French Culture* (2001).

Roger Shattuck has taught French and the humanities at Harvard; the University of Texas, Austin; the University of Virginia; and Boston University. His books include *The Banquet Years* (1958), *Proust's Binoculars* (1963), *The Innocent Eye* (1984), *Forbidden Knowledge* (1996), *Candor and Perversion* (2000), and *Proust's Way* (2000). In 1974, he received the National Book Award for his *Marcel Proust*. He has served as president of the Association of Literary Scholars and Critics.

Julie Solomon is assistant professor of French at Tufts University. She is the author of *Proust: lecture du narrataire* (1994). She has published articles on Proust, Charles Baudelaire, Colette, and Michel Leiris. She is currently completing a book manuscript entitled "Face and Figure: The Poetics of the Literary Self-Portrait."

Caroline Szylowicz is a librarian at the University of Illinois, where she directs the Kolb-Proust Archive for Research. She is the author of articles on the use of the hypertext and metadata technology in the humanities and of an inventory of Proust's manuscripts at the University of Illinois library. She is working on a bibliography of Proust criticism.

Inge Crosman Wimmers is professor of French studies at Brown University. She is the author of *Metaphoric Narration: The Structure and Function of Metaphors in* A la recherche du temps perdu (1978), *Poetics of Reading: Approaches to the Novel* (1988), and *Proust and Emotion: The Importance of Affect in* A la recherche du temps perdu (2003). She and Susan Suleiman are coeditors of *The Reader in the Text: Essays on Audience and Interpretation* (1980). She has published articles on reader-oriented approaches to narrative fiction and on literary emotions.

Kazuyoshi Yoshikawa is professor of French literature at the City University of Tokyo and president of the Japanese Society for Proust Studies. In his 1976 dissertation, he studied the genesis of *La Prisonnière* after which he published numerous articles on Proust. He is the author of *Musée Proust* (1998) and the editor of the *Index général de la* Correspondance de Marcel Proust (1998).

SURVEY PARTICIPANTS

André Aciman, *Graduate Center, City University of New York*
David Caron, *University of Michigan, Ann Arbor*
Stephanie Chastain, *University of Washington*
Marie-Magdeleine Chirol, *Whittier College*
Antoine Compagnon, *Columbia University*
Mechthild Cranston, *Clemson University*
Diane Crowder, *Cornell College*
Nicole Deschamps, *University of Montreal*
Priscilla Ferguson, *Columbia University*
Gary Godfrey, *Weber State University*
Martine Guyot-Bender, *Hamilton College*
Gerald Honigsblum, *Boston University*
Katarzyna Jerzak, *University of Georgia, Athens*
Sister Mary Helen Kashuba, *Chestnut Hill College*
Marie-Thérèse Killiam, *Sweet Briar College*
Elisabeth Ladenson, *University of Virginia*
Ursula Link-Heer, *Bergische Universität Wuppertal*
Elaine Marks, *University of Wisconsin*
Roy Jay Nelson, *University of Michigan, Ann Arbor*
Timothy Raser, *The University of Georgia, Athens*
James H. Reid, *Illinois State University*
Nathalie Rogers, *Wellesley College*
Volker Roloff, *University of Siegen*
Susan Rosenstreich, *Dowling College*
Eynel Wardi, *The Hebrew University of Jerusalem*

WORKS CITED

Aciman, André. "In Search of Proust." *New Yorker* 12 Dec. 1988: 81–85.

Adorno, Theodor W. "Short Commentaries on Proust." *Notes to Literature*. Ed. Rolf Tiedemann. Trans. Shierry Weber Nicholsen. Vol. 1. New York: Columbia UP, 1991. 174–84.

L'Affaire Dreyfus. Dir. Yves Boisset. France Télévisions, 1994.

Ahlstedt, Eva. *La Pudeur en crise: un aspect de l'accueil d'*À la recherche du temps perdu *de Marcel Proust, 1913–1930.* Paris: Thouzot, 1985.

Akerman, Chantal. "Proust." *Magazine littéraire* 2 (2000): 89.

Albaret, Céleste. *Monsieur Proust.* Paris: Laffont, 1973.

Alden, Douglas W. "Marcel Proust." *A Critical Bibliography of French Literature: The Twentieth Century*. Vol. 6. Ed. Alden and Richard A. Brooks. Syracuse: Syracuse UP, 1980. 198–350.

Andrew, Dudley. "Adaptation." *Concepts in Film Theory*. Oxford: Oxford UP, 1984. 94–106.

Aristotle. *Rhetoric.* Cambridge: Harvard UP, 1994.

Un amour de Swann. Written by Peter Brook, Jean-Claude Carrière, and Volker Schlöndorff. Dir. Schlöndorff. 1984.

Arno, Ed. Cartoon. *New Yorker* 20 Dec. 1982: 45.

Art Nouveau: 1890–1914. A National Gallery of Art Presentation. Dir. and prod. Carroll Moore. Videocassette and DVD. Home Vision Arts, 2000.

Auerbach, Erich. "Figura." *Scenes from the Drama of European Literature*. Trans. Ralph Mannheim. New York: Meridian, 1959. 11–76.

Baker, Russell. "Man with Pasty Face." *New York Times* 26 Sept. 1981: 23.

Bales, Richard, ed. *The Cambridge Companion to Proust.* Cambridge: Cambridge UP, 2001.

———. *Proust and the Middle Ages.* Geneva: Droz, 1975.

Bardèche, Maurice. *Marcel Proust, romancier.* Paris: Sept Couleurs, 1971. 2 vols.

Barthes, Roland. *Essais critiques IV: le bruissement de la langue.* Paris: Seuil, 1984.

———. "Introduction à l'analyse structurale des récits." *Communications* 8 (1966): 1–27.

———. "An Introduction to the Structural Analysis of Narrative." *New Literary History* 6 (1975): 237–72.

———. "Longtemps je me suis couché de bonne heure." Barthes, *Essais* 313–25.

———. *Mythologies.* Paris: Seuil, 1957.

———. *The Pleasure of the Text.* Trans. Richard Miller. New York: Hill and Wang, 1975.

———. "Proust et les noms." *To Honor Roman Jakobson: Essays on the Occasion of His Seventieth Birthday*. Vol. 1. The Hague: Mouton, 1967. 150–58.

———. *S/Z.* Paris: Seuil, 1970.

Bataille, Georges. *La Littérature et le mal.* Paris: Gallimard, 1957.

Bazin, André. "Adaptation; or, The Cinema as Digest." Trans. Alain Piette and Bert Cardullo. Naremore 19–27.

——. "Pour un cinéma impur: défense de l'adaptation." *Cinéma* 81–106.

——. *Qu'est-ce que le cinéma?* Collection septième art. Paris: Cerf, 2000.

Beaunier, André. "M. Marcel Proust, le traducteur incomparable de Ruskin." *Le Figaro* 19 June 1905: 3–4.

Beckett, Samuel. *Proust.* London: Grove, 1931.

Benjamin, Walter. "The Work of Art in the Age of Mechanical Reproduction." Trans. Harry Zohn. *Illuminations.* New York: Schocken, 1968. 217–51.

Bertho, Sophie, ed. *Proust et ses peintres.* Amsterdam: Rodopi, 2001.

Bidou, Henri. "*Esther* au théâtre Sarah Bernhardt." *L'Année dramatique, 1911–1912.* Paris: Hachette, 1912. 32–40.

Blanche, Jacques-Emile. "*Du côté de chez Swann.*" *L'Echo de Paris* Apr. 1914: 1.

Bonnet, Henri. *Marcel Proust de 1907 à 1914.* Paris: Nizet, 1971.

Bonnet, Henri, and Bernard Brun, eds. *Matinée chez la Princesse de Guermantes.* By Marcel Proust. Paris: Gallimard, 1982.

Botton, Alain de. *How Proust Can Change Your Life: Not a Novel.* New York: Random, 1997.

Bouchart, Francois-Xavier, and Elyane Dezon-Jones. *La Figure des pays.* Paris: Flammarion, 1999.

Boucquey, Eliane. "Les Trois Arbres d'Hudimesnil: souvenir retrouvé." *Bulletin de la Société des Amis de Marcel Proust* 38 (1988): 74–92.

Bouillaguet, Annick. *Marcel Proust: bilan critique.* Paris: Nathan, 1994.

——. *Marcel Proust*: Le jeu intertextuel. Paris: Titre, 1990.

Bouillon, Jean Paul. *Journal de l'art nouveau.* Geneva: Skira, 1985.

Bourgeois, Jacques. "Le Cinéma à la recherche du temps perdu." *La Revue du cinéma* 3 (1946): 18–37.

Bourlier, Kay. *Marcel Proust et l'architecture.* Montreal: PU de Montréal, 1980.

Braudy, Leo, and Marshall Cohen, eds. *Film Theory and Criticism: Introductory Readings.* 5th ed. New York: Oxford UP, 1999.

Bredin, Jean-Denis. *The Affair: The Case of Alfred Dreyfus.* Trans. Jeffrey Mehlman. New York: Braziller, 1986.

——. *L'Affaire.* Paris: Julliard, 1983.

Brun, Bernard, ed. *Nouvelles Directions de la recherche proustienne 2: Rencontres de Cerisy-la-Salle, 2–9 juillet 1997.* Revue des lettres modernes. 2 vols. Paris: Minard, 2000–01.

——. "Table des matières de *Contre Sainte-Beuve.*" *Bulletin d'informations proustiennes* 19 (1988): 7–14.

——. "Une des lois vraiment immuables de ma vie spirituelle: quelques éléments de la *démonstration* proustienne dans les brouillons de *Swann.*" *Bulletin d'informations proustiennes* 10 (1979): 23–38.

Brunet, Etienne. *Le Vocabulaire de Proust.* Paris: Champion, 1983.

Bucknall, Barbara, ed. *Critical Essays on Marcel Proust.* Boston: Hall, 1987.

Butor, Michel. *Les Sept Femmes de Gilbert le Mauvais.* Montpellier: Fata Morgana, 1972.

Campbell, Lawrence. Introduction. Ruskin, *Elements* v–xii.

La Captive. Dir. Chantal Akerman. Screenplay by Akerman and Eric de Kuyper. Prod. Paulo Branco. Gemini Films, 2000.

Carter, William C. *Marcel Proust: A Life*. Henry McBride Ser. in Modernism and Modernity. New Haven: Yale UP, 2000.

———. "Proust, Einstein, et le sentiment cosmique religieux." *Bulletin de la Société des Amis de Marcel Proust* 37 (1987): 52–62.

———. *The Proustian Quest*. New York: New York UP, 1993.

———, ed. *The UAB Marcel Proust Symposium: In Celebration of the Seventy-Fifth Anniversary of* Swann's Way, *1913–1988*. Birmingham: Summa, 1989.

Caws, Mary Ann, and Eugène Nicole, eds. *Reading Proust Now*. New York: Lang, 1990.

Céleste. Written and dir. by Percy Adlon. Based on *Monsieur Proust*, by Céleste Albaret. New Yorker Films, 1981.

Chantal, René de. "L'Impressionnisme de Marcel Proust." *Marcel Proust critique littéraire*. Montreal: U of Montréal P, 1967. 279–319.

Chelet-Hester, Claudie. "La Galerie des Guermantes ou la leçon de vérité d'Elstir." *Bulletin d'informations proustiennes* 22 (1991): 37–52.

Chevassu, Francis. Review of *Du côté de chez Swann*. *Le Figaro* 8 Dec. 1913. N. pag.

Cocking, John M. "Proust and Music." *Proust: Collected Essays on the Writer and His Art*. Ed. Cocking. Cambridge: Cambridge UP, 1982. 109–29.

Cohn, Dorrit. "Proust's Generic Ambiguity." *The Distinction of Fiction*. Baltimore: Johns Hopkins UP, 1999. 58–78.

Compagnon, Antoine. *Proust between Two Centuries*. Trans. Richard Goodwin. New York: Columbia UP, 1992.

———. *Proust entre deux siècles*. Paris: Seuil, 1989.

———. *La Troisième République des lettres*. Paris: Seuil, 1989.

Costil, Pierre. "La Construction musicale de la *Recherche du temps perdu*." *Bulletin de la Sociéte des Amis de Marcel Proust* 8 (1958): 469–89; 9 (1959): 83–111.

Crémieux, Benjamin. *XXième siècle: première série*. Paris: N. R. F., 1924.

Curtius, Ernst Robert. *European Literature and the Latin Middle Ages*. Trans. Willard R. Trask. Princeton: Princeton UP, 1973.

Deleuze, Gilles. Proust and Signs: *The Complete Text*. Trans. Richard Howard. Minneapolis: U of Minnesota P, 2000.

———. *Proust et les signes*. Paris: PUF, 1970.

Deleuze, Gilles, and Félix Guattari. *Mille plateaux: capitalisme et schizophrénie*. Vol. 2. Paris: Minuit, 1980.

———. *A Thousand Plateaus: Capitalism and Schizophrenia*. Trans. Brian Massumi. Minneapolis: U of Minnesota P, 1987.

Descombes, Vincent. *Proust: philosophie du roman*. Paris: Minuit, 1987.

Dreyfus ou l'intolérable vérité. Dir. Jean Cherasse. 1976.

Dujardin, Edouard. *Les Lauriers sont coupés*. 1888. Paris: Messein, 1968.

Eells, Emily. "Whistler et *Le Côté de Guermantes*." *Bulletin d'informations proustiennes* 22 (1991): 53–58.

Eisenstein, Sergei. "Beyond the Shot: The Cinematographic Principle and Ideogram." 1929. Braudy and Cohen 15–25.

Eissen, Ariane. "Les Marines d'Elstir." *Art et littérature: actes du congrès de la Société Française de Littérature Générale et Comparée.* Aix-en-Provence: U de Provence, 1988. 219–27.

Enright, D. J. "Note (1992)." Proust, *Search* 1: xix–xx.

Erickson, John D. "The Proust-Einstein Relation: A Study in Relative Point of View." *Marcel Proust: A Critical Panorama.* Ed. Larkin B. Price. Urbana: U of Illinois P, 1973. 247–76.

Fecteau, Monique L. "First- and Second-Language Reading Comprehension of Literary Texts." *Modern Language Journal* 83 (1999): 475–93.

Finch, Alison. "Love, Sexuality, and Friendship." Bales, *Cambridge Companion* 168–82.

Flaubert, Gustave. *Correspondance.* Vol. 2. Paris: Gallimard, 1980.

———. *L'Education sentimentale.* Vol. 2. Bibliothèque de la Pléiade. Paris: Gallimard, 1988.

———. *A Sentimental Education.* Trans. Douglas Parmée. Oxford: Oxford UP, 2000.

———. *Trois contes.* Ed. Pierre-Marc de Biasi. Ecole des lettres. Paris: Seuil, 1993.

Fraisse, Luc. "Les Eglises de Marcel Proust: un modèle retrouvé de Saint-André-des-Champs." *Revue d'Histoire Littéraire de la France* 89.6 (1989): 1015–30.

———. *L'Œuvre cathédrale: Proust et l'architecture médiévale.* Paris: Corti, 1990.

———. "Vinteuil et la musique à programme." *Musique et littérature au xxième siècle.* Ed. Pascal Dethurens. Strasbourg: PU de Strasbourg, 1998. 85–121.

Gandelman, Claude. "Proust as a Cubist." *Art History* 2.3 (1979): 355–63.

Genette, Gérard. "Discours du récit." Genette, *Figures* 3. 67–273.

———. *Figures of Literary Discourse.* Trans. Alan Sheridan. New York: Columbia UP, 1982.

———. *Figures 2.* Paris: Seuil, 1969.

———. *Figures 3.* Paris: Seuil, 1972.

———. *Mimologiques.* Paris: Seuil, 1976.

———. *Narrative Discourse: An Essay in Method.* Trans. Jane E. Lewin. Ithaca: Cornell UP, 1980.

———. *Narrative Discourse Revisited.* Trans. Jane E. Lewin. Ithaca: Cornell UP, 1988.

———. *Palimpsestes.* Paris: Seuil, 1982.

———. "Proust et le langage indirect." Genette, *Figures 2* 223–94.

Girard, René. *Proust: A Collection of Critical Essays.* Englewood Cliffs: Prentice, 1962.

Gombrich, Ernst. *The Story of Art.* Oxford: Phaidon, 1990.

Gordon, Linda A. "The Martinville Steeplechase: Charting the Course." *Style* 22 (1988): 391–401.

———. "Parallax as a Model of Perspective in *Ulysses* and *A la recherche du temps perdu* (Joyce, Ireland, Proust, France)." *DAI* 49.8 (1989): 2210A.

Graham, Victor. *Bibliographie des études sur Marcel Proust et son œuvre.* Geneva: Droz, 1976.

Grésillon, Almuth. *Eléments de critique génétique: lire les manuscrits modernes*. Paris: PUF, 1994.

———. "*Encore* du temps perdu, *déjà* le texte de la *Recherche*." *Proust à la lettre: les intermittences de l'écriture*. Tusson, Fr.: Lérot, 1990. 43–60.

Omaggio Hadley, Alice. *Teaching Language in Context*. Boston: Heinle, 2000.

Hay, Louis. *Essais de critique génétique*. Paris: Flammarion, 1979.

Henrot, Geneviève. *Délits/délivrance: thématique de la mémoire proustienne*. Padua: Cooperativa Libraria Editrice U di Padua, 1991.

———. "Le Fléau de la balance: poétique de la réminiscence." *Poétique* 13 (1998): 61–82.

Henry, Anne. *Proust*. Paris: Balland, 1986.

———, ed. *Schopenhauer et la création littéraire en Europe*. Paris: Klincksieck, 1989.

Heuet, Stéphane, adapt. and ill. *A la recherche du temps perdu:* "Combray." By Proust. Paris: Delcourt, 1998.

———, ill. *A la recherche du temps perdu:* "A l'ombre des jeunes filles en fleurs." By Proust. Adapt. by Stanislas Brézet and Heuet. 2 vols. Paris: Delcourt, 2000 and 2002.

Houston, John Porter. "Temporal Patterns in *A la recherche du temps perdu.*" *French Studies* 16 (1962): 33–44.

Ifri, Pascal. *Proust et son narrataire*. Geneva: Droz, 1983.

Jameson, Fredric. "Postmodernism and Consumer Society." *The Anti-aesthetic*. Ed. Hal Poster. Port Townsend: Bay, 1983. 111–25.

Johnson, J. Theodore, Jr. "*Débâcle sur la Seine* de Claude Monet: source du *Dégel à Briseville* d'Elstir." *Etudes proustiennes* 1. Paris: Gallimard, 1978. 163–76.

———. "Literary Impressionism in France: A Survey of Criticism." *L'Esprit créateur* 13.4 (1973): 271–97.

———. "Marcel Proust and Architecture: Some Thoughts on the Cathedral-Novel." Bucknall 133–61.

———. "Proust and Giotto: Foundations for an Allegorical Interpretation of *A la recherche du temps perdu.*" *Marcel Proust: A Critical Panorama*. Ed. Larkin B. Price. Urbana: U of Illinois P, 1973. 168–205.

———. "Proust and Painting." Bucknall 162–80.

———. "Proust's 'Impressionism' Reconsidered in the Light of the Visual Arts of the Twentieth Century." *Twentieth Century French Fiction: Essays for Germaine Brée*. Ed. George Stambolian. New Brunswick: Rutgers UP, 1975. 27–56.

———. "Proust's Referential Strategies and the Interrelations of the Liberal and Visual Arts." *The UAB Marcel Proust Symposium*. Ed. William C. Carter. Birmingham: Summa, 1989. 83–102.

———. *Proust Research Association Newsletter* 23 (1982): 52–53.

———. "Proust, Ruskin, et la petite figure au portail des libraires à la Cathédrale de Rouen." *Bulletin de la Société des Amis de Marcel Proust* 23 (1973): 1721–36.

Joubert, Claude-Henri. *Le Fil d'or: étude sur la musique dans* A la recherche du temps perdu. Paris: Corti, 1984.

Jullien, Dominique. "Le cathédrale romanesque." *Bulletin de la Société des Amis de Marcel Proust* 40 (1990): 443–57.

Kato, Yasue. "La Leçon d'impressionnisme d'Elstir et la vision du héros." *Etude génétique des épisodes de l'atelier d'Elstir dans* A la recherche du temps perdu. [Tokyo]: Surugadai-Shuppansha, 1998. 96–120.

Keller, Betsy. "Rereading Flaubert: Toward a Dialogue between First- and Second-Language Literature Teaching Practices." *PMLA* 112 (1997): 56–68.

Keller, Luzius. "Texte et architecture chez Proust." *Littérature et architecture.* Ed. Philippe Denon. Rennes: PU de Kennes, 1988. 109–15.

Kern, Stephen. *The Culture of Time and Space, 1880–1918.* Cambridge: Harvard UP, 1983.

Kilmartin, Terence. Introduction. Vol. 1. *Remembrance of Things Past.* By Marcel Proust. Trans. C. K. Scott-Moncrieff and Kilmartin. 3 vols. New York: Random, 1981.

———. *A Reader's Guide to* Remembrance of Things Past. New York: Random, 1984.

Kracauer, Siegfried. "Basic Concepts." Braudy and Cohen 171–82.

Kramsch, Claire. *Context and Culture in Language Teaching.* Oxford: Oxford UP, 1993.

———. "Literary Texts in the Classroom: A Discourse." *Modern Language Journal* 69 (1985): 356–66.

Kramsch, Claire, and Olivier Kramsch. "The Avatars of Literature in Language Study." *Modern Language Journal* 84 (2000): 553–73.

Kristeva, Julia. *Le Texte du roman.* The Hague: Mouton, 1970.

Lacan, Jacques. "La Fonction de l'écrit." *Séminaire* 20. Paris: Seuil, 1975. 29–38.

Lacoue-Labarthe, Philippe. *Musica ficta: figures de Wagner.* Paris: Bourgois, 1991.

Ladenson, Elisabeth. *Proust's Lesbianism.* Ithaca: Cornell UP, 1999.

Larcher, P. L. *Le Temps retrouvé d'Illiers.* Luisant: Imprimerie Durand, 1971.

Lee, James F. "The Relationship of Verb Morphology to Second Language Reading Comprehension and Input Processing." *Modern Language Journal* 82.1 (1998): 33–48.

Lee, James F., and Bill VanPatten. *Making Communicative Language Teaching Happen.* New York: McGraw, 1995.

Lefrançois-Tourret, Catherine, and Denis Gombert, with Geneviève Chourreu. *Marcel Proust: l'ecriture et les arts: cahiers pédagogiques des expositions.* Paris: Bibliothèque Nationale, 1999.

Leonard, Diane. "Ruskin and the Cathedral of Lost Souls." Bales, *Cambridge Companion* 42–57.

Le Pichon, Yann. *Le Musée retrouvé de Marcel Proust.* Paris: Stock, 1990.

Leriche, Françoise. "Marcel Proust. A l'ombre des jeunes filles en fleurs." *L'Œuvre d'art: un thème, trois œuvres.* Eric David, Leriche, and Raymond Mahieu. Paris: Belin, 1993. 55–122.

Leriche, Françoise, and Catherine Rannoux. Sodome et Gomorrhe *de Proust.* Neuilly: Altande, 2000.

Levinas, Emmanuel. "The Other in Proust." *The Levinas Reader.* Ed. Seán Hand. Oxford: Blackwell, 1989. 160–65.

Lewis, Pericles. *Modernism, Nationalism, and the Novel*. Cambridge: Cambridge UP, 2000.

Lydon, Mary. "Pli selon pli: Proust and Fortuny." Caws and Nicole 167–84.

Lyotard, Jean-François. *La Condition postmoderne: rapport sur le savoir.* Paris: Minuit, 1979.

Mâle, Emile. *L'Art religieux du XIIIe siècle en France: étude sur l'iconographie du Moyen Age et sur ses sources d'inspiration*. Paris: Leroux, 1898.

Marcel Proust: A Writer's Life. PBS, 1992; Films for the Humanities, 1998. <www.films.com>.

Marcel Proust: Remembrance of Things Past. Ten Great Writers of the Modern World. Films for the Humanities, 1987. <www.films.com>.

Marc-Lipianski, Mireille. *La Naissance du monde proustien dans* Jean Santeuil. Paris: Nizet, 1974.

Marrus, Michael R. *The Politics of Assimilation: A Study of the French Jewish Community at the Time of the Dreyfus Affair*. Oxford: Clarendon, 1971.

Marvell, Andrew. "To His Coy Mistress." *The Norton Anthology of English Literature*. Gen. ed. M. H. Abrams. New York: Norton, 1979. 1361–62.

Matoré, Georges, and Irène Mecz. *Musique et structure romanesque dans* la Recherche du temps perdu. Paris: Klincksieck, 1972.

Mauriac, Claude. *Le Temps immobile*. Paris: Grasset, 1974.

Mauriac, Nathalie, and Etienne Wolff, eds. "Avant-propos." *Albertine disparue*. By Marcel Proust. Paris: Grasset, 1987. 11–19.

Mauriac Dyer, Nathalie. "*Albertine disparue, Les Œuvres libres* et l'oubli," *Bulletin d'informations proustiennes* 19 (1988): 85–101.

McHale, Brian. *Postmodernist Fiction*. New York: Methuen, 1987.

Méjean, Annie. "Inventaire du Cahier 26." *Bulletin d'informations proustiennes* 10 (1979): 45–49.

Merleau-Ponty, Maurice. *Le Visible et l'invisible*. Paris: Gallimard, 1964.

Metz, Christian. "Some Points in the Semiotics of the Cinema." Braudy and Cohen 68–74.

Mézaille, Thierry. "'Combray': analyse microsémantique et génétique." *Bulletin d'informations proustiennes* 23 (1992): 107–36; 24 (1993): 83–96.

Michaudon, P., and J. Chabot. "Les clochers de Martinville." *Information littéraire* 44.2 (1992): 32–39.

Miguet-Ollagnier, Marie. "Le 'père Norpois' et le roman familial." *Revue d'histoire littéraire de la France* 90 (1990): 191–207.

Milly, Jean. *La Longueur des phrases dans "Combray."* Paris: Champion, 1986.

———. *La Phrase de Proust*. Paris: Larousse, 1975.

———. *La Poétique des textes*. Paris: Nathan, 1992.

———. *Proust et le style*. Paris: Minard, 1970.

———. "Sur quelques noms proustiens." *Littérature* 14 (1974): 65–82.

Monbrun, Estelle. *Meurtre chez Tante Léonie*. Paris: Hamy, 1994.

———. *Murder chez Proust*. Trans. David Martyn. New York: Arcade, 1995.

Monnin-Hornung, Juliette. *Proust et la peinture*. Geneva: Droz, 1951.

Moraru, Christian. "Exploring Names: Notes on Onomastics and Fictionality in Marcel Proust's *Remembrance of Things Past*." *Names* 43 (1995): 119–30.

Mortimer, Armine, and Katherine Kolb, eds. *Proust in Perspective: Visions and Revisions*. Urbana: U of Illinois P, 2001.

Muller, Marcel. *Les Voix narratives dans* A la recherche du temps perdu. Geneva: Droz, 1965.

Mulvey, Laura. "Visual Pleasure and Narrative Cinema." Braudy and Cohen 833–44.

Naremore, James, ed. *Film Adaptation*. New Brunswick: Rutgers UP, 2000.

Nathan, Jacques. *Citations, références et allusions dans* A la recherche du temps perdu. Paris: Nizet, 1953.

Nattiez, Jean-Jacques. *Proust as Musician*. New York: Cambridge UP, 1989.

Newman, Pauline. *Dictionnaire des idées dans l'œuvre de Marcel Proust*. The Hague: Mouton, 1968.

Nicole, Eugène. "Genèses onomastiques du texte proustien." *Cahiers Marcel Proust* 12. *Etudes proustiennes* 5. Paris: Gallimard, 1984. 69–125.

———. "L'Onamastique littéraire." *Poétique* 54 (1983): 233–53.

———. "Personnage et rhétorique du Nom." *Poétique* 46 (1981): 199–216.

102, Boulevard Haussmann. Written by Alan Bennett. Dir. Udayan Prasad. Prod. Innes Lloyd. Dist BBC. 1991.

Painter, George Duncan. *Marcel Proust: A Biography*. 2 vols. London: Chatto, 1959.

Pasco, Allan H. "Reading the Age of Names in *A la recherché du temps perdu*." *Comparative Literature* 46 (1994): 267–287.

Pautrot, Jean-Louis. *La Musique oubliée*. Geneva: Droz, 1994.

Piégay-Gros, Nathalie. *Introduction à l'intertextualité*. Paris: Dunod, 1996.

Pinter, Harold, with Joseph Losey and Barbara Bray. *The Proust Screenplay:* A la recherche du temps perdu. New York: Grove, 1977.

Pinter, Harold, and Di Trevis. *Remembrance of Things Past*. London: Faber, 2000.

———. *Remembrance of Things Past*. Cottesloe Theatre, London. 23 Nov. 2000.

Piroué, Georges. *Proust et la musique du devenir*. Paris: Denoël, 1960.

Placella Sommella, Paola. *Proust e i movimenti pittorici d'avanguardiâ*. Rome: Bulzoni, 1982.

Portoghesi, Paolo, Luca Quattrocchi, and Folco Quilici. *Baroque et art nouveau: le miroir de la métamorphose*. Trans. Anne Guglielmetti. Paris: Seghers, 1988.

Portrait souvenir: Marcel Proust. Prod. Roger Stéphane and Roland Darbois. Ten Great Writers of the Modern World. 1962.

Poulet, Georges. *L'Espace proustien*. Paris: Gallimard, 1963.

———. *Proustian Space*. Trans. Elliott Coleman. Baltimore: Johns Hopkins UP, 1977.

Proust, Marcel. Against Sainte-Beuve *and Other Essays*. Trans. and ed. J. Sturrock. Harmondsworth, Eng.: Penguin, 1988.

———. *A la recherche du temps perdu*. Ed. Jean-Yves Tadié. Bibliothèque de la Pléiade. 4 vols. Paris: Gallimard, 1987–89. Vol. 1: *Du côté de chez Swann*. Vol. 2: *A l'om-*

bre des jeunes filles en fleurs / *Le Côté de Guermantes.* Vol. 3: *Sodome et Gomorrhe* / *La Prisonnière.* Vol. 4: *Albertine disparue* / *Le Temps retrouvé.*

———, trans. *La Bible d'Amiens.* By John Ruskin. Paris: Mercure de France, 1904.

———. *Le Carnet de 1908.* Ed. Philip Kolb. *Cahiers Marcel Proust* 8. Paris: Gallimard, 1976.

———. *Combray.* Ed. Germaine Brée. New York: Prentice, 1952.

———. Contre Sainte-Beuve *précédé de* Pastiches et mélanges *et suivi de* Essais et articles. Ed. Pierre Clarac and Yves Sandre. Bibliothèque de la Pléiade 229. Paris: Gallimard, 1971.

———. Contre Sainte-Beuve; *Suivi de* Nouveaux mélanges. Ed. Bernard de Fallois. Paris: Gallimard, 1954.

———. *Correspondance.* Ed. Philip Kolb. 21 vols. Paris: Plon, 1970–93.

———. "Impressions de route en automobile." *Le Figaro* 19 Nov. 1907.

———. *In Search of Lost Time.* Trans. and rev. D. J. Enright. 6 vols. New York: Mod. Lib., 1993. Vol. 1: *Swann's Way.* Vol. 2: *Within a Budding Grove.* Vol. 3: *The Guermantes' Way.* Vol. 4: *Sodom and Gomorrah.* Vol. 5: *The Captive* and *The Fugitive.* Vol. 6: *Time Regained.*

———. *In Search of Lost Time.* Ed. Christopher Prendergast. London: Penguin, 2003.

———. *Jean Santeuil.* Ed. Pierre Clarac and Yves Sandre. Bibliothèque de la Pléiade. Paris: Gallimard, 1971.

———. "La Mort des cathédrales." *Le Figaro* 16 Aug. 1904.

———. *On Reading Ruskin.* Trans. and ed. Jean Autret. New Haven: Yale UP, 1987.

———. *Pastiches et mélanges.* Paris: N. R. F., 1919.

———. *Les Plaisirs et les jours.* Pref. Anatole France. Illus. Madeleine Lemaire. Music pieces by Reynaldo Hahn. Paris: Calmann-Levy, 1896.

———. *Selected Letters.* Ed. Philip Kolb. Vol. 1, 1880–1908. Trans. Ralph Manheim. Garden City: Doubleday, 1983. Vol. 2, 1904–09. Trans. Terence Kilmartin. London: Collins, 1989. Vol. 3, 1905–17. Trans. Terence Kilmartin. New York: Harper, 1992. Vol. 4, 1918–22. Trans. Joanna Kilmartin. New York: Harper, 2000.

———, trans. and ed. *Sésame et les lys.* 1906. By John Ruskin. Ed. Antoine Compagnon. [Brussels]: Complexe, 1987.

Proust: Œuvres romanesques complètes. CD-ROM. Champion, 1998.

Proust vivant: Marcel Proust du côté des lecteurs. Written by Jérôme Prieur. L'INA, La Sept, et ARTE. Sept. 2000.

Pudovkin, Vsevolod. "On Editing." 1926. Braudy and Cohen 9–14.

Quémar, Claudine. "L'Eglise de Combray, son curé et le Narrateur (trois rédactions d'un fragment de la version primitive de 'Combray')." *Cahiers Marcel Proust* 6. *Etudes proustiennes* 1. Paris: Gallimard, 1973. 277–342.

Rabaté, Dominique. *Le Roman depuis 1900.* Paris: PUF, 1998.

Racine, Jean. *Esther. Théâtre complet.* Ed. Maurice Rat. Paris: Garnier, 1960. 595–647.

Rancœur, René. "Bibliographie de Marcel Proust." *Cahiers Marcel Proust.* Nouvelle série. *Etudes proustiennes* 1–6. Paris: Gallimard, 1973–87.

Richard, Jean-Pierre. *Proust et le monde sensible.* Paris: Seuil, 1974.

———. "Proust et la nuit mérovingienne." *Cahiers Marcel Proust.* Nouvelle série. *Etudes proustiennes* 1. Paris: Gallimard, 1973. 21–34.

Ricœur, Paul. *Temps et récit.* Paris: Seuil, 1983.

———. *Temps et récit II: la configuration dans le récit de fiction.* Paris: Seuil, 1984.

———. *Temps et récit III: le temps raconté.* Paris: Seuil, 1985.

Riding, Alan. "A Debut to Remember in the Comics." *New York Times* 3 Oct. 1998, late ed.: B7.

Riffaterre, Michael. *La Production du texte.* Paris: Seuil, 1979.

Rivière, Jacques. *Quelque progrès dans l'étude du cœur humain.* Paris: Libraire de France, 1926.

Robbe-Grillet, Alain. *La Jalousie.* Paris: Minuit, 1957.

Rolland, Romain. *Jean-Christophe.* 1904–12. Paris: Michel, 1931.

Ropars-Wuilleumier, Marie-Claire. *Ecraniques.* Lille: PU de Lille, 1990.

Rorty, Richard. *Contingency, Irony and Solidarity.* Cambridge: Cambridge UP, 1994.

Rosenbaum, Jonathan. "The Sweet Cheat." *Chicago Reader* 2000: sec. 1.

Rosenthal, Leon. *Carpaccio, biographie critique.* Paris: Laurens, 1906.

Ruskin, John. *La Bible d'Amiens.* Trans. Marcel Proust. Paris: Mercure de France, 1904.

———. *The Bible of Amiens. Complete Works* 33: 1–187.

———. *The Elements of Drawing.* Introd. Lawrence Campbell. *Illustrations* 51. New York: Dover, 1971.

———. *Sesame and Lilies. Complete Works* 18: 1–187.

———. *The Seven Lamps of Architecture.* 14 plates by Ruskin. New York: Dover, 1989.

———. *The Complete Works of John Ruskin.* Ed. E. T. Cook and Alexander Wedderburn. Library edition. 39 vols. London: Allen, 1903–12.

Saito, Yoshiko, Elaine K. Horwitz, and Thomas L. Garza. "Foreign Language Reading Anxiety." *Modern Language Journal* 83.2 (1999): 202–18.

Sandre, Yves. "Notices, notes et choix de variantes." Proust, *Pastiches* 694.

Schuré, Edouard. *Le Drame musical.* Paris: Sandoz et Fischbacher, 1875.

Schwab, Gabriele. *The Mirror and the Killer Queen: Otherness in Literary Language.* Bloomington: Indiana UP, 1996.

Scott, Virginia M. "An Applied Linguist in the Literature Classroom." *French Review* 74 (2001): 538–49.

Sedgwick, Eve Kosofsky. *Epistemology of the Closet.* London: Harvester, 1991.

Serça, Isabelle. "Solutions de continuité dans *Sodome et Gomorrhe*." Ed. Evelyne Grossman and Raymonde Coudert. *Lectures de* Sodome et Gomorrhe *de Marcel Proust. Cahiers textuels* 23 (2001): 43–69.

Shattuck, Roger. *Proust's Way: A Field Guide to* In Search of Lost Time. New York: Norton, 2000.

Simon, Claude. *Les Corps conducteurs.* Paris: Minuit, 1971.

Soucy, Robert. "Bad Readers in the World of Proust." *French Review* 44 (1971): 677–86.

Souza, Sybil de. "L'Importance de la musique pour Proust." *Bulletin de la Société des Amis de Marcel Proust* 19 (1969): 879–87.

———. "Pourquoi le 'Septuor de Vinteuil.'" *Bulletin de la Société des Amis de Marcel Proust* 23 (1973): 1596–1608.

Spitzer, Leo. "Zum Stil Marcel Proust's." *Stilstudien*. Vol. 2. Munich: Hueber, 1961. 365–497.

Sprinker, Michael. *History and Ideology in Proust:* A la Recherche du temps perdu *and the Third French Republic.* Cambridge: Cambridge UP, 1994.

Stam, Robert. "Beyond Fidelity: The Dialogics of Adaptation." Naremore 54–76.

Stock, Janet C., ed. *Marcel Proust: A Reference Guide, 1950–1970.* Boston: Hall, 1991.

Suleiman, Susan Rubin. "The Parenthetical Function in A *la recherche du temps perdu.*" *PMLA* 92 (1977): 458–70.

Tadié, Jean-Yves, ed. *Lectures de Proust.* Paris: Colin, 1971.

———. *Marcel Proust.* Paris: Gallimard, 1996.

———. *Marcel Proust: A Biography.* Trans. Euan Cameron. London: Viking, 2000.

———. *Marcel Proust: une découverte multimédia de l'œuvre de Marcel Proust.* CD-ROM. Paris: Gallimard, 1999.

Tadié, Jean-Yves, and Florence Callu, eds. *Marcel Proust: l'écriture et les arts.* Paris: Gallimard, 1999.

Le Temps retrouvé. Dir. Raoul Ruiz. Prod. Paulo Branco. Kino Intl., 1999.

Turner, Joan F., and Glynis Cowell. "A Cognitive Model for the Teaching of the Literary Elements in the Second-Year Language Class." *Patterns and Policies: The Changing Demographics of Foreign Language Instruction.* Ed. Judith E. Liskin-Gasparro. Boston: Heinle, 1996.

Uenishi, Taeko. "L'Affinité cubiste de l'écriture de Proust." *Le Style de Proust et la peinture.* Paris: Sedes, 1988. 83–168.

Ushiba, Akio. "Les correspondances proustiennes: à propos des églises." *Etudes de lexicographie et stylistique offertes en hommage à Georges Matoré.* Textes réunis par Irène Tamba. Paris: Société pour l'information grammaticale; U de Paris–Sorbonne, 1987. 89–102.

Valéry, Paul. "Hommage à Marcel Proust." *Œuvres complète.* Paris: Gallimard, 1957.

Valesio, Paolo. "Levels of Phonological Admissibility." *Linguistics* 106 (1973): 28–53.

Vaudoyer, Jean-Louis. "Le mystérieux Vermeer." *L'Opinion* 30 May 1921.

Vendryès, Joseph. "Marcel Proust et les noms propres." *Mèlanges de philologie et d'histoire littéraire offerts à Edmond Huguet.* Paris: Boivin, 1940. 119–27.

Vogely, Maxine A. *A Proust Dictionary.* Troy: Whiston, 1981.

White, Edmund. *Marcel Proust.* New York: Viking, 1999.

Wilson, Edmund. *Axel's Castle.* New York: Scribner's, 1931.

Yoshikawa, Kazuyoshi, ed. *Index général de la* Correspondance de Marcel Proust. Kyoto: PU de Kyoto, 1998.

———. "Proust et Carpaccio: un essai de synthèse." *Travaux de littérature* 13 (2000): 271–86.

———. "Proust et le Greco." *Bulletin de la Société des Amis de Marcel Proust* 44 (1994): 29–41.

———. "Proust et Moreau: nouvelles approches." Brun, *Nouvelles directions* 97–114.

———. "Proust et Vermeer: nouvelles approches." *L'Histoire littéraire: ses méthodes et ses résultats, mélanges offerts à Madeleine Bertaud.* Geneva: Droz, 2001. 793–802.

———. "Vinteuil ou la génèse du Septuor." *Etudes proustiennes 3. Cahiers Marcel Proust* 9. Paris: Gallimard, 1979. 289–347.

INDEX

Modern Language Association of America

Approaches to Teaching World Literature

Joseph Gibaldi, series editor

Achebe's Things Fall Apart. Ed. Bernth Lindfors. 1991.
Arthurian Tradition. Ed. Maureen Fries and Jeanie Watson. 1992.
Atwood's The Handmaid's Tale *and Other Works*. Ed. Sharon R. Wilson, Thomas B. Friedman, and Shannon Hengen. 1996.
Austen's Pride and Prejudice. Ed. Marcia McClintock Folsom. 1993.
Balzac's Old Goriot. Ed. Michal Peled Ginsburg. 2000.
Baudelaire's Flowers of Evil. Ed. Laurence M. Porter. 2000.
Beckett's Waiting for Godot. Ed. June Schlueter and Enoch Brater. 1991.
Beowulf. Ed. Jess B. Bessinger, Jr., and Robert F. Yeager. 1984.
Blake's Songs of Innocence and of Experience. Ed. Robert F. Gleckner and Mark L. Greenberg. 1989.
Boccaccio's Decameron. Ed. James H. McGregor. 2000.
British Women Poets of the Romantic Period. Ed. Stephen C. Behrendt and Harriet Kramer Linkin. 1997.
Brontë's Jane Eyre. Ed. Diane Long Hoeveler and Beth Lau. 1993.
Byron's Poetry. Ed. Frederick W. Shilstone. 1991.
Camus's The Plague. Ed. Steven G. Kellman. 1985.
Cather's My Ántonia. Ed. Susan J. Rosowski. 1989.
Cervantes' Don Quixote. Ed. Richard Bjornson. 1984.
Chaucer's Canterbury Tales. Ed. Joseph Gibaldi. 1980.
Chopin's The Awakening. Ed. Bernard Koloski. 1988.
Coleridge's Poetry and Prose. Ed. Richard E. Matlak. 1991.
Conrad's "Heart of Darkness" and "The Secret Sharer." Ed. Hunt Hawkins and Brian W. Shaffer. 2002.
Dante's Divine Comedy. Ed. Carole Slade. 1982.
Dickens' David Copperfield. Ed. Richard J. Dunn. 1984.
Dickinson's Poetry. Ed. Robin Riley Fast and Christine Mack Gordon. 1989.
Narrative of the Life of Frederick Douglass. Ed. James C. Hall. 1999.
Eliot's Middlemarch. Ed. Kathleen Blake. 1990.
Eliot's Poetry and Plays. Ed. Jewel Spears Brooker. 1988.
Shorter Elizabethan Poetry. Ed. Patrick Cheney and Anne Lake Prescott. 2000.
Ellison's Invisible Man. Ed. Susan Resneck Parr and Pancho Savery. 1989.
English Renaissance Drama. Ed. Karen Bamford and Alexander Leggatt. 2002.
Dramas of Euripides. Ed. Robin Mitchell-Boyask. 2002.
Faulkner's The Sound and the Fury. Ed. Stephen Hahn and Arthur F. Kinney. 1996.
Flaubert's Madame Bovary. Ed. Laurence M. Porter and Eugene F. Gray. 1995.
García Márquez's One Hundred Years of Solitude. Ed. María Elena de Valdés and Mario J. Valdés. 1990.

Gilman's "The Yellow Wall-Paper" and Herland. Ed. Denise D. Knight and
    Cynthia J. Davis.
Goethe's Faust. Ed. Douglas J. McMillan. 1987.
Gothic Fiction: The British and American Traditions. Ed. Diane Long Hoeveler
    and Tamar Heller. 2003.
Hebrew Bible as Literature in Translation. Ed. Barry N. Olshen and
    Yael S. Feldman. 1989.
Homer's Iliad *and* Odyssey. Ed. Kostas Myrsiades. 1987.
Ibsen's A Doll House. Ed. Yvonne Shafer. 1985.
Works of Samuel Johnson. Ed. David R. Anderson and Gwin J. Kolb. 1993.
Joyce's Ulysses. Ed. Kathleen McCormick and Erwin R. Steinberg. 1993.
Kafka's Short Fiction. Ed. Richard T. Gray. 1995.
Keats's Poetry. Ed. Walter H. Evert and Jack W. Rhodes. 1991.
Kingston's The Woman Warrior. Ed. Shirley Geok-lin Lim. 1991.
Lafayette's The Princess of Clèves. Ed. Faith E. Beasley and
    Katharine Ann Jensen. 1998.
Works of D. H. Lawrence. Ed. M. Elizabeth Sargent and Garry Watson. 2001.
Lessing's The Golden Notebook. Ed. Carey Kaplan and Ellen Cronan Rose. 1989.
Mann's Death in Venice *and Other Short Fiction.* Ed. Jeffrey B. Berlin. 1992.
Medieval English Drama. Ed. Richard K. Emmerson. 1990.
Melville's Moby-Dick. Ed. Martin Bickman. 1985.
Metaphysical Poets. Ed. Sidney Gottlieb. 1990.
Miller's Death of a Salesman. Ed. Matthew C. Roudané. 1995.
Milton's Paradise Lost. Ed. Galbraith M. Crump. 1986.
Molière's Tartuffe *and Other Plays.* Ed. James F. Gaines and
    Michael S. Koppisch. 1995.
Momaday's The Way to Rainy Mountain. Ed. Kenneth M. Roemer. 1988.
Montaigne's Essays. Ed. Patrick Henry. 1994.
Novels of Toni Morrison. Ed. Nellie Y. McKay and Kathryn Earle. 1997.
Murasaki Shikibu's The Tale of Genji. Ed. Edward Kamens. 1993.
Pope's Poetry. Ed. Wallace Jackson and R. Paul Yoder. 1993.
Proust's Fiction and Criticism. Ed. Elyane Dezon-Jones and
    Inge Crosman Wimmers. 1993.
Rousseau's Confessions *and* Reveries of the Solitary Walker. Ed. John C. O'Neal
    and Ourida Mostefai. 2003.
Shakespeare's Hamlet. Ed. Bernice W. Kliman. 2001.
Shakespeare's King Lear. Ed. Robert H. Ray. 1986.
Shakespeare's Romeo and Juliet. Ed. Maurice Hunt. 2000.
Shakespeare's The Tempest *and Other Late Romances.* Ed. Maurice Hunt. 1992.
Shelley's Frankenstein. Ed. Stephen C. Behrendt. 1990.
Shelley's Poetry. Ed. Spencer Hall. 1990.
Sir Gawain and the Green Knight. Ed. Miriam Youngerman Miller and
    Jane Chance. 1986.

Spenser's Faerie Queene. Ed. David Lee Miller and Alexander Dunlop. 1994.
Stendhal's The Red and the Black. Ed. Dean de la Motte and Stirling Haig. 1999.
Sterne's Tristram Shandy. Ed. Melvyn New. 1989.
Stowe's Uncle Tom's Cabin. Ed. Elizabeth Ammons and Susan Belasco. 2000.
Swift's Gulliver's Travels. Ed. Edward J. Rielly. 1988.
Thoreau's Walden *and Other Works*. Ed. Richard J. Schneider. 1996.
Tolstoy's Anna Karenina. Ed. Liza Knapp and Amy Mandelker. 2003.
Vergil's Aeneid. Ed. William S. Anderson and Lorina N. Quartarone. 2002.
Voltaire's Candide. Ed. Renée Waldinger. 1987.
Whitman's Leaves of Grass. Ed. Donald D. Kummings. 1990.
Woolf's To the Lighthouse. Ed. Beth Rigel Daugherty and Mary Beth Pringle. 2001.
Wordsworth's Poetry. Ed. Spencer Hall, with Jonathan Ramsey. 1986.
Wright's Native Son. Ed. James A. Miller. 1997.